5.59
Amaza

Chris Horrie is the author of seven books, including the bestselling *Stick it Up Your Punter!* and *Live TV*. He is a national newspaper and magazine journalist.

Also by Chris Horrie

Disaster!:
The Rise and Fall of the News on Sunday
Anatomy of a Business Failure

Stick it up Your Punter!:
The Rise and Fall of the Sun

Sick as a Parrot:
The Inside Story of the Spurs Fiasco

Fuzzy Monsters:
Fear and Loathing at the BBC
(with Steve Clarke)

Live TV:
Tellybrats and Topless Darts

Citizen Greg:
The Extraordinary Story of Greg Dyke
and How He Captured the BBC
(with Steve Clarke)

PREMIERSHIP

Chris Horrie

POCKET BOOKS

LONDON · SYDNEY · NEW YORK · TOKYO · SINGAPORE · TORONTO

First published in Great Britain by Pocket Books, 2002
An imprint of Simon & Schuster UK Ltd
A Viacom Company

1 3 5 7 9 10 8 6 4 2

Simon & Schuster UK Ltd
Africa House
64–78 Kingsway
London WC2B 6AH

www.simonsays.co.uk

Simon & Schuster Australia
Sydney

A CIP catalogue record for this book is available
from the British Library

ISBN 0-7434-4065-X

Typeset by Palimpsest Book Production Limited,
Polmont, Stirlingshire
Printed and bound in Great Britain by
Clays Ltd, St Ives plc

For Lynn

Contents

'If one day I should return to soccer, it would mean it has changed. I've been through the system. I left it because it was no longer similar to my vision of the game. Because of all the financial interests at stake, the sport is turning into a mafia.'

Eric Cantona
February 2001

Acknowledgements

This book has its origins in a proposed series of TV documentaries commissioned by Channel Four under the provisional title *The Other Side of Football*. The idea was that the series would 'lift the lid on the darker side of a national obsession' and provide some sort of investigative counterpoint to the overwhelmingly – and sometimes oppressively – positive coverage of the Premiership in the rest of media. For a host of technical, budgetary and logistical reasons the series never made it to the screen. A huge amount of work was nevertheless done on the project by Roy Ackerman and Ed Crick of Diverse Production, and so the first thanks go to them.

In the course of ten years of writing about and researching the business side of football and, in particular, the relationship between TV and football which forms the core of the Premiership story, I have been helped by many people at all levels of the game, many of whom have been extremely generous with their time and advice. In no particular order they include Gordon Taylor, Rick Parry, Alex Fynn, Irving Scholar, Sheila Kronert, Andreas Herren, Steve Double, Dennis Campbell, David Dein, Kate Hoey, John Adams, Chris Nawrat, Charlie Wheelan, Mihir Bose, Harry Harris, Henrik Madsen, Jeff Randall, Johnson Fernandez, Graham Sharpe, David Yallop, Greg Dyke, Stephen Fotterell, Michael Crick, David Conn, Stefan Szymanski and many others.

I would also like to thank my agent Robert Kirby at Peters, Fraser and Dunlop and both Martin Fletcher and Andrew Gordon, my editors at Simon & Schuster.

Final thanks go to Clare, Lotte and Tom, for their patience.

Preface

In April 1991 Graham Kelly, then head of the Football Association, emerged into the spring sunshine from the darkened corridors of the FA's Mayfair headquarters clutching a thick document called 'The Blueprint for the Future of Football'.

The Blueprint was a suitably worthy document from the FA – a crusty conservative organization which had its roots in Victorian amateurism. And Kelly himself, a softly-spoken former bank clerk and failed Blackpool FC reserve goalkeeper, hardly looked or sounded like a revolutionary.

Amid all the usual talk about tending the grass roots and helping the England national team, Kelly had included in his Blueprint a bombshell – the ruthless proposal that the FA should set up a rival competition to the long-established ninety-two club Football League. Twelve of the country's most popular clubs joined up at once. Within weeks another half-dozen followed suit. The Premier League was born.

The motivation was, of course, money. As members of the Football League, the best supported clubs had to share the revenue they got from TV with all the other League clubs. It meant the likes of Manchester United earned less than £40,000 a year as their share of the TV rights sales negotiated centrally by the Football League.

Manchester United chairman Martin Edwards, one of the moving spirits behind the breakaway, complained that the smaller clubs among the League's ninety-two were 'bleeding the game to death'. They were not viable as businesses and ought to be 'put to sleep'. For almost a decade he had been looking for a way

Chris Horrie

of paying off the £500,000 debt he had taken on in order to consolidate his control of the club. He turned to Sir Roland Smith – the first major figure to be brought into a football boardroom from the City – to prepare United for flotation.

The City was sceptical. Tottenham Hotspur had gone public in 1983, but had bombed as a business. Football clubs were seen as the ultimate basket cases, beset with the soaring cost of players' wages and, in addition, facing the vast expense of rebuilding their stadiums in the wake of the Hillsborough disaster.

The only way forward was to exploit the linked areas of TV rights sales, merchandising and sponsorship, crucial new sources of revenue. And that meant breaking away from the Football League.

Edwards' predicament coincided with Kelly's arrival at the FA from the League, during a bitter bureaucratic turf-war between the two governing bodies. Divisions were deep, and stretched back to the League's embrace of professionalism a century or more before. Now the League was proposing a merger, an idea popular among many fans and at the game's grass roots, but less so with the amateur worthies who ran the FA council. They saw it as a threat – nothing less than an attempted takeover.

Kelly, keen to make his mark at the FA, saw off the merger and then turned the tables. Throughout the 1980s, plots hatched by Edwards and others to form a breakaway league had partly foundered due to opposition from the FA as well as the Football League.

Kelly, once the gamekeeper, turned poacher with a vengeance. Irving Scholar, chairman of Tottenham and a man as eager as Edwards to break away, was later to say that it was the FA's stamp of respectability which had enabled the Premier League to get off the ground.

From the start Kelly had seen that TV money would be crucial to the finances of the new 'Premiership' (the inevitable legal tussle with the rump Football League – which briefly went into receivership when the big clubs left – meant that the FA could not use 'League' in its title). The Blueprint specified that 'one live game every week' would be shown on TV. At the time it was thought that this would mean a deal with ITV, who had held the rights to the old League, where Greg Dyke was handling negotiations.

The outline of a deal was already clear. Dyke was prepared to pay at least £20 million for the rights. This was roughly double what ITV had paid in the past. More importantly, the money would be shared by the Premiership clubs only, giving them £1 million each, compared with the few tens of thousands they had got when the money had been split between all ninety-two Football League clubs.

At Manchester United, Edwards and Smith thought this vast leap in TV revenue would be enough to interest the City. The flotation, held back on the grounds that United were playing in the European Cup Winners' Cup final until after the Blueprint was published, went ahead in May 1991. The float valued the club at £47 million, but it was not a great success. Some of the shares remained unsubscribed.

A year later the City's enthusiasm for Manchester United plc began to pick up after the TV rights deal awarded the Premiership not to ITV, as expected, but to BSkyB, who had paid what was then regarded as the staggering sum of £304 million for a five-year rights deal. This guaranteed United around £3 million a year – a hundred-fold increase on the previous Football League deal. A thirty percent increase in ticket prices, a new multi-million sponsorship deal and investment in the goldmine of replica shirt sales meant that the plc was soon one of the darlings of the city, boosted by success on the pitch and weekly dollops of free positive publicity in the sports sections of the papers.

Manchester United's amazing turn-round encouraged others to pile in. Within days of the deal with Sky, Sir John Hall bought a controlling stake of Newcastle United for about £3 million. Five years later, after flotation, the club was valued at over £100 million. New and financially astute directors ousted or joined the traditional worthies in club boardrooms up and down the country.

It was the age of the 'football fat cats'. But the real winners were to be BSkyB. Before buying the Premier League rights the company had been facing bankruptcy. After the deal, chief-executive Sam Chisholm announced that it was 'like Christmas every day' as subscriptions rolled in. Football's role as the most valuable rights property in the TV business was confirmed: it was the 'driver', the only type of programming that could be guaranteed to sell dishes. Sky's effective owner, Rupert Murdoch, described the Premiership as the 'battering ram' which had got pay TV off the ground in the UK. In 1996 the deal was renewed, with Sky paying £670 million to hang on to the 'crown jewels' of the pay TV business.

The 1996 deal with Sky saw football shares soar. Aggressive marketing and branding operations led to talk of vast new revenues from the innovation of pay-per-view. Manchester United began to describe itself as a 'world brand' to rival McDonalds and laid plans for chains of shops, branded fast-food outlets and even theme parks around the world. Eventually Sky moved to protect its investment by bidding to buy Manchester United. All football shares went through the roof as Sky's rivals lined up to buy other clubs – the cable TV operator NTL bought into Newcastle; Granada took a stake in Liverpool; Carlton eyed up Arsenal – the attraction being access to the all important screening rights.

But as the City's love affair with football peaked, Graham Kelly was having difficulty riding the tigers he had helped release from their cages. Some clubs began to act as though the Premiership and the FA needed them more than they needed the Premiership. They demanded more power, especially over TV rights negotiations, and became ever more fixated on European competitions, where there were even greater profits to be had.

Kelly was eventually forced out in November 1998 after admitting making unauthorized payments to the Welsh FA to secure their votes as part of the FA's imploding bid to stage the 2006 World Cup in England. But he had been under pressure before that, annoying some clubs by enforcing rules on irregular payments to players, and others by interfering with TV negotiations. Kelly, in the end, was devoured by the revolution he had unleashed.

In many ways it is surprising that English football continues to enjoy such an overwhelmingly popular media image. The fact is that the game, through the decade of its commercial transformation, was beset with the sort of 'sleaze' which would have created massive outcry had it been found in any other walk of life.

By the middle of the nineties the FA woke up to the fact that the player transfer system was riddled with irregular payments which openly flouted its own rules. But it took the Inland Revenue to discover that tax avoidance was taking place on a massive scale and that, in some cases,

Chris Horrie

League managers accepted 'unsolicited gifts' – more commonly known as 'bungs' – from grateful agents after spending huge sums of club money on buying their players.

The 'bungs scandal' – centred on George Graham of Arsenal – coming at the same time as allegations of match-fixing, led the FA to take action. But unlike the American NFL, which has a ramified system of commissioners who oversee individual clubs' financial dealings, the FA appointed just a single official – ex-Yorkshire policeman Graham Bean – as its 'sleaze-buster'.

The redoubtable Mr Bean soon found that he had his work cut out for him. Increasingly, the transfer dealings of English Premiership clubs were linked to countries like Italy, Spain and, above all, South America and Eastern Europe, where corruption is endemic.

The new commercial leaders of football clubs claimed that the greater financial accountability entailed by plc status spelled an end to corrupt practices in the English game. But they were powerless to control the activities of illegal betting syndicates who, it is widely believed, have corrupted the very international competitions on which English football's prospects for further financial growth increasingly depend.

Virtually every major European League has been tainted with allegations of match-fixing, and several European Champions League games have been shown to have been targeted by match-fixers. In the Far East, national leagues have had their results annulled and there have been mass arrests of players for bribery and fraud. The game's greatest exponent, Pelé, has claimed that Brazilian football has been corrupted from top to bottom. It has recently been revealed that some transfers of South American players to clubs throughout Europe have involved forged passports and other types of fraud.

All the evidence suggested organized crime was turning its attention more and more to the reputedly 'clean' Premier League, now that it had been sold to cable and satellite TV throughout the world. Despite all this, criticism of the way the game was being run was mainly restricted to what remained of the fanzine 'fanpower' movement of the 1980s. Individuals might be singled out for criticism from time to time – when there were allegations of match-fixing for example – but coverage of the game on TV and in the press was overwhelmingly positive. This was hardly surprising. The country's biggest selling papers – the *Sun*, *News of the World* and *The Sunday Times* – belonged to Rupert Murdoch, the owner of Sky. Having paid over £1 billion for the rights to show the Premiership, it was unlikely that another branch of the same company would say that things in the garden were anything but rosy.

There were honourable exceptions, but most of the press and TV had some sort of vested interest in putting a positive spin on the progress of the Premiership – either because they had a slice of the action or wanted to buy the rights themselves. Even the BBC had *Match of the Day* – until the Corporation lost the rights to ITV. Its coverage of football tended to be less hysterically positive than other broadcasters, but its fastest growing radio channel – Five Live – depended on a thriving Premiership. As part of its deal for exclusive radio rights the BBC had formally agreed to 'show the Premiership in a generally positive light'. In 2001, the BBC ran a documentary series called *The Men Who Changed Football*, which basically presented the new commercial rulers of the game as visionaries and towering business geniuses who had dragged football out the dark ages.

The greatest claim was that they had tackled the

related problems of hooliganism and racism and, with impeccable right-on credentials, made stadiums safe and more welcoming for women and children. It was unfortunate that only a few months later the entire Premiership was castigated in an official report for 'institutional racism' in its backroom employment practices. There were plenty of black stars – some of them even from the UK – fitting Nike-style stereotypes of black physical prowess, but very few in the boardroom or in management.

Hooliganism continued to flare up at England matches, at smaller clubs and in town centres before and after games. The clubs, rather than 'solving' the problem, swept it out of their grounds by means of saturation use of closed circuit TV and other heavy-handed security measures – so that somebody else could deal with it.

The City and financial world's love affair with football is now well and truly over. Manchester United continues to plough ahead, but the plc, to use the cliché, is now 'in a league of its own'.

But even for United the future looks far from certain. The main danger is the soaring cost of players' wages, set to reach a standard £100,000 a week for top players. Already City analysts and institutional shareholders are complaining that the football plcs spend a much higher proportion of their revenues on salaries than on any other type of business.

Despite their much higher turnovers, English clubs are finding it difficult to compete with salaries offered by European clubs which are, in general, privately owned. In some cases, billionaires like AC Milan owner Silvio Berlusconi are even prepared to run their clubs at a vast loss.

Worse than this, the leading players have realized, just as the leading clubs once did, that TV does not pay to show football 'in general'. Manchester United and the others became rich by insisting that TV only wanted their games and insisted that they, therefore, should keep most of the money. Now the players are applying the same logic. Increasingly, it is no longer Manchester United or Arsenal who are the attraction – especially to world audiences – it is individual stars like David Beckham.

The stars are starting to throw their weight about. Contract freedom introduced by the EU in wake of the Bosman case means that players could, in theory, change clubs week by week, offering their services like professional boxers, golfers, or pop stars, to the highest bidder. They are doubtless aiming for the sort of salaries earned by individual American sports stars – perhaps £1 million a week. 'Post-Bosman' salaries heading in this direction have already crippled many football clubs.

At the same time there are signs of growing boredom with the game. It is no longer the sure-fire audience 'driver' that it once was. The transfer of Premiership highlights from the BBC to ITV at the start of the 2001/2 season became one of the greatest ratings disasters in recent TV history. TV ratings for the 'made for TV' UEFA Champions league are disappointing. A plan, two years ago, to repeat the Premiership trick on a continental scale by setting up a breakaway European Super League foundered on the realization that few people would pay to watch it.

The danger is that the new commercial version of the game, made for TV and performed by individual stars paid millions ('mercenaries' in fan-speak), will fail to recruit the next generation of addicted consumers.

Chris Horrie

The vast increase in football's capital value was driven by the clever commercial exploitation of 'brand loyalty' built up over generations. It was said that while people might change their politics or religion, betray their country or get divorced, there was no known case of a person changing the club they supported.

But TV audiences are notoriously fickle. How will football, saddled with its massive overheads, recruit a new generation of addicted customers when replica shirts become last year's fashion, about as attractive as Pokemon cards, and viewers switch to the latest TV sensation as easily as they switch between Playstation games or zap from *Who Wants to Be a Millionaire?* to *Big Brother?*

Chris Horrie, London, October 2001

Part 1.

Origins

1.
Camera, Action . . . Floodlights

January 1966

It is a freezing night at Turf Moor, a strip of ground clinging to the Pennines above the unlovely mill town of Burnley. The collection of crudely painted sheds in shades of muddy purple claret and clashing blue keep out the worst of the sleet, but offer little protection from the cutting gusts of icy wind rolling down from the surrounding dark and sodden hills. A crowd of 10,000 or less is gathering on the terraces of Burnley FC's ground, warmed only by the prospect of a Cup replay against Bournemouth – that and the savoury delights of Bovril and a Lord's Meat Pie, a local delicacy noted for its flavoursome gristle, rock-hard pastry and glutinous gravy.

Outside the ground a drama is developing. A BBC outside broadcast unit has arrived and is demanding entry. They have instructions from the Corporation to film the impending action (expected to be a walk-over since Burnley are one of the top teams in the country, enjoying their Golden Age, lately playing in the European Cup as English league champions). But they have reckoned without Burnley's Bob Lord, also known as 'Lord Bob' or 'Barrow Boy Bob', a no-nonsense self-made northern Lard Mogul, owner of and monopoly pie supplier to Burnley Football Club.

The groundsmen will not let cameramen into the ground. The BBC team produce a letter from the FA promising them access and help in bringing FA Cup ties (and replays) to the nation in line with a contract binding together the Corporation and English football's governing body. But it does no good. Finally the startling sheepskin-coated, fur-collared figure of Lord Bob himself emerges from the gloom. He grabs the FA's letter, rips it up and tells the BBC team where they can stick their cameras. Attendance is low enough, the chairman thinks, without the BBC enabling people to watch the game from the comfort of their living rooms, escaping the bracing conditions of Turf Moor, evading the two shilling admission price and, most important of all, remaining beyond the clutches of his claret and blue Burnley pie salesmen.

The next day Lord Bob is all over the newspapers berating the FA for inviting the BBC to his football club without permission and, worse still, castigating the BBC for announcing that the game would be shown on TV. The attendance, Lord Bob maintained, was directly affected as a result, and he was out of pocket. The reason for this outrage, the FA swiftly accepted, was a cock-up. Dennis Fallows, the FA secretary, had forgotten to tell the BBC that Burnley was one of only two clubs (the other was Everton) out of the ninety-two in the Football League, who were not party to an agreement for televising the FA Cup, agreed the year before. Bob Lord had forgone the £250 per game fee, plus £75 inconvenience money paid in return for erecting the usual death-trap gantry/scaffold under the main stand for the cameras, reckoning that the loss of gate money – and pie sales – would be far greater.

The John Bull of Football – 'Yes, that's what they call me' – has a visceral dislike of television anyway. He thinks the medium is controlled by 'showbusiness Jews' who are somehow plotting to undermine the national game or, at least, are working to stitch up the football clubs over payment for screening rights and compensation for lost gate money. (At the time it was conventional wisdom that televising football in any form would mean fewer paying customers at the grounds.)

The deal from which Bob Lord had dissented had its origins in the arrival on the national scene of ITV, the new commercial wing of British broadcasting, in 1956. Until then the exposure of football on television had been limited to the FA Cup final, some FA Cup ties, amateur games, friendlies and internationals, all broadcast by the BBC on the grounds of national significance in return for a purely nominal fee. The companies bidding for ITV franchises, a network of strongly localized broadcasters established by law to serve an audience in a particular region, had immediately targeted football as the ideal type of programming. The attraction of football was that many games were of great local appeal. And with the advent of the new technological wonder of floodlighting, matches could take place for the first time on winter evenings – which was when the ITV companies needed them. In the run-up to the great ITV switch-on the new franchises began courting the football authorities, offering what were by the standards of the time huge sums for the rights to show live games.

The football authorities had always been divided over how much football should be shown on television. The Football Association, custodians of the game's rules, the national team and the FA Cup, had welcomed the arrival of television and its ability to get a greater national audience for the sport. But since the 1930s power had shifted away from the game's origins in southern public school amateurism towards the professionalism of the Football League, the independent and distinctly northern association of clubs which organized the game's other main competition under FA rules. The league clubs functioned as local businesses and were far less concerned than the FA about the larger role played by the game in national life. Money came from paying customers at the turnstiles and, importantly, from catering contracts. Many of the owners of clubs ran catering companies, breweries or, like Lord and the Edwards dynasty who had just taken control of Manchester United, were butchers eager to offload their perishable product to the captive audiences gathered in football grounds after pouring out of the local mills and factories every Saturday afternoon.

By the spring of 1955, with ITV's regional companies due to go on air one by one over the following twelve months, rumours began to circulate that the League was about to sign a big-money deal with ITV companies in football-mad areas such as the North West, London and the Midlands. From the start ITV was interested in screening only selected games. The money on the table was huge: companies were willing to pay up to £1,000 per match. At the time the average First Division game generated about £3,000 at the turnstiles and the TV money represented around 10,000 extra paying customers at the gate. ITV deal-makers, many with a background as showbiz, cinema or boxing promoters and impresarios, had been buttering up the chairmen of glamour clubs such as Arsenal, Aston Villa and Manchester United – making it clear that most of the money would go to them. Newcastle were so keen on getting TV money that they even offered to stage extra floodlit evening games against local rivals Sunderland just for the benefit of the new service.

Crucially, the ITV offers were made directly to individual clubs and not, as was later to be the case, to the League itself. The smaller clubs affiliated to the League were understandably alarmed – not to say jealous – that their already more successful rivals were planning to leave them out of the bonanza. To chairmen such as Bob Lord the development seemed even more threatening. The danger was that visiting supporters might stay at home to watch the match on TV. Manchester United, which could draw on support from several million 'local' supporters from the Manchester conurbation, might not find their home gates hit too badly by the arrival of such 'armchair supporters' (as they were to be called). But Burnley's gate numbers could be devastated. The town of Burnley had only some 40,000 male inhabitants and, as Lord knew only too well, the regular gates of 20,000 crammed into Turf Moor depended on the large numbers of fans who came with the visits of better supported rivals. Since it was the case that until the 1980s clubs kept almost all the money from the home gate, the large clubs subsidized the smaller ones.

Months of internal League politicking in the spring of 1955 led to a special conference of all ninety-two club chairmen, which took place in Manchester. Arthur Drewery, the League chairman, had recommended that individual clubs be given the right to negotiate with ITV companies. But, not for the last time, the small clubs revolted. Fretting over a decline in attendances of two million in a single season, and supported by the chairmen of Everton, Manchester City and Stoke City plus a united front of all the clubs in the lower divisions, Lord managed to push through a total ban on televised league football. The big clubs were told that if they tried to do their own deals with ITV they would face expulsion from the League – in effect their destruction as businesses. The response from some of the larger clubs was immediate and remarkably similar to the events which led to the formation of the Premier League almost forty years later – they threatened to walk out of the Football League and set up their own, rival TV-funded competition.

In 1955 the breakaway threat was led by Newcastle United, whose Stanley Seymour proposed a British floodlit league composed of ten clubs who would play each other four times a season with every game taking place in the evening under floodlights and televised live. Seymour told the papers: 'If clubs cannot get the co-operation they want from the League over TV money, the time is not far off when commercial TV will approach leading clubs, and the players' union, to form either a TV league or a TV cup. The money will be so good that few clubs could afford to refuse.' By January 1956 Seymour was claiming that Sunderland, Arsenal and Spurs from England, together with Hearts and Hibs, were prepared to join Newcastle and go ahead with the breakaway. The other invited clubs – Aston Villa, Manchester United, Celtic and Rangers – had not committed themselves. Seymour claimed that ITV were very keen on televising at least thirty-five of the forty games in an 'ITV Floodlit League' and were prepared to pay as much as £50,000 a year to do so.

Seymour's breakaway 'made for ITV' British league was an idea at least thirty years ahead of its time. A version was revived in the late 1980s by ITV sport boss Greg Dyke who was to propose an 'ITV Ten' made-for-TV league, consisting of the ten best supported English teams. The idea was to be taken much more seriously then and would lead directly to the formation of the Premiership. But in 1956 it was destroyed by a combination of political lobbying by the smaller clubs, the opposition of the FA, and vacillation on the part of ITV, which had begun to doubt that matches would get the audiences needed to justify such massive investment.

There was another decisive factor. Manchester United and Celtic came out against the idea of a British Floodlit League because it conflicted with their preoccupation with the European Cup – the newfangled evening football competition that was to become Manchester United manager Matt Busby's obsession.

Matt Busby, a softly spoken, tough-minded former coalminer from Motherwell, took over as manager of Manchester United in 1945. It was he who created the modern United, bringing the club out from under the shadow of its often more successful rival, Manchester City, and laying the foundations for its domination of English and, in financial terms at least, world club football at the end of the twentieth century.

Before the television age transformed the economics of the football industry there was a natural rise and fall among a group of around twenty clubs, each of which had a run at the top with a good young team, or with the touch of an inspired coach or manager, before falling back down the league, allowing another club to have its few years of glory. What locked Manchester United into a position of dominance, which even two decades of often pitiful mismanagement in the 1970s and 1980s could not shake, was the simple fact that United happened to be the top team at the moment television arrived. Had TV come in the 1920s, the power centre of English football would have been Huddersfield or Sheffield; the 1930s or 1940s would have given predominance to Arsenal, or possibly Portsmouth.

It was thus a tremendous stroke of good luck for

Chris Horrie

United that Busby's 'Babes' team came into its own in 1955 and 1956 when ITV was being set up, ready to pay large sums to fill its yawning hours of airtime with football. Busby, able to lead the lacklustre Manchester United chairman Harold Hardman and his geriatric board by the nose, grasped the importance of televised football at once, and was reportedly intrigued by the plan for a breakaway ITV British Floodlit League put forward by Newcastle United's Stanley Seymour. The attraction of Seymour's idea was of course financial. ITV was offering £1,000 per televised game, not to the League to be divided equally between the participating clubs but directly to the clubs themselves. It was likely that, as reigning champions, United would attract most of the attention from TV just when the new medium was beginning to establish its grip on the average Briton's increasing leisure time and to provide, through advertising, a direct line to every wallet and purse in the country.

In an additional stroke of luck Granada, the free-spending Manchester-based ITV company, was turning out to be the most powerful in the network.

But already United and Granada had their eyes on a bigger prize – the European Cup, set up in 1955 on the initiative of the French sports newspaper *L'Équipe*. Chelsea, who had won the English First Division in May 1955, had been invited to take part as English champions. They had turned down the offer under pressure from the Football League who were still opposed on principle to floodlit evening games. The competition had gone ahead anyway and had proved to be a hit, the final between Real Madrid and Reims in May 1956 gaining a vast European-wide TV audience.

United won the First Division title in the summer of

1956, by which time ITV and Granada had gone on the air and the League had adopted Bob Lord's ban on televised football. United and Busby found themselves in a strong position. Seymour's breakaway televised British league had its attractions – both to United and ITV, but the European Cup looked an even better bet. As a business proposition it was very similar to Seymour's British league, but one with even greater financial potential. The format of the new competition was two-legged ties (one home game and one away) in every round including the final, with matches being played in the evening under floodlights.

Qualification for the European Cup would virtually guarantee a run of ten or so evening games which were perfect for ITV, and the new network would pay handsomely to screen them. The home legs were certain to be all-ticket sell-outs and so there was no danger of losing gate money to hordes of armchair supporters who, given the fact that United would be representing England in the competition, would be drawn from all over the country. Even better, in an age when foreign travel was virtually unheard of, away games could, in practice, be seen only on TV, profitably enough for both the club and the broadcaster. Although Chelsea had not taken part in the inaugural European Cup, the Scottish champions, Hibernian, had done so and had earned £25,000 in extra gate money and their share of TV screening rights by reaching the semi-final.

If Hibernian could reach the semis, Busby told the United directors, then his young team had 'an excellent chance of winning the competition'. He urged the board to grab the opportunity, even if it meant upsetting the League, who had written to warn that 'participation is not in the best interests of the League, having regard to the possible effect on League match attendances'. United went ahead.

Busby's foresight was borne out in the winter and spring of 1956–57. United's first home game in Europe was played against Anderlecht of Belgium at Manchester City's Maine Road stadium in front of 43,635 people. Old Trafford, only recently rebuilt after wartime bombing, still had no floodlights. United won 10–0. The scale and style of the victory banished an initial feeling that the new floodlit competition was a gimmick and a distraction from the real business of the Football League. More than 75,000 turned up for the next game, also at Maine Road, to see United beat Borussia Dortmund 3–2. After a further victory against Athletic Bilbao, United sealed a TV deal with Granada, getting £2500 for the rights to show each of their home matches, on top of a share of money already being paid by foreign broadcasters for the away legs.

United's first televised home European game could not have been better for ITV. Under newly installed floodlights they drew 2–2 in a dramatic semi-final against the reigning European champions, Real Madrid. United had lost the away leg 3–1, and so were now out of the competition. Real Madrid, who again went on to be European champions, had struggled to beat the still young United side, although Busby said of the semi-final defeat that 'a great, experienced team will always triumph over a great, inexperienced team'. The away game had attracted a British TV audience of 6.5 million – by far the biggest for any ITV programme in the new service's first year of broadcasting. Importantly for the relationship between football and television, there were signs that large numbers of people had bought a television for the first time just to watch the game. Football, right from the start, had established itself as what the TV industry would later call a 'driver' – a way of getting people to invest in the sets (and later dishes) needed to see the matches.

A few weeks later United gained another massive TV audience for their appearance in the 1957 FA Cup final. Already First Division champions, for the second time in a row (which was then a rare achievement for any club), they unexpectedly lost the final to Aston Villa.

United's progress in their first campaign in Europe had earned them at least £60,000 in extra gate and TV rights money. By the start of the following season, which would again see them play in Europe as champions of England, TV exposure had already started to work its magic. Busby told the club's annual general meeting that television and the European Cup had made Manchester United a 'household name throughout the universe'. The odds were that they would once again reach at least the semi-finals and they looked a good bet to reach the final itself.

2.
Birth of a Legend

20 February 1958, Rechts der Isar Hospital, Munich

Duncan Edwards, twenty-one years old, eighteen caps for England, the heart of the Manchester United 'Busby Babes' team lies in a coma, hooked up to a kidney machine. There is massive damage to his internal organs. He is not expected to survive. Suddenly, after fourteen days of unconsciousness, his eyes flicker and he comes round. He peers at the cluster of people surrounding his bed, as though searching for Matt Busby, team manager and father figure. But Busby is not there. The manager is along the corridor in an oxygen tent, almost as close to death as Edwards. More than once a priest has been called to administer the last rites to Busby.

Edwards recognizes Jimmy Murphy, Busby's deputy. Suddenly strangely coherent, the young player asks quietly, 'What time's the kick-off against Wolves on Saturday?' Murphy replies, 'Two thirty – as usual.' Edwards smiles, whispers, 'Get stuck in, lads . . .' then drifts off again, his eyes closing for the last time. Moments later he sighs peacefully. Duncan Edwards is dead, joining seven other United players killed when a plane bringing them back to Manchester after a European Cup game in Belgrade crashed during takeoff after a refuelling stop at Munich airport. Eleven others are dead. Most of the survivors, including Bobby Charlton and Matt Busby, are seriously injured.

Charlton would later say of Duncan Edwards that future generations would never realize just how good Edwards had been as a player. 'He had everything. He didn't have a fault. I feel terrible trying to explain to people how good he was. They just expect to be able to see what he was like on television – but they are never going to see it.' Busby said simply that Edwards had been 'incomparable'.

It had been raining all day in Munich on 6 February 1958. By night time the temperature had dropped and it was snowing. The United team's plane, a British European Airways liner called the *Lord Burghley*, twice abandoned attempts to take off. The plane taxied back and the players returned to the departure lounge. When it was decided to make another attempt, the players reboarded. As the plane raced along the runway for the third time, snow was coming off the wheels. The plane started to lift but then bumped down again, skidding off the runway, crashing through barriers and smashing into a wooden hut before exploding into a fireball.

The Munich disaster established Manchester United as the first football team of the television age. The tragedy, the funerals and the slow recovery of the survivors, including Matt Busby himself, were given saturation coverage, relayed to the nation every night on TV. In Manchester there was a mass outpouring of grief.

But not everyone joined in the mourning. Bob Lord, the Burnley pie salesman who was still leading the Football League's rearguard action against television and its effects on the game, achieved notoriety by complaining about all the 'sob-stuff' on TV after Munich. The disaster, he implied, was some sort of divine retribution for the 'greed' United had displayed by playing in Europe against the wishes of himself and the League Management Committee he dominated. An unsentimental man, Lord refused to help United by loaning or transferring players, as several other clubs did. 'Lord Bob' then accused the patched-up United team of crash survivors, reserves and volunteers of behaving 'like a bunch of thugs and Teddy Boys'.

Lord had no control over the televising of the European Cup, but he had been remarkably successful in keeping League football off the screens. In 1955 a meeting of League club chairmen had rejected ITV's original pre-launch rights offer and had imposed a total ban on televised League football. The BBC made an improved counter-offer of £1,500 per game, as opposed to ITV's proposed £1,000. The Corporation wanted to show only ten live games per season – playing on the small clubs' fears of losing gate money. Viewers did not want 'the airwaves to be awash with too much football,' the BBC said. But Lord and the League Management Committee maintained their hard line. The BBC's offer was rejected out of hand.

ITV was left only with shared access to the FA Cup and its coverage of the European Cup. Its entry into the world of televised football seemed ill starred. The new network's coverage of its first live FA Cup game – the second half (only) of a third-round replay between mighty Arsenal and non-League Bedford played on a Thursday afternoon in January 1956 (due to lack of flood-lights), ended in farce. Tens of thousands who took the afternoon off work to watch at home were disappointed because the cameras broke down a few minutes before the second half kick-off leaving the screens blank.

There was more trouble later in the same year when the players' union demanded extra payments for taking part in televised games. Now that ITV was offering serious money, they wanted their share. At the time the union was fighting a separate campaign for the abolition of the maximum wage, the last remnant of the old battle between the League and the FA over amateurism. In the mid-1950s the maximum wage that could officially be paid to a top First Division player was £15 per week during the season and £12 during the summer – a sum which, within a generation, a top-flight player would earn in twenty seconds. The players' union saw the arrival of both floodlit evening matches in general and televised games in particular as a lever they could use. In March 1956 the union threatened a total ban on evening and televised games unless bonuses were paid.

The League split along the increasingly familiar fault line of small versus large clubs. Big-city clubs generally favoured paying star players more money since they also generally favoured televising league matches and calculated that the extra TV revenue would allow them to carry a higher wage bill. Birmingham City led the campaign for bonuses to be paid for TV games and, with support from London clubs including Chelsea and Fulham, also proposed an across-the-board increase in the maximum wage from £15 to £20. Tommy Trinder, the TV comedian and director of Fulham, told the papers: 'Footballers are television entertainers now, and they should be paid as such.'

The smaller clubs, again led by Bob Lord, took a harder line. They were opposed to televised league games and so the players' threatened ban suited them just fine. The maximum wage worked in their favour and they were determined to keep it in place. The danger of a free market was that the richer clubs, bolstered by TV money, would attract all the best players, leaving small clubs unable to compete. Something like this had already happened in Spain and Italy where 'superclubs' such as Real Madrid and Milan were paying top players hundreds of pounds per week. There was yet another factor. A big part of a club like Burnley's business involved scouting for good young players (mostly from the North East), locking them into iron-clad maximum wage contracts and making money by selling on their registrations to bigger clubs for transfer fees. Burnley had become so expert at this that the club, after investing in the best training facilities in the league, had become known as 'Bob Lord's Sausage Machine'. Any move in the direction of contract freedom threatened not only Burnley but all the smaller clubs and, with their huge built-in majority in the League policy-making bodies, they made sure that the maximum wage stayed in place.

ITV tried to defuse the crisis created by the threat of a player strike by upping their offer, at the same time running a noisy press campaign to the effect that they would pump money into the clubs, enabling them to meet the players' legitimate and reasonable demands for an end to the 'feudal' maximum wage rule. In an important new move ITV tried to outmanoeuvre Lord by offering to pay some of the money into a pot to be shared by all clubs. This more than doubled the sum to be paid to individual clubs from £1,000 per game to £3,000 per full game, or £1,500 per half game – much more than the £2,500 paid by Granada for Manchester United's European games. Fears that televised live games might affect attendances at other matches were addressed by offering to move televised games to Saturday evening, and even showing only the second half if there were signs of a dip in gate money. ITV offered to create a compensation pot of £60,000 a season to be claimed by clubs who could show that attendances had fallen as a result of competition for TV. The fund, it was claimed, would cover reductions in gates of up to 1,000,000 in a season. To cap it all, the network offered to pay overnight hotel and other expenses incurred by away teams playing in Saturday evening games.

But ITV's tactics did not work. Their offer was again rejected. The grip of Lord and the small clubs on the League was so tight that the anti-TV and pro-maximum wage stance actually hardened. The League was even able to lean on the FA, getting the senior football organization to ban TV cameras from a midweek evening FA Cup replay between Chelsea and Burnley. W. J. Harrop, chairman of the FA Committee, said the ban had been imposed 'after representations from Mr Bob Lord and the League Management Committee' because there was a danger that 'attendance might be affected at the League Division Three (North) match between Stockport County and Grimsby Town' taking place at the same time. Then the FA gave in again to the League by banning TV cameras from a fifth-round FA Cup tie between West Bromwich Albion and Birmingham City because of 'the likely effect on gate receipts at many matches taking place in the Midlands including Wolves, Leicester City and Coventry City'. Significantly, ITV had planned to show the West Brom–Birmingham game – which was an all-ticket sell-out with attendance capped by the police at 57,000 – on the first day of its Midlands service.

The BBC was now on the sidelines because of the amount of money on the table. ITV could always afford to pay more because the extra viewers brought in by live football – as demonstrated by the vast armchair audiences for Manchester United's European games – led directly to extra advertising revenue. In contrast the Corporation received the same income from the licence fee regardless of the number of viewers.

The commercial network came back with another

Chris Horrie

improved offer – a reduction in the proposed number of live Saturday games to be shown from the original bid for thirty-five to a mere sixteen programmes a year featuring the second half only of selected games. The offer was designed to appeal to the small clubs right across the four leagues and allay their fear of direct competition from TV with their normal Saturday afternoon games.

The sum offered to featured clubs was the same as before – £1,500 for each second-half game shown. The main new feature was the hardening up of the £60,000 compensation pot that Lord and the small clubs had regarded with suspicion, doubting they would ever be able to claim it in practice, into a firm offer of £5,500 to be paid directly to the League and shared between all ninety-two clubs, regardless of what happened to their attendances. Many of the smaller clubs were tempted and, importantly, the principle of TV paying the League as a whole rather than individual clubs – the basic position up to and including the creation of the Premiership – for the right to show games was established for the first time. But the money on the table was not enough.

In 1960 ITV came up with the offer of a total package of £15,000 a year for ten years with most of the money to be paid to the League and shared by the ninety-two clubs. The small clubs who were anyway enjoying increasing gates after the decline of the mid-1950s, decided it was an offer too good to refuse and their representatives on the League Management Committee voted in favour of acceptance. The objection this time came from the big clubs, who demanded that all the money available from ITV should go to them – since without them TV would not have been interested in the first place. Despite League Management Committee approval the deal was abandoned when Arsenal, Spurs and Sheffield

Wednesday said they would take legal action to establish that they owned the rights to their home games and that they would prevent cameras from entering their grounds, unless they and not the League received all the money.

The football authorities and TV companies remained deadlocked for a further four years in the early 1960s during which the basic shape of the politics of televised football deals took shape. What television wanted, especially ITV, was live coverage of big evening floodlit matches, the audience-pulling power of which had been demonstrated by Manchester United's European games. The League, dominated by small clubs like Burnley, would always oppose any such deal unless the money was paid to the League and shared equally between all ninety-two clubs. But if this happened the big clubs would get so little money that it would not be worth their while.

One way out of this conundrum was for TV to increase the sum it was willing to pay for live football. If ITV valued a live First Division game between two top teams at £5,000, then they would have to pay something like half a million to the League if all the other clubs were to receive an equal share. Even if ITV could find the money it still might not work. Clubs such as Tottenham Hotspur and Manchester United objected to sharing television cash with other less glamorous clubs, who were, after all, rival businesses. Spurs had spent heavily buying players after the abolition of the maximum wage in January 1961, winning the League and Cup 'double' that year with the country's first million-pound football team. It made sense for TV to pay to show Spurs' games. But why should Spurs share the money with other clubs who had invested nothing and might use the cash to compete for players in the newly inflated transfer market?

Chris Horrie

The solution came not from the clubs, but from television and it was again driven by advances in the TV business itself. New technology meant that it was easier to record and edit outside broadcasts (a difficult and expensive business in the 1950s). The BBC, faced with filling up a lot of extra airtime following the launch of BBC 2, came up with the idea of producing a highlights show – effectively an extension of the snippets of live games that had long been shown in the sports sections of news bulletins on Saturday evening. In 1964 they offered about £3,000 a year – to be shared equally between all ninety-two clubs – for the rights to produce a Saturday evening highlights programme featuring several League games. This would become *Match of the Day*, the country's longest-lived and best-loved football TV show.

The BBC was offering far less than ITV because it was not demanding live coverage, evening games or any alternation to the League programme. Instead the Corporation would show a maximum of twenty edited minutes of a game on Saturday night and, moreover, the match chosen would remain a closely guarded secret until at least 5 p.m. when all the day's games would be over. The BBC further agreed that the programme would not go out before 9.30 p.m., the latest time, it was reckoned, that fans visiting an away game in any part of the country would arrive home (some clubs pressed for the show to go out on Sundays for this reason).

The BBC also acquired the right to show snippets of up to ten minutes of other matches so that *Match of the Day* could be scheduled to last fifty minutes. (When it was shown that being on *Match of the Day* did not affect attendance at the chosen game, the BBC was allowed to extend the highlights to forty-five minutes if it wanted.) There was then a further deal allowing ITV to show snippets of two or three minutes in the extended sports sections of its Saturday night and Sunday news bulletins.

The first *Match of the Day* was shown on BBC2 on 22 August 1964 and featured highlights of Liverpool beating Arsenal 3–2 at Anfield. The programme was an immediate hit and at the peak of its popularity in the 1970s, having switched to BBC 1, attracted fully a quarter of the adult population of the country.

The success of *Match of the Day* showed that highlights could get an audience as big as live football. In many ways it was more attractive than watching a whole game, much of which could be boring. The editor of the programme at the time said that making it was simplicity itself: 'You just cut out all the rubbish, point the camera at the most crowded part of the ground and turn up the sound level.' The style of production introduced another element into the story of modern football. At a time when youngsters in particular could hardly see anything unless the ground was half empty or they stood on a soap box, the games on television looked much better and exciting than they often were in cold reality.

As far as the FA Cup was concerned, in the summer of 1965 FA secretary Dennis Fallows proposed a total ban on televising live Cup ties (except for the final) unless television came up with a much increased offer for the games they had been used to showing for next to nothing. 'More and more people are sitting at home watching football instead of going to matches,' he complained. League secretary Alan Hardaker agreed: 'The money clubs are getting from TV is immaterial. The damage done to attendances is far more important.'

There had indeed been a slight decline in overall football attendance in the 1964–65 season, the first year

Chris Horrie

of *Match of the Day*. But this was not the whole picture. Fewer people had turned up at FA Cup matches, especially in the earlier rounds, and at lower division league matches, but things were different in the First Division, where games were featured every week on *Match of the Day*. Overall attendances in the First Division had gone up by some 300,000, with the average First Division gate moving up to 27,500 – the highest figure for six years.

The increase was biggest for the glamour clubs such as Spurs and, above all, Manchester United, who appeared most often on *Match of the Day*. United's average attendance in the first *Match of the Day* season was 46,000, up by an average of almost 3,000 per week and the best since the Munich disaster in 1958. It became a commonplace to think that these extra paying customers at the grounds were being attracted – rather than put off – by *Match of the Day*. Many fans liked the idea that the game they were watching was also on TV; it added a sense of occasion. At a time when grounds consisted of mainly open terraces where people could move from place to place if it was not too crowded, a trend emerged for fans – especially kids – to place themselves where they thought they might appear on TV in the background of a close-up of a player taking a throw-in or a corner. The great game was to watch *Match of the Day* and try to spot yourself on the telly.

The fact was that United's gates grew by leaps and bounds during the *Match of the Day* era, peaking at 58,000 in the European Cup-winning 1967–68 season. The average gate did not drop below 50,000 until 1974, when the club was relegated to Division Two and thus did not feature quite so often on the programme. Within a couple of years of the launch of *Match of the Day* exposure on it could reasonably have been calculated to have been earning United £3,000 a week in extra gate revenue – a much more important sum than their minuscule share of the money paid to the League as a whole for the rights.

Match of the Day was such a success that ITV immediately became interested in making a counter-bid, offering more money. Emboldened by the show's popularity, the League and the FA for once presented a united front designed to get the BBC and ITV to bid against each other for *Match of the Day*-style highlights. They reduced the number of FA Cup ties that could be broadcast live and so pushed up the price of the main live football 'product' – England international games in the run-up to the World Cup finals due to take place in England in the following season. Round one went to the Football League. After a brief bidding war the BBC ended up increasing the amount it paid for *Match of the Day* from £3,000 to £60,000, a vast one-off increase the like of which would not be seen again until the arrival of satellite TV in the 1990s.

But round two, the battle for the rights to show the approaching World Cup, went to the television companies. The FA tried to play hardball. But, licking their wounds after the massive hike in the price of League football, the BBC and ITV decided to get together and agree the maximum either would pay. The two TV companies decided in advance which games in the World Cup fixture list they wanted to show and made low 'take it or leave it' bids for each one. Negotiations ended in total humiliation for the FA and victory for the TV business. Secretary Denis Follows had started off by complaining that TV exposure was killing the live game, but he ended up allowing BBC and ITV to show a massive fifty hours of World Cup football, bought very cheaply.

Chris Horrie

The coverage of the 1966 World Cup was a triumph for television, culminating in England's 4–2 win against Germany in the Wembley final. Kenneth Wolstenholme's famous 'they think it's all over . . . it is now!' phrase was broadcast by the BBC at the climax of a match that had been watched by a worldwide audience of 400 million. The moment was later voted the greatest in British TV history.

3.
Fame

George Best slouches around a Birmingham hotel bed-room on some drunken night in the mid-1970s, his football career on the slide. Earlier in the evening he had won £25,000 at a casino and the cash is spread out on the bed. His latest girlfriend, the reigning Miss World Mary Stavin, is on the bed as well. Room service arrives with a bottle of vintage champagne. The porter plucks up his courage and asks, 'Mr Best . . . where did it all go wrong?'

The story is a legend, often told by the former Manchester United player against himself as he did the chat-show round once most of his fortune had evaporated. There are lots of legends about George Best. In the year 2000, finally hospitalized as the result of years of hard drinking, he was voted British 'Footballer of Century' by the massed pundits and soccer hacks assembled for the Rothmans Annual Football Awards. Duncan Edwards – eighteen England caps, 'incomparable' according to Matt Busby, 'faultless' in the opinion of Bobby Charlton – did not get a look in.

George Best was doubtless a great player – a genius even. But there had been plenty of skilled players before him and a good few afterwards. What was different about George Best was his fame. And, unlike Edwards and others of whom no video recording existed, his fame was created by television. Best started playing and scoring regularly in the Manchester United first team in 1963. The greatest years of his playing career coincided with the early boom years of *Match of the Day*, when Manchester United were virtually ever-present on the screen. He scored some remarkable, individual goals – all of them broadcast to an audience of millions on Saturday evenings. *Match of the Day* in the late '60s often seemed more like the *George Best Show*.

Manchester United had started the first *Match of the Day* season as the previous year's runners-up and ended it as champions. The club was popular not only with its own fans, but also with almost everybody else in the country – in stark contrast with the club's image in later decades. Many fans, it was said, held an affection for United as their second team. United were seen as a side embodying the wholesome, northern grassroots spirit of the game, battling against Tottenham, the 'moneybags' team who threatened to dominate English football in the 1960s and who stood accused of buying success with a series of record-breaking transfers.

There was also the reservoir of sympathy dating from the Munich disaster and tremendous admiration for the way Matt Busby had put together a second highly talented team. To the dignified, tragi-heroic aura of Munich survivor Bobby Charlton was added the glamour of George Best and Dennis Law. Then, in 1966, two United players – Charlton and the lovable toothless rogue Nobby Stiles – were among the national heroes of England's 1966 World Cup triumph. For a while it was said that Bobby Charlton had become the most famous Englishman on earth. According to legend explorers meeting tribesmen deep in the Amazon rainforest would find that if they knew any words of English at all they would be 'Bobby Charlton'.

In the first four seasons following the arrival of *Match of the Day*, United won the championship twice and were runners-up once. This run of success culminated with United winning the European Cup – the first English club to do so – live in front of another massive British and international TV audience in 1968.

And TV loved George Best – an individualist rather than a dedicated team player, whose several seconds of skill or lovable 'bad boy' arrogance could be clipped out of ninety minutes of football, showcased on *Match of the Day* and repeated over and over in replays. George Best was a celebrity in a football shirt, the first player to feature regularly on TV outside his role as a footballer. He made the news bulletins and became a regular on the chat shows. Documentaries were made about him. Rock groups sang songs about him. A long-haired rebel, he was 'El Beatle', a symbol of the 'baby boomer' TV generation with money to spend. Older supporters on the terraces at Old Trafford would worry about his work rate, his lack of contribution to the team effort. When he started drinking some thought him a liability. But the fact was that in the late 1960s and early 1970s it was hard to find a working-class lad kicking around a football on any piece of rough ground anywhere in the country who did not want to be George Best.

It is doubtful if Bob Lord of Burnley would ever have allowed George Best house room at Turf Moor, let alone entrust him with a claret and blue shirt. Lord had railed against the influence of the Beatles by insisting that all his players had military-style short back and sides. He instituted a club ban on the effeminate practice of players hugging each other 'like bloody big girl's blouses' after scoring a goal, a virus, he reckoned, that had spread to England as a result of youngsters watching too many Italian – 'Eye-tie!' – footballers cavorting about during televised coverage of the World and European Cups. Meanwhile Burnley had been League champions in 1960,

Chris Horrie

and had continued to do well in the four years up to the start of *Match of the Day*. In 1962 the team had come within an ace of doing the League and Cup double but ended up second in the League and losing the FA Cup final to Tottenham.

Lord was one of only four major club chairmen to have voted against the BBC deal that led to the creation of *Match of the Day* and in favour of maintaining a total ban on televised league football. The others were the chairmen of Everton, Stoke and Manchester City. Significantly, three of these die-hard clubs were in the hinterland of Manchester United, while the fourth, Everton, was in the shadow of Liverpool, another rising football superpower of the television age. The danger was that the rising generation of fans in towns such as Burnley and Stoke might identify themselves with nearby United or Liverpool, seeing so much of them on TV, rather than with their own local team.

Choice of allegiance to a football team was a complicated and emotional business – a sort of pubescent psychological epiphany according to a later generation of football intellectuals of the Nick Hornby school. But there was little doubt that many working-class boys would support the team they fantasized about playing for in some magical grown-up future. The prospect of playing for Burnley, and thus becoming a local hero and celebrity, might have packed the local teenagers of the 1940s and 1950s into Turf Moor. But by the 1960s more and more wanted the sort of celebrity offered by turning out for Manchester United – local enough now that many people had cars and motorways had been built, and ineffably heroic and romantic after the Munich disaster – where players were 'household names throughout the universe' in Matt Busby's phrase. Burnley were not enjoying the new age of televised football, and the writing was on the wall when, to general amazement, it was reported in the local paper that the high street school outfitter had sold more red football shirts trimmed with the white piping of Manchester United than Burnley's claret and blue.

As United forged ahead, Burnley and other small clubs went into steep decline. The Turf Moor club never finished in the top half of the First Division after 1967 and were to progress beyond the third round of the FA Cup only rarely. In 1972, with falling gates and no longer able to compete for the best players, Burnley were relegated to the Second Division. They bounced back for three seasons in the mid-1970s, but by that time the club was mired in debt. In 1977 they dropped back into the Second Division. By 1981 they were in the Third Division and in 1986 sunk to the Fourth Division. At the end of the following season Burnley finished in twenty-second place in the bottom division and were facing bankruptcy.

Other north-western teams in the 'fan base' hinterland of United and Liverpool suffered a similar fate. Once mighty Preston North End, frequent Cup finalists in the pre-TV era and First Division regulars since the inception of the League, dropped into the Second Division in 1962 and began a steady descent eventually ending up in the Fourth Division. The story at Blackburn, Bolton and Blackpool – all First Division and Wembley regulars in the 1950s and early 1960s – was similar. Local rivals such as Bury, Chester, Stockport and Rochdale who had never achieved much but had established themselves as more or less viable small-time businesses were likewise affected.

In 1960, before the advent of the *Match of the Day* and

televised European Cup era, Bury averaged a home gate of around 10,000 – fully a quarter of Manchester United's home gate, even though they were playing in the deeply inferior Third Division. A decade later Bury's crowd, despite the club moving up to the Second Division for much of the 1960s (and even having an outside chance of promotion to the same league as United in some years), amounted to less than one tenth of those turning up at Old Trafford. But there was another and more important factor in the yawning gulf emerging between televised glamour teams such as United and small fry such as Bury. By 1970, United's fan base, including armchair TV supporters (even though an efficient way of tapping them for money had not yet been devised), meant that in the space of a single decade United had moved from being four times the size of Bury to being 40,000 times as big.

In January 1969, less than a year after winning the European Cup, Matt Busby resigned as Manchester United manager. He had been in the job for twenty-four years. In that time he had taken a club saddled with debt and with a bombed-out stadium and turned it into what was to become one of the most famous and profitable clubs in the world. Busby had always been well paid by the standards of the time. Since 1967 he had enjoyed a salary of £10,000 a year and was provided by the club with a company Rover, upgraded to a Mercedes after the European Cup win and the ensuing knighthood. Busby planned for his retirement by paying £2,000 to buy the lease to the small shed in the Old Trafford car park which functioned as the Manchester United souvenir shop, which he was allowed to operate for a weekly rent of £5.

Under Busby, United had managed to recover from the

catastrophe of Munich, but the club was to take far longer to recover from the departure of Busby. The loss of the man who created Manchester United came just a few years after a boardroom coup that brought the club into the ownership of Louis Edwards, a Manchester butcher very much in the mould of Burnley's Bob Lord. Much of the Busby inheritance was squandered under the regime of Edwards and his son Martin, who inherited the club after Louis's death in 1978. After the dynamism of the Busby years United pretty much went to sleep through the 1970s and 1980s. A series of underachieving managers failed to win the League championship and thus United was locked out of the all-important European Cup. Vast sums were wasted in the transfer market and, in the wake of George Best, indiscipline was such that United became known as 'the drinking club', the haunt of demoralized, overpaid and cosseted players who could turn it on for the TV cameras in live FA Cup games – United appeared in a Wembley Cup final five times in the 1970s and 1980s, a better record than any other team – but did not have the stomach for the grind of the long championship season.

For one season, 1974–75, United even dropped into the Second Division. But the locked-in fan base acquired in the glorious Busby years was so loyal that even when playing in the Second Division United had an average home gate of 48,000 – the biggest in the country and almost twice the average for the First Division from which they had been relegated. Before the advent of *Match of the Day* United's home gates had hovered just above the average for the First Division as a whole with, usually, between three and five other clubs gaining greater support. After the *Match of the Day* effect got into its stride United had the biggest crowds in all but five of thirty-five seasons and its gates moved inexorably towards double those of the rest of the First Division. By the year 2000 the club was plausibly claiming that it would attract crowds of 100,000 or more, if Old Trafford could be expanded to cater for the demand.

While United failed to win the League, rivals Liverpool dominated the championship and therefore hogged the English place in the European Cup. It was partly because of the languid way in which United, the biggest club, was managed that football as a whole did not change much as a business during the 1970s. The biggest failure was not to capitalize on the relationship with television, which had been pioneered by Busby in the early years of the European Cup.

The importance of football to television had been demonstrated over and over since the triumph of the 1966 World Cup. The 1970 FA Cup final between Leeds and Chelsea had set a new ratings record with an audience of 20 million. The 1982 World Cup was to beat even that, and Liverpool's outings in Europe also drew huge audiences. But the main event of the English League was proving to be less attractive. Audiences for *Match of the Day* levelled off and even dipped in some seasons. Various reasons were put forward: the new problem of hooliganism tarnishing the game's image; the boredom of watching Liverpool win the competition year in, year out; and the fact that the best English footballers now tended to be transferred to much richer clubs in Italy and Spain, giving the English league a distinctly second-rate feel.

Edwards, as the man in charge of the League's biggest gun, made sporadic attempts to get a better deal from the television companies. But ITV and the BBC had learned to operate as a cartel. With only the odd hitch, such as the time ITV's Michael Grade made an improved 'Snatch of the Day' offer without telling the BBC (the deal was soon called off and reversed), the TV companies had managed to hold the price at the 1966 level, despite soaring inflation. By 1980 the First Division clubs were still getting only about £10,000 a year each from television, which, when adjusted for inflation, was far less than what they had been offered by ITV a quarter of a century earlier.

With United locked into a strange lethargy and football starting to slip from its central place in the nation's affections, the game's centre of gravity began to shift away from its traditional heartland in the north towards the media and financial power centres of London and the South. Within a few years, when the word 'City' was used in United's boardroom the club's directors would not be thinking about their footballing rivals a few miles down the road.

4.
Floating

Irving Scholar cut a strange figure in the traditional and insular world of English football. By the age of thirty-four, the former tea boy in a north London estate agent's had risen from standing on the Shelf, the terrace where the hard core Tottenham Hotspur fans gathered, to making millions as a property developer and taking ownership and control of the club.

His method of gaining control had been controversial. In sharp contrast to many other football chairmen Scholar was not especially interested in the social status attached to chairmanship. He was a razor-sharp modern business-man and deal-maker who roared around town in a flashy Range Rover with the number plate FA H1T. Unmarried, he liked the high life, lived for part of the year in Monte Carlo and had a reputation as something of a playboy.

In 1982 Irving Scholar and his business partner Paul Bobroff decided to buy Tottenham Hotspur, even though the existing regime of the Richardson family had no intention of selling it to them. To some it might have looked like an impossible task. The fact that football clubs did not run at a profit – and had never been designed to do so – combined with FA regulations disallowing the payments of dividends meant that their shares were rarely traded. Changes of ownership did take place, but almost always this was done on a friendly basis, with one local dynasty giving way to another at the invitation of the existing board. Hostile takeovers were unknown. The system was underpinned by an FA regulation that required all clubs participating in their competitions to insert a 'poison pill' into their articles of association, signing over their assets to the FA if the club ever stopped playing football. The intention was to prevent a businessman from buying a club, closing it down and selling off the assets to make a quick profit. Another regulation strictly limited the dividends that could be paid to shareholders and the remuneration that could be paid to directors. A final rule, also designed to keep clubs stable and in the 'right hands', specified that the existing chairmen had to approve any major transfer of shares – an arrangement unique in British business and one that ensured that clubs generally stayed in the hands of the original directors or their approved nominees for generations. All this was designed to protect the idea that club chairmen, directors and shareholders were selfless custodians of the club. Clubs were incorporated as limited companies only so that they could pay bills and borrow moderate amounts of money from banks.

The first breach in these formidable defences was made in the early 1960s when Louis Edwards began quietly buying small packets of Manchester United shares. Many of the holders – often elderly second- or third-generation descendants of the original shareholders – were delighted to be offered hundreds, or in some cases a few thousands, for the certificates they had previously assumed to be of only antique or sentimental value. Eventually Edwards bought a majority stake. But even then the ageing, outgoing chairman, Harold Hardman, might have been able to block a takeover if he had chosen to put the FA's regulations to the test. He decided not to do so and ownership of Manchester United passed to the Edwards family.

Louis Edwards would have had to have been psychic to envisage that the £45,000 he invested to buy control of United would, a single generation later, give his family

Chris Horrie

control of a complex leisure and entertainment company worth £1 billion. But it was a shrewd move anyway. After Louis's death in 1980 the chairmanship passed to his son Martin, who, after investing a further £600,000 in a rights issue, was eventually to reap a personal 'paper' profit in the region of £200 million. But the prospect of capital gain could not, back in 1964, have been Louis Edwards's main motivation. He was still of the generation who saw chairmanship of a football club as the highest form of civic honour – financially useful only in so far as it gave him personal and political clout and added prestige, and brought contracts for his main business, the wholesale meat trade.

It was Louis Edwards's example that Scholar and Bobroff now copied in order to gain control of Tottenham, after discovering that the rule giving existing chairmen a veto over share transfers was not as tight as many had assumed. A careful reading indicated that Richardson could veto share dealing only by members of the Tottenham board of directors. He had no control over the hundreds of others who might not even take much interest in the club's affairs any more, but who between them owned a majority of the shares. Scholar and Bobroff started poring over the dusty Tottenham share register, and set about contacting shareholders and buying their stakes stealthily in small parcels. One day Scholar turned up in the club's boardroom and declared himself – to considerable astonishment – to be the new chairman.

But unlike Edwards, Scholar had put the next part of the new financial equation in place. This was the simple but brilliant brainwave of setting up an entirely new company, free from League rules and restrictions, that would own the existing football club as a subsidiary. Tottenham was to be the first football PLC, issuing shares that, unlike those of the original FA-regulated football companies, paid dividends and entitled the holder to a share of the assets – in other words, shares that were as valuable as shares in any other publicly floated company and could be traded just as easily. It was this piece of clever financial engineering by Irving Scholar which ushered in a new financial age for football and opened the door to people who wanted to get involved in the game with an eye to making profits, and not just for the fun or glory of it.

Scholar's first task was to deal with Tottenham's massive debt. The old regime had overspent by about £1 million on building a prestigious but badly thought-out £3.5 million main stand. They had allowed Tottenham to accumulate what was routinely called 'the biggest debt mountain in British football'. Scholar was shocked by the scale of mismanagement. Simple matters such as VAT records had not been kept up to date, and one of his first acts was to fend off a court summons for non-payment. Rummaging around White Hart Lane the new owners found great wads of banknotes lying in the ticket office. Scholar listened with horror to the story of how a great pile of fivers handed over at the turnstiles had once spilled on to the office floor and had to be swept up by the cleaners. The only firm indicator of the club's position was the raw bank balance – and that was so bad that he had to ring the bank manager in Tottenham High Street to get permission for any spending over and above petty cash.

The position at Tottenham was made worse by the fact that in 1982 Britain was in the middle of its worst economic recession since the 1930s. There had been riots in the streets around Tottenham where unemployment, especially youth unemployment, was reckoned to be as high as 50 per cent. At the same time inflation was roaring. Football was far from unaffected. In just five years average First Division home gates had fallen by a third from around 30,000 to 20,000. As the economic crisis continued, the gap between soaring costs and declining incomes widened by the week.

Selling off players was the traditional option for a club in Tottenham's predicament. But Scholar, the fan from the terraces, did not want to do that. Besides, it was not really an option. The Richardson board had bought players at the top of the market – authorizing the spending of a record £1.4 million on two players (Steve Archibald and Garth Crooks) in 1980. Scholar was now stuck with the high wages and bonus payments which always form part of big transfer deals. Although Archibald was later sold on at a profit to Barcelona, in 1982 Scholar could safely reckon that the asset value of Spurs' players had halved in just a few years. With even Manchester United feeling the pinch, few English clubs had the money to buy players. It was a buyer's market and the only real buyers were the big Italian and Spanish clubs who, for most of the 1980s, found they could take their pick of the best English players.

Scholar decided that the only way forward for Tottenham was to develop a ramified leisure business with the football club at its core but by no means its most profitable activity. His radical first step was to create a new company – Tottenham Hotspur PLC – which would own the football club – Tottenham Hotspur Ltd – as just one of several subsidiaries in areas such as catering, publishing and branded sportswear. Since gate money was falling and the player transfer market was dead, Spurs would need all of these new sources of income to pay off the debts. Moreover, right from the start, Scholar also believed that all football clubs, including Spurs, could get more money from television if there were reforms to the management of the League and the FA and if a more aggressive and professional stand were taken in negotiations with the TV companies. But his most radical step of all was to float Tottenham Hotspur on the Stock Exchange, making it the first of what would become a clutch of football businesses.

Standing in the way of Scholar's master plan were the Football League and the regulations of the FA. The rule decreeing that if a club went bust its assets became the property of the League meant that no serious investor, especially no City institution, would put money into Tottenham because it did not have full control over its assets. Scholar side-stepped the problem by proposing that only the holding company, and not the club itself, would be floated. This arrangement stayed within the letter of the League's regulations, but definitely broke their spirit. Scholar expected a fight. But it never came. 'We kept waiting for somebody to tell us we couldn't do it, the League, the FA or somebody,' he later said. 'But nobody did. It just seemed that nobody had ever wanted to, so nobody had tested the rules.'

The flotation was a success. On 13 October 1983 3,800,000 shares in Tottenham Hotspur PLC, costing £1 each, sold out within minutes and the issue was four times oversubscribed. The flotation provided the new PLC with £3.8 million which, together with a previous £1.3 million from a rights issue in the still privately owned Tottenham Football Club, wiped out all the debts Scholar had inherited from the old regime. Scholar immediately started looking for new sources of income to fuel the brave new financial structure. The most obvious one was television.

*   *   *

Things had not changed much in the relationship between football and TV since the launch of *Match of the Day* in 1964. The League's Management Committee had maintained its ban on the screening of live League games. The issue continued to be the smaller clubs' fear that televised football would hit what remained of their gates, and since they had an equal say in the League's annual meetings, they always got their way.

Big clubs such as Liverpool, Arsenal and Manchester United – already getting large sums of money for one-off European games over which the League had no control – would have dearly liked to sell their League games as well. But the danger was that they would be thrown out of the League or, at least, massively fined if they tried. One possibility was for the big clubs to break away and set up their own 'Super League', an idea first aired at the time of the birth of ITV in 1957. For the big clubs there were two attractions: first, television companies would be prepared to pay far more for live games than for highlights; and second, that money could be kept by the big clubs and not shared with the rest.

In 1982 Manchester United joined forces with Everton, and threatened to break away and form the nucleus of a rival Super League, negotiating their own TV deal for live games and inviting other clubs to join them in a new competition. In order to appease United, Everton and other big clubs tempted by the breakaway, the League agreed to important changes. Firstly they conceded that clubs could keep all their home gate money, instead of sharing it with the visitors, bringing a significant immediate increase in income for well-supported clubs.

But the big clubs failed to get their own way over television rights. The League at last relented on the ban on live TV coverage, allowing a small number of live games to be shown on Sunday afternoon so that they did not present any threat to attendances on the traditional Saturday match day. This made football far more valuable to the TV companies but, still working as a cartel, BBC and ITV were able to hold the cost down, in 1983 making a 'take it or leave it' offer of only £2.5 million. The amount was tiny but worse still was the League's insistence that even this small sum should be shared equally between all the League clubs. Despite being the main attraction for TV, United's share of the money would be exactly the same as that due to Rochdale or Scunthorpe – a measly £30,000 a year. It was less than ITV had been prepared to pay for a single live European Cup tie twenty years earlier and amounted to less than one per cent of United's turnover at the time.

Edwards was naturally depressed about Manchester United's prospects after the débâcle of the 1983 TV negotiations. The club was still by far the best supported in the country and gate money was much higher now that it did not have to give away half the takings to visiting teams. But having a lot of supporters brought its own cost. United had not won the League championship for sixteen years. The vast crowds were frustrated and blamed Edwards. There were even signs that United's original TV-generated fan base was under threat from Liverpool, routine League winners in the 1970s and 1980s and now the club that a new generation of teenage TV-watching fans were more used to seeing play live in Europe. United's latest free-spending manager, Ron Atkinson, as well as the papers and various fan-power movements, were constantly on Edwards's back, demanding that he go even further into debt to buy players that might win the League, winning the right to play in the European Cup – the competition that really mattered.

Edwards had brought more money into the club by putting up ticket prices as much as he dared. But United still made a loss most years and Edwards did not have enough money even to redevelop the Old Trafford stadium, now shabby (and, possibly, dangerous). New sources of revenue had come from catering, corporate entertainment and sponsorship, but these activities alone could not turn United around and, anyway, depended like gate income on buying players in order to win trophies.

In desperation Edwards had turned to Sir Roland Smith, a Manchester business professor and corporate troubleshooter who had previously worked for the Edwards family's meat business. Smith joined the United board and at once began preparing the club for a stock market flotation – the only way in the short term to get more money into the club (and, as it happened, into Martin Edwards's pockets). The flotation plan naturally brought Edwards into close contact with Irving Scholar, who was preparing Tottenham's market flotation. Edwards and Scholar hit it off at once, both men seeing themselves as pioneers – modern, thrusting businessmen up against an elderly football establishment who, in Edwards's opinion, had arranged things so that the small clubs could cash in on the popularity of football as a TV sport created by United and other big clubs and 'bleed us to death'. In the summer of 1983 Scholar and Edwards went on a joint Tottenham–United tour to Swaziland where, among other things, both men took part in a football match staged between the management and non-playing staffs of the two clubs (Scholar's team beat Edwards's 8–0).

As things were to turn out Edwards's dealings with Scholar did not lead to an immediate market flotation for United. After Scholar's original triumph, Tottenham's share price had bombed, increasing scepticism in the City for the time being at least. But, crucially for the future of football, Edwards found that Scholar had done a great deal of detailed work aimed at increasing revenue from areas such as merchandising, publishing and TV rights. At once the alliance was cemented with joint publishing deals. To their horror Tottenham fans found that Scholar's Spurs-linked publishing company was soon pumping out tomes dedicated to the greater glory of Manchester United as well as their own team. Other initiatives included a plan for Scholar's Hummel sportswear subsidiary to produce United's kit. (Hummel's bid was not accepted by the United board, but proved useful when the club negotiated an improved deal with its traditional supplier, Umbro.) Scholar, hyperactive as usual, was full of useful advice on how United could follow his own example and make more money from catering, merchandising and even computerized ticket sales.

The most important result of the Edwards–Scholar relationship, however, was a tough new approach to TV rights negotiations. In 1983 Edwards had threatened the Football League with the prospect of a rival Super League that would do its own TV deal if they did not hold out for a vastly improved payment and, furthermore, then allow United and the other big clubs to keep most of it. The League had simply called Edwards's bluff and carried on as before. Now, in the run-up to the next round of negotiations, Edwards found that Scholar, with his better contacts in the London-based worlds of advertising, marketing and the media, had done much more detailed work on a possible breakaway.

After taking over at Tottenham, Scholar had immediately lined up the club with the Super League possibility – seeing it at least as a way of strengthening his hand against the League. But he had arrived too late to play much of a role in the 1983 negotiations. To move things on he now hired Alex Fynn, a consultant working for Saatchi and Saatchi, who, it was later claimed, first came up with the plan for what was to become the Premier League. Fynn took as his model the USA where sports such as American football received massive sums of money from sponsorship, merchandising and, above all, TV rights. English football had the potential to do the same, but was light-years behind America.

Advertising agencies such as Saatchi and Saatchi were expert at working out the exact value of programmes to ITV, based on knowledge of what was charged for adverts and how much ITV needed to spend on popular programmes – football for instance – that attracted the audiences advertisers wanted. There was no doubt that football was important to ITV. And, thanks to the League's cowardice and incompetence, as the likes of Edwards and Scholar saw it, they were getting it incredibly cheaply. England's campaign in the 1982 World Cup had attracted domestic audiences of over 10 million. It would have cost ITV at least £500,000 to buy in programmes (for example, recent Hollywood movies) that could be reliably expected to get that sort of audience. All the rest was simple arithmetic. A package of, say, twenty games between really big clubs such as Tottenham and United was worth £10 million. Moreover, just five clubs – the 'Big Five' in the First Division at the time: United, Liverpool, Everton, Arsenal and Tottenham – whose home gates accounted for more than a quarter of all football fans in the country – that could generate the sort of ratings ITV needed.

Instead of the £30,000 a year the likes of Tottenham and United were receiving, the Saatchis said they should be getting over £2 million each. That was just for starters. By creating a smaller Super League, with perhaps ten clubs instead of the twenty-two in the First Division, the Big Five could reduce the total number of games, hyping each one like a cup final. By reducing supply the price was bound to go up. And the vast television audiences likely for the new Super Games ('event-like' matches as the Saatchis put it) would lead to vast additional revenues from increased ticket prices, the value of sponsorship and pitch-side advertising, catering, corporate entertaining and TV-boosted American NFL-style merchandising.

All of this was based on the assumption of the Super League working with ITV where, ultimately, all the money would come from advertising. But by the early 1980s experience in America was showing that popular sport worked well on satellite and cable pay-TV. In the UK satellite and cable TV were just starting up. It would be a few years before they were serious players but, even at this stage, the Saatchis and more media-conscious figures such as Scholar had worked out that the pay-TV business could only put up the value of TV rights – perhaps enormously so.

The fact that five out of the ten clubs in the new League might get no television money in future was no great worry. They stood to lose only the £30,000 a year they were getting from the current arrangements. The big clubs could pay an equivalent sum, or perhaps much more, as an appearance fee for playing against the Big Five. Scholar's partner at Tottenham said that he was sure that the Big Five would be 'magnanimous and give some money to other clubs'. But he also stressed that it was 'essential that we keep the lion's share'.

Edwards was much more blunt. He said that the small clubs should be 'put to sleep'.

5.
Hooligans

It was called the 'English disease' – football hooliganism. Violence, death and disaster were nothing new at British football grounds, but in the 1984–85 season the sporadic tussles between gangs of supporters exploded into fighting on a scale not seen before.

It started with a pitched battle between Millwall skinheads and heavily outnumbered police at a live, televised FA Cup game at Luton. The toll of forty-seven injured established a new record in the unofficial hooligan league. The abiding image of the riot was of a Millwall skinhead putting the boot into a policeman who was trying to give the kiss of life to a collapsed colleague.

Next into the fray were the Chelsea mob, who smashed up the stands at Stamford Bridge, throwing seats and other debris on to the pitch during a League Cup semifinal against Sunderland. Ken Bates, the newly installed owner of Chelsea, announced that he was going to put a 12-foot electrified fence up around the pitch at Chelsea's stadium, similar to the one he used to control cattle at his Home Counties farm, to deal with the problem. (Only a veto from the Greater London Council prevented him from doing so.) Events at Luton and Chelsea were followed by a riot organized by a Manchester City gang at Notts County. A fight between Leeds and Birmingham supporters left a fifteen-year-old boy dead. A few weeks after that seventy England supporters were arrested after taking part in mass looting before an England international match in Finland.

The outcry following all this mayhem was such that on 1 April 1985 Prime Minister Margaret Thatcher called

FA and League chiefs to Downing Street and asked them what they were going to do about it. Put simply, the people running football had no idea. After the meeting FA Secretary Ted Crocker told the press that the hooligans were 'society's problem'.

But despite this pronouncement, the violence that seemed to be present to a lesser degree at or around every football ground in the country in the second half of the 1984–85 season was to continue. On the last day of the season an ancient, barely maintained and litter-strewn wooden stand at Valley Parade, home of Bradford City, caught fire. The flames spread quickly. Although most fans managed to escape on to the pitch, hundreds were trapped in the blaze and fifty-six died in the most horrific circumstances. The tragedy was shown on television and the following day the papers carried sickening pictures of traumatized victims crawling out from the billowing clouds of thick black smoke.

And the horror was not yet over. A few days later a fight during the European Cup final between Liverpool and Juventus at the Heysel stadium in Brussels led to the collapse of a wall which crushed hundreds and killed thirty-nine. Liverpool fans were blamed for the deaths and all English clubs were banned from European competitions until they sorted out the 'English disease'.

This series of catastrophes had an immediate financial effect on Manchester United and Tottenham, the two clubs making the running in the financial modernization of the football industry. The problems only confirmed the thinking of Martin Edwards and Irving Scholar that their old foes at the top of the FA and the Football League, as well as most other club chairmen, were not fit to run the modern game. The failure to make football profitable meant that there had been no money to invest in making stadiums safer. Many grounds were almost as dilapidated as Valley Parade. It made their pursuit of money all the more urgent.

The problem, as ever, was where the money would come from. The troubles of 1984–85 meant that Edwards's plan to follow Tottenham with a market flotation was ruled out completely. Tottenham's share price had been weak even before the season of disasters. It now hit the floor. The European ban was a particular blow for Tottenham and United. Scholar had spent millions in the previous season using part of his flotation money to buy players, including a record transfer fee to bring Chris Waddle to Spurs. The aim was to win the League and thus access some of the TV riches that could be claimed by qualifying for the European Cup. Edwards had spent even more on a series of record-breaking transfers with the same thing in mind. Now the money had been wasted. With no European places at stake, the English League was, in financial terms, hardly worth winning.

Edwards's depression, which started with the fiasco of the 1983 television rights negotiations, intensified. He had actually considered selling the club, rather than merely diluting his holding with a flotation, the previous year. Robert Maxwell, the owner of the *Daily Mirror*, two smallish football clubs (Derby and Oxford) and, coincidentally, a close media contact of Scholar, had tabled a £10 million offer. Edwards had been tempted but backed out thinking, before all the mayhem started, he might be better off with the flotation. Now he was stuck with ownership of a football club apparently doomed, like most of the others, to carry rising overheads and disastrously declining income. The impact of the European ban and the backwash of the hooligan problem led to a collapse in gates; even the crowd at United was well down. In a final irony, alcohol, the very foundation of

Scholar's and Edwards's plans for increased income from hospitality and catering, was banned at football grounds as part of the half-baked response to the hooligan problem. (The ban was later lifted for those with tickets to expensive executive boxes, and applied only to the hoi poloi.)

Bleak prospects for traditional areas of income placed more importance than ever on the campaign to get more money for TV rights. Here Edwards's dealings with Maxwell, as well as Scholar and his Saatchi advisers, were important. Maxwell knew more about TV finance and the cost and value of programming than any other football club chairman. He was a director of Central TV, the ITV franchise in the Midlands, and bought a lot of TV advertising designed to promote the *Daily Mirror*. What is more, he had lately bought into cable TV in anticipation of the launch of pay-TV in the 1990s and was already developing a pay channel linked to the *Mirror*, called SelecTV.

Maxwell had been as disgusted by the spineless performance of the League Management Committee during the 1982 TV negotiations as Scholar and Edwards and, like them, he was determined to get a much better deal when the contract came up for renegotiation in 1985. He had already managed to get a TV ban on shirt advertising lifted after a legal tussle with the BBC. Scholar and, especially, Edwards were deeply grateful. The fact that teams could turn themselves into human advertising hoardings exposed for periods much longer than the usual ad breaks every week on *Match of the Day* and on live ITV games vastly increased the value of shirt sponsorship. United had cashed in at once, signing the first multimillion long-term shirt sponsorship deal with the Japanese electronics firm, Sharp.

After this triumph Maxwell had barged his way on to

a special League subcommittee preparing the way for the 1985 contract renegotiation. Engaging in his usual megaphone diplomacy, using the back page of the *Daily Mirror*, which was read by millions of football fans, Maxwell immediately started castigating League chiefs as the 'Football Mismanagement Committee'. The paper's line never varied. The money needed to buy star players – the only thing the fans really cared about – could come only from a big TV rights deal. The *Mirror*'s (and Maxwell's) line was that football was worth at least £10 million, the figure arrived at by Scholar and the Saatchis. The *Mirror* started reporting rumours that unless the League managed to obtain this amount of money and, just as importantly, allowed the big clubs to keep all or most of it, the big clubs would walk out, and set up their own rival competition.

With Maxwell leading the way in public, Edwards and Scholar started to put some flesh on the bones of the Super League idea. They were determined that if they were forced in the 1985 negotiations to use the threat of a breakaway, they would have to be ready to carry it out if they did not get their way. A crucial event was the arrival of David Dein as the effective financial power at Arsenal. Dein, like Scholar, was a self-made millionaire who shared Scholar's, Maxwell's and Edwards's dim view of the existing League Management Committee. It meant that the number of clubs now seriously prepared to contemplate a break away had expanded from the original partnership of United and Everton in 1982 to include Tottenham and Arsenal. Furthermore, unlike in 1982, this powerful group had the detailed research and planning commissioned from the Saatchis by Scholar and powerful media and legal support from Maxwell and the *Daily Mirror*. With the addition of Everton's

Chris Horrie

Philip Carter and Liverpool's Noel White the Big Five chairmen began to meet regularly at the Park Lane Hotel in Mayfair to compare notes over issues such as market flotation, merchandising, sponsorship and, most important of all, getting a better TV deal backed by the serious threat of a breakaway.

Television executives, getting wind of all this, entered the negotiations in an equally determined frame of mind. Working more closely than ever, John Bromley of ITV and Jonathan Martin of the BBC offered only £4.5 million for a package of nineteen live games and an unlimited number of *Match of the Day* highlights – a mere £2 million more than they had paid in the humiliating 1983 deal. Maxwell's *Daily Mirror* propaganda machine was pumped up to full blast, but the TV team remained resolute. 'Football rates itself far too highly,' Jonathan Martin told the papers. 'It has no God-given right to be on television. It is not our job to underwrite and subsidize the game.' Martin said that in many ways football, especially after the horrors of the 1984–85 season with collapsing attendances, the sale of star players to Italian and Spanish clubs together with the European ban, was less attractive than ever as a TV spectacle. He then issued what amounted to a threat. If the League did not accept the improved offer the BBC and ITV had put on the table, they would walk away. Football would not get a penny from television and it would disappear from the nation's screens, hitting pitch-side advertising income. 'We don't depend on football and if it loses its slot there is no knowing if it will ever get it back.'

The League Management Committee collapsed at once and recommended acceptance of the joint BBC–ITV offer to a meeting of all 92 League chairmen. The small clubs were, as ever, inclined to accept what was on offer and think themselves lucky. But the Big Five let it be known that they were deeply unhappy and might be forced to move ahead with the breakaway Super League. Inspired leaks printed all over the back pages of Maxwell's *Daily Mirror* convinced many that the Big Five were serious. The prospect of a sort of reverse ejection from a league including the Big Five clubs put the fear of God into many small club chairmen. Also, backed by these threats, Maxwell produced a performance of such violent verbal force at the meeting, denouncing the 'Mismanagement Committee' for selling out too cheaply and 'killing the game', that the cowed chairmen decided to reject the offer, allowing Maxwell and the TV subcommittee to go back and see if they could negotiate a better deal.

The approach Maxwell took was the basic business tactic of getting ITV and the BBC to bid against each other. At a meeting between the Big Five chairmen and television executives Maxwell said that he had insider information from the TV companies which showed that football was worth 20 times what they were offering to pay. £90 million a year to them. When Philip Carter of Everton doubted this, Maxwell raged: 'Don't give in to these mad people from television.' But the TV executives were having none of it. They called Maxwell's bluff and announced failure to reach agreement. Their offer was still on the table, but unless the League accepted it no games at all in the 1985–6 season, due to start in just a few weeks, would be shown. In a final insult Jonathan Martin said that the BBC would fill the gap by showing more snooker, the new televised sport sensation, which, it was pointed out, got higher ratings than most football matches for a fraction of the cost.

Chris Horrie

The threat of a TV 'blackout', as it was called, immediately plunged the League into crisis. Norwich City chairman Sir Arthur South demanded that Maxwell and the Big Five back down and accept what was on offer. When they would not, Sir Arthur resigned. The television companies carried out their threat to drop football from the schedules and, for the first time since 1964, there was no League football – not even highlights – on TV.

The effect was dramatic. Ever since TV had arrived on the scene the conventional wisdom in the League was that screening a game would lead to a drop in gate money as fans stayed at home to watch the match in the comfort of their living rooms. Back in the 1950s fees offered by TV were described as 'compensation' for potential dips in gate money. What happened in August 1985 was to destroy that myth for good and prove the new reality – that football had become in effect a form of television entertainment. The total absence of TV coverage was followed by the biggest single drop in gates, especially in the First Division, in the history of football. The Big Five, who were most used to being on *Match of the Day*, were the hardest hit. Tottenham's home gate collapsed from well over 20,000 to under 15,000 – despite the team having finished third in the League the previous season. As the untelevised season went on, Tottenham's gates started to drop towards 10,000 and a home game against Birmingham City established a new record low of 9,359. The violence of the previous season doubtless played its part in deterring people from turning up. But many of the worst affected and most hooligan-ridden clubs were in the lower divisions where gates did not decline to anything like the same extent.

Maxwell, Scholar, Edwards and the other Big Five chairmen were fingered as the villains of the piece. It was their hard line which had resulted in the disappearance of football from the screens. The small clubs had always been against them, but now even medium-sized clubs rose in revolt and started campaigning for an immediate capitulation in order to get the TV cameras switched back on. Many were still smarting over the 1983 decision to allow the big clubs to keep all their gate receipts. Now it looked as if 'greedy' upstarts such as Edwards, Scholar and Dein were trying to cut the financial lifeline of television income. Fifty thousand pounds – which was roughly the figure each club stood to receive from the offer – might be peanuts to the likes of Manchester United or Arsenal, but it was a huge sum to the likes of Grimsby Town or Exeter City and a significant amount even for smaller First Division regulars such as Coventry City or Southampton.

By September the pressure to settle with the TV companies was becoming intense. Scholar reacted by sounding out the possibility of a new deal. The £4.5 million was still on the table and there was now no chance of getting the offer increased. But this did not mean that the big clubs could not end up better off if they played their cards right. It was time to activate the Super League plan. A breakaway of ten top clubs could take the £4.5 million and divide it up between themselves instead of sharing it with the others. That way each Super League club would get £450,000, compared with the £30,000 they received under the 1983 deal.

The Big Five held a special meeting at Old Trafford at which, after all the years of talk, the momentous decision to put the Super League plan into action was made. The proposed breakaway was immediately leaked to the *Daily Mail*, which splashed the story under the headline 'SUPERLEAGUE REBELLION'. The paper's report detailed the Saatchis' plan for the Big Five to resign from the Football League – which was entirely within their individual power – and form a new association to run an alternative competition. The report added that the Big Five would be inviting 'between six and thirteen' other teams to join them, meaning that the new league would consist of all the best supported and TV-friendly clubs in England. The decision to expand membership of the proposed breakaway from the ten originally envisaged in the Saatchi plan to as many as eighteen was a clever political move. It meant that as many as fifty clubs might think – in tune with their eternally optimistic attitude – they had an outside chance of getting one of the non-Big Five places in the new set-up, at least within a couple of seasons.

There was consternation at the League's headquarters in the genteel but run-down northern seaside resort of Lytham St Anne's. League secretary Graham Kelly, a plump, bespectacled and quietly spoken bureaucrat, began chanting the word 'compromise' like a mantra. If the existing Football League could prevent clubs from being promoted to or relegated from the new breakaway competition, they might be able to strangle the Premier League at birth. Many clubs, including within living memory Manchester United and Tottenham, had been relegated from the First Division, and the threat of this happening was the main attraction for many supporters in seasons when their team had little chance of winning the championship. In the mid-1980s the Big Five clubs were starting to move away from the others, although the gap was not as great as it was to become in the 1990s.

Kelly and the League's other main card was European competition. The European Cup and subsidiary competitions such as the European Cup Winners' Cup and the

UEFA Cup were organized by UEFA, the European federation of national football associations. The selection of who took the places allocated to English clubs was technically in the gift of the FA, UEFA's affiliate in England. Winning the FA Cup entailed automatic qualification for the European Cup Winners' Cup, which was the senior UEFA competition in the same way that the English FA Cup predated the League championship. It was up to the FA to nominate a club to play in the European Cup (later Champions' League). In theory members of the FA's Management Committee could pick any club they liked, though in practice they always chose the winners of the existing First Division. It was possible that they would ignore the proposed breakaway Super League and continue to nominate the champions of Kelly's denuded Football League. If that meant Oxford United, winners of the Second Division in 1985, instead of First Division champions Everton that would doubtless cause a furore. But with English teams banned from playing in Europe for the next five years, there would be plenty of time for rival sets of lawyers and committee fixers to get to work.

With all these threats and counter-threats in the air an additional element of drama was introduced by Gordon Taylor, the secretary of the Professional Footballers' Association, in effect the players' trade union. Taylor was dead set against the Super League because, he believed, it would lead to dozens of small clubs going bust, making hundreds of his members redundant and, in addition, forcing down wages in non-Super League clubs. The strike threat was taken seriously and was to prove an important deterrent to Scholar, Edwards and the others.

Taylor and Graham Kelly organized a meeting at

a hotel near Heathrow to thrash out a compromise between the Big Five and the others. The Five were represented by Scholar, Edwards and Philip Carter of Everton. They lined up against a small-club delegation led by Lawrie McMenemy of Sunderland, Bill Fox of Blackburn and Ron Noades, the combative chairman of Crystal Palace. There were no members of the League Management Committee present. Agreement on the first point came quickly. Scholar, Edwards and Carter persuaded Taylor to call off the strike threat in return for which they would stop any immediate move towards a Super League. The Big Five were prepared to do this because they had already decided that there was no need for a breakaway with all the potential complications over promotion, relegation and European places. They proposed, in effect, detaching the First Division from the rest of the league and making it function in more or less the same way as a Super League.

The new 'Super' First Division now being proposed would still technically be under the control of the Football League in Lytham but in reality the power would pass to the big clubs. Instead of each of the ninety-two clubs having a single vote in League meetings the Big Five demanded that those in the First Division be given two votes each, giving them, as things stood in 1985, forty-eight votes against sixty-eight. It meant they would have to persuade only ten or so small clubs to vote with them on any matter to gain a majority. This in itself was a huge shift in power. But, in addition, the Big Five insisted that the League Management Committee should be reorganized to give the First Division clubs a majority.

This was as near to complete independence for the First Division as the Big Five dare go. And there were to be other changes. The original Saatchi idea was that the Super League should have ten clubs, each playing each other four times (instead of the existing twenty-four playing each other twice). This arrangement would have maximized the potential revenue from TV by creating more of the 'event-like' games (producing twice as many Manchester United–Arsenal type fixtures) that attracted a large TV audience, while cutting out all the dross. But it had already been decided that such a dramatic reduction in the number of clubs was politically impossible – at least for the time being. For now the Big Five proposed a reduction in the number of teams in the Super First Division from the existing twenty-four to twenty-two over three years, followed by a vaguer prospect of reducing the number to twenty and then eighteen or fewer in the future. But the most important change concerned what had caused the drama in the first place – television money. The Big Five wanted the new First Division to keep half of whatever ITV and the BBC came up with.

Taylor for the PFA, McMenemy and the other small club representatives agreed to all these demands, and they were set out in what became known as the 'Heathrow Agreement'. The proposals were put to a meeting of all club chairmen, who were told that unless they agreed the threat to break away would be revived. The Heathrow Agreement was accepted. The existing members of the League Management Committee put themselves up for a vote of confidence and, with the First Division clubs using their new voting power for the first time, they were all booted out. The outgoing League president, Jack Dunnett of Notts County, was replaced by Philip Carter, who had emerged as the main spokesman of the Big Five (being less objectionable to the minnows than Scholar or Edwards). It was the first time in the

Chris Horrie

League's history that an incumbent president had not been re-elected.

Carter went back to the television companies and announced the League was now prepared to accept the 'insulting' £4.5 million offer for live ITV games and *Match of the Day* made before the start of the season. The agreement that the First Division clubs would keep half of the total pot of TV money meant that the Big Five (like all other First Division clubs) would receive around £100,000 each – well short of the £1 million they thought they should be getting, but a step in the right direction. But the TV companies were still playing hard-ball. The collapse in gates and the fact that their ratings had hardly suffered at all from the absence of football from the screens meant that they were prepared to offer just £1.5 million for the rest of the season, take it or leave it. Carter, thoroughly humiliated in his first outing since the triumph of the Heathrow Agreement, had no choice but to accept.

After all the fuss, the Big Five received about £30,000 each from the deal – exactly what they had got in 1983. Football returned to the nation's television screens and, significantly, crowds at live games increased immediately and dramatically; by the end of the season, which had started with a collapse in attendances, total gates were hardly down on the previous season. The effect of the recovery was to strengthen the hand of the TV executive who said that the blackout had shown that television acted as a form of advertising for the game. Some even claimed that the football clubs should pay television – and not the other way round – for the privilege of being televised. With their hand strengthened in this way the television companies were able to hold down the price for the next full season at £3.1 million. ITV insisted on showing eighteen games instead of the ten they had bought in 1983. Although the total sum had gone up slightly, television companies had actually reduced the amount they were paying per game.

Edwards at Manchester United was so distraught that he again considered selling the club. But it was unlikely that there would be many buyers. The Super League project had failed to unlock the huge new revenues he needed if anyone was ever going to be able to redevelop Old Trafford, win the championship and, most important of all, interest the City in a flotation.

Others, including Scholar and Robert Maxwell – now increasingly entangled in Tottenham's finances as well as in League affairs – were prepared to be more patient. The pitiful TV deal of 1986 had just two years to run. When the time came to renegotiate it, changes in the TV industry would shift the balance of power massively towards football and the Big Five in particular. If they hung on in there, massive sums of money would soon be there for the taking.

Meanwhile, over on the tropical north-eastern coast of South America, an event was about to take place which would put a rocket under English football, changing it for ever.

6.
Destiny

11 December 1988, Kourou, French Guiana

After four days of torrential rain and high winds the black tropical storm clouds roll away, revealing brilliant blue skies. Sunlight glints on the sleak silver lines of the European Space Agency's commercial space rocket, Ariane 44. Following several days of nerve-jangling delays Ariane's thrusters finally burst into life with an enormous explosion, flames shooting in all directions. The unmanned rocket begins to lift into the air, slowly straining against gravity and somehow, unbelievably, stays upright. After a few moments it seems to wobble. The hearts of those watching skip a beat. Images of the implosion of NASA's manned Challenger space-shuttle two years before are still fresh in everyone's mind. But the rocket continues on its way and soon is nothing more than a wisp of twisting vapour trail disappearing into the blue.

ESA cargo flight V27 carried in its nose-cone the 1768 kg Astra 1A telecommunications satellite owned by a consortium of British broadcasters including the ITV company Thames Television and Rupert Murdoch's Sky Television. Richard Dunn, managing director of Thames, later remembered the moment: 'I watched £7 million of my shareholders' funds tied around the nose-cone of that damn rocket. Fortunately it worked. It did what it was supposed to do. It opened its little solar panels and everyone breathed a huge sigh of relief.' Hours later the Astra satellite took up its stationary position at 19.2° East, ready to transmit up to sixteen subscription/television channels to anyone in western and central Europe who had a satellite dish and a box of electronics to decode the signals. The age of British satellite television had arrived.

Rupert Murdoch, owner of the *Sun* and a string of other newspapers around the world, had always wanted to break into British television. In the 1970s he had owned a slice of the London ITV company, London Weekend Television. But British media regulation law meant that he could not have outright ownership or control over a TV company unless he sold off his newspapers. Since Murdoch's *Sun* was to become probably one of the most profitable newspapers in the world there was no chance of him doing that.

But by the early 1980s developments in technology would enable him to become a key part of the British broadcasting establishment by the back door. The new technology was cable and satellite TV and, better still, it allowed operators to charge viewers for subscriptions instead of relying on the more unpredictable business of collecting advertising revenues. And so Murdoch's Sky TV was born. In the mid-1980s Sky was established as a pan-European broadcaster – a very small-scale operation, broadcasting a single channel consisting largely of cheap American imports and endless repeats of low-budget British comedy shows, watched mainly, if at all, on European subscription-only cable TV stations (most of its viewers, at one point, were in Belgium).

The technology continued to increase in sophistication, and by the time of the launch of the Astra satellite, the opportunity was there to broadcast a whole clutch of channels branded together as 'pan-European' Sky (to get round the rule preventing Murdoch from owning a British TV operation) and, possibily, sold to subscribers for a lot of money.

Chris Horrie

Murdoch's strategy for Sky was simple from the start. He wanted the rights to show live football exclusively on the system. His experience of pay-TV in America, alongside endless detailed market research reports, showed that anywhere in the world there were only three things that people would pay to watch on television: pornography, 'hot' live sport and recent Hollywood movies. In the UK porn was out for regulatory reasons. Murdoch had bought a huge number of Hollywood films, and the few people who had signed up for Sky had done so mainly to watch the films. But in Britain films alone could not do the trick. The UK had the largest number of video recorders of any country in the world. If people wanted to watch a film on TV they tended to pop down to the local video hire shop rather than pay a much bigger sum up-front for a satellite movie channel. That left sport. And in England sport meant league football.

One problem for Murdoch was that another pay-TV operator, British Satellite Broadcasting, had also entered the market, backed by big blue-chip companies such as Granada TV. BSB, with its rival 'squariel' system, made the early running, buying up the rights to many of the best Hollywood movies and announcing the company's arrival on the scene by also making a massive offer for rights to show live League football.

This was the moment that Irving Scholar, Robert Maxwell and some of the more astute club chairmen had been waiting for. The arrival of pay-TV, delayed though it was for various political and technical reasons, meant that the rights to live football would go through the roof.

But the chairmen were not the only ones watching these developments. Greg Dyke, the ITV executive in charge of football negotiations for the whole network, had been tracking developments since the early 1980s. His experience of the television business in America had convinced him that an operator like Sky could quickly make a deep impact on a country like the UK, at a time when many others at the top of ITV and the BBC tended to dismiss satellite and cable as gimmicks that presented little threat to the existing system. Dyke realized that the battle with pay-TV would be fought over access to football. It was football that had persuaded many to buy their first TV sets in the 1950s; and it was football that could persuade people to now buy a satellite dish. Dyke, aware of the threat, tried to convince others in ITV that the network would have to give football a much better deal if they were to stop the sport defecting to one or other of the new pay-TV operators.

Dyke also made it his business to stay close to the Big Five chairmen. He impressed them on a personal level, presenting himself as a self-made man who had risen, like them, through sheer talent and energy. He was a modernizer and innovator who hated pomposity, embraced change and was prepared to think the unthinkable – the launch of a breakaway Super League, for example. He was also a Manchester United fan (later joining United's board to advise on television matters) and so was naturally close to Martin Edwards. As a Londoner, and playing the streetwise Cockney wheeler-dealer, Dyke became very friendly with David Dein of Arsenal and, especially, Irving Scholar, winning their trust by admitting that ITV and the BBC had operated as a cartel in the past (something still officially denied at the time) and promising to treat them more fairly in future. Dyke was absolutely determined that football should not be bought up by satellite TV, which would present a serious threat to his main preoccupation – the financial health of ITV.

In June 1988, as Dyke had feared, British Satellite Broadcasting fired the opening salvo by publicly offering £11 million a year to the League for the rights to a number of live games to be shown on the new satellite service when it went on air, as planned, in a few years' time. But that was just for starters. BSB was offering to pay up to £25 million a year, more than ten times the amount then paid by ITV and the BBC, as its audience grew. If things went according to plan, the satellite station would easily be able to afford it since every new punter who bought a dish to watch live football paid a subscription. There was a direct link between the number of people watching, the revenue the channel collected and the amount it could afford to pay for the rights. On the other hand, without live football BSB might sell hardly any dishes at all.

The economics were entirely different for ITV. Football attracted a decent audience and was worth showing if it could be obtained cheaply enough. But the experience of the TV blackout of 1985 had shown that the ratings would not collapse if there was no live League football in the schedule. Buying football was not a matter of life and death, as it was for BSB.

There was no way Dyke could match the £25 million a year BSB was talking about paying when the system was properly up and running with a decent number of subscribers. Even matching the seed corn £11 million on offer for the first year would involve more than doubling what ITV and the BBC combined had previously paid. But there was another way forward. Dyke focused not on the League as a whole, but on the Big Five clubs, the only ones ITV was really interested in screening and the only ones, in reality, whose games were worth anything to ITV. BSB's bid looked massive, but under the terms of the Heathrow Agreement the £25 million would be split 50/50 between the First Division and the rest of the League and then split again equally between the twenty-two First Division clubs. That meant that the Big Five would get £500,000 a year each (at the same time as clubs in the bottom divisions, the Rochdales, Scunthorpes and Northamptons, who United's Martin Edwards wanted to have 'put to sleep', would siphon off about £200,000 a year each – perhaps equivalent to ten years' gate money and enough to put them back on their feet).

Dyke immediately revived Scholar's original Saatchi-inspired ten-club Super League plan. If the TV deal was done between the Big Five and five other clubs invited to join any new Super League, he could afford to pay each of the ten double what they would get from BSB. It would cost him only five or six million a year but would give the big clubs more than what they would get as their share of BSB's four-year deal – which is exactly what he now offered the Big Five chairmen over dinner at the headquarters of LWT. Newcastle, Nottingham Forest, Sheffield Wednesday, Aston Villa and West Ham were chosen to join the original Big Five, creating an 'ITV Ten'. The Big Five had fewer qualms about upsetting the League and the FA than in 1985, when they had first threatened a breakaway in anger. They had decided that there was no chance of the FA being able to persuade UEFA that European places belonged to the winners of the rump Football League when the breakaway would include all the best known English clubs. The attraction of the ITV Ten League, Arsenal's David Dein told the press, was that it 'placed us in control of our own destiny'. The big clubs were simply fed up with making compromises with the rest of the League and now, more than ever, saw no reason why all the money being put into football by television should not be channelled to them.

But once the ITV Ten plan was made public the Football League, under pressure from small clubs naturally much more inclined to accept the riches being offered to them by BSB, took out an injunction to prevent the breakaway going ahead. Events followed the same pattern as in 1985. Dyke attended an emergency meeting of First Division clubs (only) held at Aston Villa at which it was agreed to completely outmanoeuvre the League by extending the ITV Ten to all twenty-two First Division clubs. After this clever political move what might have been called the 'ITV First Division' threatened to walk out of the Football League unless the Heathrow Agreement was altered to allow them to keep 75 per cent of the TV money as opposed to the 50 per cent they had won in 1985. This meant that the First Division clubs would get £8.5 million a year between them, compared with the £1.8 million they had got from the previous deal. The amount each non-First Division club received doubled yfrom around £20,000 to £40,000, but was much less than what they had stood to get from a deal with BSB.

The 1988–89 season started with live football taking place every Sunday afternoon under the title of *The Big Match* at ITV's preferred time in the schedule, 5 p.m. on Sundays. What was not made public at the time was the existence of a secret protocol between Dyke and the Big Five chairmen guaranteeing them a certain number of appearances. This had been agreed when the decision was made to extend the threatened breakaway from ten to all twenty-two First Division clubs. The effect was to give the Big Five a much bigger share of the £8.5 million pot (since payment was made partly on the basis of the number of appearances), as well as extra revenue from pitch-side advertising, shirt sponsorship and merchandising resulting from prime-time exposure on screen.

The domination of *The Big Match* and the hogging of appearance money by the Big Five came to be deeply resented by the chairmen of smaller First Division clubs, some of whom formed the view that they had in effect been conned and were being treated as barely tolerated make-weights. Dyke had a difficult job keeping the Big Five chairmen in line. Martin Edwards thought the big clubs should be getting all of ITV's money and clashed with ambitious smaller club chairmen such as Ken Bates of Chelsea and Ron Noades of Crystal Palace who were starting to throw their weight about and wanted a bigger share. Things were not helped by Dyke's habit of boasting about his own cleverness in outmanoeuvring the League chairmen. At the Edinburgh festival Dyke claimed that he had 'paid £5 million more than football merited in order to prevent BSB scheduling forty-two League games a season which might persuade people to buy a dish'.

But almost as soon as the new arrangements were in place and the threat of a breakaway appeared to be history, the smaller clubs began to reassert their power. At a League meeting in September 1989 Philip Carter of Everton was voted out of his position as League president and David Dein was ousted from the League Management Committee, accused of showing too much bias towards the Big Five. There followed damaging rows with Dyke over the timing of *Big Match* games. They were played at the untraditional time of 5 p.m. to suit ITV's schedule, resulting in away fans sometimes not getting home much before midnight. There was an especially fierce row over Dyke's refusal to postpone a particularly enticing audience-grabbing fixture between Arsenal and Liverpool, due to take place three days before an England international. All the other teams had agreed to give their players a rest. But Dyke would not relent. Weak in diplomatic skills, the ITV chief said that he had paid for the matches and he would show them when it suited him, not the rest of football. His approach did nothing to quell the growing feeling that ITV had bought football and was determined to turn it into a television show run for the benefit of the Big Five and the TV business.

Ken Bates, owner of Chelsea, had been to the fore in the anti-Big Five and anti-ITV agitation and was to play an even bigger role after Chelsea were promoted back into the First Division in 1989. He immediately tabled a demand that the First Division should return to being a twenty-two-club competition. A reduction to twenty clubs had been agreed in 1988 with, if anything, an intention to go down to eighteen clubs in future as part of the settlement which persuaded the Big Five to call off the breakaway. A return to a twenty-two-club league was a step in the direction of re-establishing the old order. The effect would be to allow more clubs to share the TV money and, coincidentally, lessen the chances of Chelsea being relegated back to the Second Division. The Big Five voted against the proposed re-enlargement, but it went through anyway.

For the Big Five, still fuming over the removal of Carter and Dein from the League Management Committee, the re-enlargement was a turning point. They still felt that they were giving away far too much of the TV money to the likes of Chelsea. Now they would have to share even more. As they saw it, the League was welching on the 1988 agreement which had led them to call off the breakaway. In the interests of compromise they had agreed to an eighteen-club league, instead of the ten-club set-up arranged with Dyke and ITV. The result had been the sacrifice of almost half the television income they were individually due. Now, with Edwards at United desperate to increase revenues in advance of his planned flotation and all the others in need of a cash infusion, they decided for the third and final time to organize a breakaway.

7.
Moment of Truth

Brian Clough marches up and down the echoing changing room buried deep underneath the stand at Hillsborough football stadium, home to Sheffield Wednesday and venue of the 1989 FA Cup semi-final between Liverpool and Nottingham Forest. It is a pleasant, spring Saturday afternoon. Clough has been looking forward to the match. He has already been twice the winner of the European Cup, three times the winner of the Football League and has a host of other trophies on the shelf, but the FA Cup is the one competition he has never won as a manager. But now Clough is irritated, impatient, irascible. The players sit in facing rows, fidgeting, annoyed, waiting, full of tension.

Ten minutes earlier his team, Nottingham Forest, had been on the pitch, psyched up for kick-off. Play had started, prompting an almighty surge among the Liverpool fans tightly packed on the standing-only Leppings Lane terrace behind the Liverpool goal. For a minute or two it looked as if the rowdiness and ructions might pass, but then large numbers of Liverpool supporters started climbing over the high security fence screening off the terrace from the field of play to prevent pitch invasions. But this time the 'invaders' did not seem very interested in what was happening on the field. They just wanted to get away from the terrace. As more Liverpool fans poured on to the pitch the referee stopped the match and ordered the teams back to their dressing rooms until order could be restored.

Clough paces and looks at his watch, waiting for the referee to call them back to resume the game. The minutes tick by. If the situation is not sorted out soon the match might have to be called off. The players have to warm up and go through exercises before it is safe to put their muscles through the physical crunch of a top-flight football game. But it is not the referee but a ground official who eventually appears. 'They think there are casualties,' he says. 'They think there are people dead.' Nobody says very much. Even Clough is lost for words. More reports come. It is true. There are dead bodies. Five dead . . . seven . . . ten . . . fourteen . . .

A similar scene is unfolding in the Liverpool dressing room. Manager Kenny Dalglish had taken his team off first and had not even noticed any problems beyond a policeman running on to the pitch and speaking agitatedly to the referee just before the game was stopped. He led the players back to the dressing room and told them to stay there while he set off to find out what was going on. The moment he closed the door he spotted a small group of Liverpool fans further down the corridor. 'Kenny! Kenny!' they yelled in anguish. 'There are people dying out there.' The garbled news that the crush has led to hundreds of injuries in the Leppings Lane stand hits Dalglish like a sledgehammer. His own son Paul was in the crowd. Sick with fear, he can hardly function until he spots the boy wandering safely on the pitch.

The police gathered both managers and they made their way out on to the field to call for calm over the PA, but either the microphone was not working or their appeals were drowned out in the developing mayhem. The police led the two managers back into the bowels of the stand, through a maze of corridors, towards the police control room to use the main Tannoy system. The mind plays funny tricks at moments of great trauma and Clough later said that his most vivid memory of the day was passing through the kitchens and seeing row upon row of meat pies and pasties set out neatly on trays ready for half-time. 'I can still see the icing-sugar on rows of fruit pies,' he remembered many years later. 'And the chefs still working on refreshments to be sent up to the restaurants and VIP quarters. They were not to know what was happening outside.'

Outside, Forest fans were by now climbing over the fences at their end of the ground, rushing towards the Liverpool supporters – either to join in the excitement or looking for a fight. They had seen the Liverpool fans apparently 'vandalizing' the security fence and pitch-side advertising hoardings, tearing them down and carrying them off. The Forest fans had no idea that the Liverpool pitch invasion was in fact a desperate attempt to escape from being crushed to death. The advertising hoardings were being pulled down to be used as make-shift stretchers to carry away the dead and injured, many of whom were the smallest and weakest – children pushed to the front, right up against the fences. The reality was that far too many people had been let into the Leppings Lane terrace. The police had then closed the exits and the terrace's design had funnelled a massive weight of flesh and bone down the steep incline, crushing those up against the security fence at the bottom. One small mercy was that the fences were not electrified – as they might have been if Chelsea chairman Ken Bates had been given his way. The final death count was 96.

Clough, worshipped by the fans and seen as a virtual father-figure by many, appealed to them to behave themselves. 'Don't let's have any more trouble,' he said over the loudspeaker system. But by then everyone in the ground was aware that a catastrophe had taken place. There was no danger of any fighting. Clough went back to the dressing room and told the Forest team: 'Get straight in the bath – we're not going out there again.' The referee and the police advised him to remain where he was and 'stay calm'. He was even told that the game might restart. But Clough was having none of it, briskly telling the players to get dressed quickly and get ready to leave. His order was enough. No explanations were needed; they would find out what had happened soon enough. The police, trained to prevent people from leaving the scene of a crime or accident and probably with the routine idea of taking statements in mind, told Clough and the players to stay where they were. But the manager more or less barged past them, leading his team away and on to their coach, in which they travelled, silent, back to Nottingham, listening stunned to news reports of the mounting death toll. By the time the game was officially called off at 3.30 p.m. they were already on the motorway.

As the survivors made their way back home the city of Liverpool closed ranks in shocked disbelief. Crowds began to gather at the Shankly Gates outside Liverpool's ground to place tributes of flowers. The scene gave a terrible poignancy to Bill Shankly's famous aphorism: 'Football isn't a matter of life and death – it's more important than that.' But, in an age of mass media, the pain was not yet over. The next day, as the city struggled to pull itself together and get on with the business of organizing an endless series of funerals, the world's media turned up in force, focused on the grisly business of prizing pictures and tear-jerking stories from parents, relatives and friends of the dead. The *Sun* newspaper alone was reckoned to have sent eighteen reporters to Liverpool. The following day's tabloid front pages would later be remembered as some of the most shameful in newspaper history. Usually, during a tragedy – plane crash, mining disaster, earthquake or fire – it was rare to have photographers and journalists in place and even rarer to have them capture the actual moment of death. But at Hillsborough the usual contingent of sports photographers was present in force and, the moment the disaster began to unfold, they had turned their lenses on the crowd.

The *Mirror* caused the most anguish, leading off sixteen pages of photographs with a massive front-page picture showing a pile of bodies of the dead or dying lying on top of each other. Other pictures showed the faces of youngsters in their death throes, their faces turning blue as they were crushed against the fence. The insensitivity was astounding. At the time there was no official list of those dead. Some families had not been notified that their relatives were among the fatalities and were clinging on to the desperate, irrational hope that their failure to come home might have another explanation. Real anger was now mixed with the grieving. Why had they printed the photos? What did it add to the understanding of what had happened? How could they be allowed to make money by selling pictures of the dying? There was the chilling thought that the last thing some of the dying would have seen on earth was a tabloid photographer pointing a camera at them, and excitedly clicking away. Moreover, even though the photographers might not have been in a position to help, why had they stood there taking pictures instead of trying – somehow, anyhow – to rescue the victims who were only inches away. Unconfirmed stories started to circulate that some of the photographers had been seen kicking over the corpses to get pictures of their lifeless faces. Reporters from the *Sun* were accused of posing as Salvation Army helpers or relatives and parents demanding information, in order to get better pictures or quotes.

But the tabloid press, which had such a close relationship with football and derived so many sales and so much profit from writing about it, was to inflict yet more pain on Liverpool. This time the culprit was to be the *Sun*, Rupert Murdoch's most profitable newspaper, the jewel in his crown and the very cornerstone of his media empire. The paper, disappointed by the way the *Mirror* had beaten it in the race to increase circulation in the immediate aftermath of the disaster, decided to add a new opposition-crunching twist to the story. It was already being murmured that the Liverpool fans had caused the accident by indulging in heavy drinking before the game and then turning up looking for trouble. At the *Sun*'s Wapping headquarters editor Kelvin MacKenzie decided to run a front-page 'story' squarely blaming the Liverpool supporters for the deaths. The original version of the front page MacKenzie had planned to print directly addressed the Liverpool supporters and had the massive headline:

YOU SCUM

Underneath that appeared further, smaller headlines which said Liverpool fans had:

PICKED POCKETS OF VICTIMS
URINATED ON BRAVE COPS
BEAT UP PCs GIVING KISS OF LIFE

Fortunately for MacKenzie, cooler heads at the newspaper persuaded him to change the main headline to

Chris Horrie

'THE TRUTH' and insert the words 'some fans' into the accusation that Liverpool supporters had attacked rescuers and robbed corpses – all of which was a tissue of lies as Lord Justice Taylor's official report into the disaster was later to show.

Underneath these headlines the *Sun* 'revealed' that 'drunken Liverpool supporters viciously attacked rescue workers'. An unnamed high-ranking policeman was quoted as saying the Liverpool fans had 'acted just like animals'. Filling in the detail the paper said that one group of fans had spotted a dead woman with her breast exposed from her clothes and had shouted to a rescue worker, 'Throw her up here and we will fuck her.' It was all found to be lies, based on sheer prejudice and a desire to boost circulation. The *Daily Mirror* tried to justify printing its intrusive pictures of the dying, saying that by bringing home the true horror of the disaster it might prompt more effective action to improve ground safety. But the *Sun* did not even have this excuse. It had libelled the dead in order to make a profit out of them.

When copies of the paper arrived in Liverpool, they were burned on the streets. People seen reading the paper in the days or weeks that followed found themselves confronted; they even had the paper snatched from their hands and torn up in front of them. Many newsagents refused to stock it and others who did found it wise to keep the copies under the counter. A spontaneous boycott of the *Sun* led to an average 30 per cent drop in sales in the wider Merseyside area, with much higher falls reported in the city itself. The boycott began to slip as time passed and memories faded, but even a decade later the *Sun*'s circulation was well down relative to other circulations, especially in its strongholds in London and the South.

When the scale of the commercial disaster that editor MacKenzie's story had caused was realized, Rupert Murdoch personally called a crisis meeting aimed at repairing some of the damage and improving the *Sun*'s image in Liverpool and with football fans generally. This was now crucial. Murdoch was already planning to move into football in a major way, intending to win the rights to screen live matches on his recently launched satellite system, Sky TV. If the Liverpool fans, and perhaps others, found out that he was the man ultimately responsible for printing 'THE TRUTH', there could be problems. Murdoch's paper was already controversial in the football world and with some fans, for the way in which it preyed on the game: hyping transfer deals at the behest of players' agents; villifying managers; encouraging the 'lager lout' mentality by engaging in continual racial abuse of Krauts, Argies, Frogs and Wops in its coverage of international matches; and making non-stop hysterical demands that clubs should spend more and more on players, despite the fact that it would leave clubs with little money to redevelop dilapidated and unsafe stadiums.

None of this really mattered to the *Sun*, or Rupert Murdoch, so long as he had no direct financial interest in football. But by the time of Hillsborough Murdoch was planning to move into football in a big way and was, in fact, to end up as paymaster to the entire English branch of the football industry from top to bottom. Ask Liverpool fans – salt of the earth, what the 'beautiful game' is all about, football more important than life and death – or the supporters of many other clubs who would be the last person on earth they would want to end up virtually owning football and in all probability they would reply the owner of the *Sun*, the man responsible for putting the boot into English football during its darkest hour.

The rest of the emerging football industry had no qualms about doing business with Rupert Murdoch or taking his money – star players and managers (including Clough himself and, amazingly enough, Dalglish's successor as Liverpool manager, Graeme Souness) took lucrative contracts to ghost write columns or give exclusive interviews to Murdoch's *Sun*; chairmen and directors, meanwhile, could not wait to grab his money, giving him considerable control over the game.

As Lord Justice Taylor was to write in his report on the Hillsborough disaster, it was 'legitimate to wonder whether the directors are genuinely interested in the welfare of their grass-roots supporters. Boardroom struggles for power, wheeler-dealing in the buying and selling of shares, and indeed of whole clubs, sometimes suggests that those involved are more interested in personal financial benefits or the social status of being a director than in directing the club in the interests of supporter customers'.

The estimated total cost of carrying out the safety improvements set out in the Taylor Report ranged from a minimum of £120 million to as much as £200 million. One of the main recommendations was that stadiums should be made all-seater but, importantly in the light of what was to happen in subsequent years, it also said that clubs should not use this as an opportunity to put up prices excessively. Instead what was effectively public money was made available to the football clubs by a reduction in the tax on football pools and diverting the money into a fund operated by the Football Trust. It was an official sign from the government that football was not just like any other business. There was no way that, for example, a chain of supermarkets would be given a slice of the country's tax income to improve the layout of their stores to make them safer.

Over the following twelve months the Trust received 120 applications for money and paid out almost £80 million. Most of it went to the big clubs. Manchester United got £3.4 million, Ken Bates's Chelsea got £4 million and Sheffield Wednesday £3.6 million. But it was clear that the clubs would have to shoulder most of the cost at a time when almost all of them were running at a loss.

Even Manchester United was in the red most seasons, the result of the latest player-buying binge. New manager Alex Ferguson had spent £12 million on players since arriving at the club in 1986 and the wage bill had risen to over £5 million a year. Now that English clubs were back in Europe after the lifting of the Heysel ban, Ferguson and the fans were loudly demanding even more spending to acquire the sort of international stars that would be needed to have a good chance of winning first the league championship and then a European trophy.

Now – after Hillsborough and the Taylor report – Edwards was saddled with the cost of effectively knocking down the mostly ancient Old Trafford ground which, but for luck, could easily have been the scene of a disaster on the scale of Hillsborough, and rebuilding it as a smaller but more modern, all-seater stadium. Capacity would go down, perhaps halving attendances at a time when gate money still accounted for by far the largest source of income. The solution, of course, was to put up admission prices. But it was reckoned there would be a limit to what the punters might be prepared to pay unless the team started winning major trophies. That seemed to mean any increases in ticket prices would be swallowed up buying players and paying inflated wages.

The 1988 *Big Match* deal had put United's TV income up to around £500,000 a year – a handy sum, but dwarfed by the £15 million taken at the turnstiles. Edwards was still pessimistic about the future and, following the abortive takeover talks with Robert Maxwell in the early 1980s, had again tried to sell the club, this time to small-time property developer Michael Knighton, who was offering £22 million.

Edwards told Alex Ferguson that he wanted out, complaining that he was sick of the way the United fans were always on his back, demanding more expenditure on players when the club did not have the money. There had been a particular furore when Ferguson had wanted to sign Paul Gascoigne, then seen as the most talented midfield player in Europe, but Edwards had failed to come up with the transfer fee, resulting in the player going to Tottenham instead. One day during the closed season Edwards marched up to Ferguson and said, 'I'm going to sell. If you know anyone who would be prepared to buy my shares for £10 million, with a guarantee that he will spend another £10 million on renewing the Stretford End, then he can have it.' Knighton was not mentioned. Ferguson said he would 'put out feelers' and went off on his annual holiday.

When he returned, Ferguson was shocked to find that United had apparently been sold already, without him being consulted, to Knighton. Ferguson, nonplussed, prepared to adjust to the new regime. But then matters descended into farce. It seemed that Knighton might have difficulty coming up with the cash. Edwards and Knighton were lambasted in the press, especially in Maxwell's *Daily Mirror* (Maxwell still had a significant stake-holding in United and was ready to mount a renewed takeover bid if things looked up). The takeover was off. One effect was to damage the image of Edwards with those fans who already blamed him for United's failure to win the League championship.

After the Knighton fiasco Edwards again looked at the possibility of a stock market flotation – the financial move first considered in 1984 but effectively ruled out by negative City reaction in the wake of the hooligan crisis. Now, despite the Hillsborough tragedy, things looked a little better. But there were still problems. Edwards' friend Irving Scholar had floated Tottenham in 1983 and, seven years later, it remained the only top flight publicly floated football business. But Tottenham Hotspur PLC had failed to prosper. Scholar had been hit by all the same problems as United: tarred with the brush of hooliganism and dilapidation (despite the fact that Spurs had some of the best facilities and most enlightened anti-hooligan policies in football); saddled with soaring player costs as a result of giving in to fan power and huge spending plans of an ambitious manager, Terry Venables; hit by the European ban and, worst of all, by the failure to unlock the TV riches that Scholar had thought would be the rock on which his new Tottenham leisure brand would be built.

As Tottenham was the only PLC on the stock exchange, the City was bound to base their estimation of United's prospects on the actual financial performance of Tottenham. And by 1989 Tottenham was in deep financial trouble. Scholar, meanwhile, was struggling to keep his board under control while at the same time being lambasted by a fan power group who blamed him for the team's failure to win anything and wondered innocently why money from the vastly increased ticket prices Scholar had instituted was not being used to buy star players. Now Tottenham, like everyone else, would have to face up to the cost of carrying out the recommendations of the Taylor Report. But Scholar was still convinced that television would eventually come up with a step change in the amount of money they would pay for football. It was only due to cruel fate and the ineptitude of the League that the bonanza had been delayed. Casting around for money to tide him over until the gravy train arrived – probably in two years' time when the rights contract again came up for renegotiation – Scholar managed to persuade Robert Maxwell to secretly provide a £1.1 million loan. The understanding was that Maxwell might take on a more formal role at Tottenham in future – especially in helping to unlock the Aladdin's cave of TV riches. For the time being his involvement was kept quiet. Since his family already owned Oxford United and Derby County (he also had an undisclosed stake in United and had even considered Arsenal as another possible takeover target), the League's rules prevented him from having an open involvement with Tottenham or any other club.

Despite the lack of City enthusiasm Edwards and the United board decided to go ahead with a flotation anyway. Between December 1990 and February 1991 a new legal and financial entity called Manchester United PLC was created as a holding company and was given all the shares in the existing Manchester United Football Club Ltd, a move necessitated by League rules preventing a football club from becoming a PLC. Sir Roland Smith, the former Maxwell adviser who had planned the abortive early 1980s United flotation, took the post of non-executive chairman on the board of the new PLC.

The City institutions, the people who would actually come up with the money in return for shares in

Manchester United PLC, were invited to Old Trafford to trawl over the books and the offer prospectus. Edwards and Smith had assured potential investors that profits would rise, stipulating a 30 per cent increase in ticket prices after flotation, as well as forecasting increased revenue from merchandising, catering, sponsorship and, above all, television.

After the 1989 revolt of the small clubs, which had resulted in the re-expansion of the 'Super First Division' back to twenty-two clubs, Edwards and the rest of the Big Five had finally realized that they would never get what they wanted within the League. For the third time since 1982 they were involved in preparations for a breakaway. This time they were determined to make it work.

One key development this time round was the move of League secretary Graham Kelly to take over as chief executive of the FA. Kelly had joined with the Big Five chairmen in voting against the re-enlargement of the First Division, ostensibly on the grounds that the top English clubs played far too many matches, leaving no time for the best players to train with the FA's England national team. Beyond this he shared the general view of the Big Five that the League was a reactionary organization dominated by old-fashioned and small-minded chairmen who were holding back the national game.

After detailed talks with the Big Five chairmen soon after the 1988 breakaway crisis, Kelly began working on a report which became known as *The Blueprint for the Future of Football*. It was a detailed plan, and for the first time an entirely workable one, for an eighteen-club Super League. Previous breakaway plans had foundered on the opposition of the League and the FA, a venerable institution with 100 years of history (the League celebrated its centenary in 1989; the FA itself was even older), and depended on setting up a new Super League Federation of some sort. Any new federation faced the danger of not being recognized by the FA, who could apply all kinds of sanctions. Even if they did not, the politics of setting up a central organization which would not be seen merely as the creature of the Big Five was a nightmare.

Kelly's involvement solved all these problems at a stroke. The FA would run the Premier League, adding the competition to its control of FA Cup and England internationals and pushing Kelly's old employers at the Football League to the margins. Irving Scholar later explained the significance of the simple brainwave of allowing the FA and not the League or some new organization to run the breakaway. 'Our previous attempts,' he said, 'could always be brushed off as the work of greedy chairmen of the big clubs. We needed the FA, the governing body, on-side.'

Throughout 1990 Kelly worked away quietly, putting flesh on the FA-sponsored plan. Sponsors were found for the breakaway, which was, therefore, to be called the FA Carling Premiership. Eventually it was decided that the Premiership would consist of the twenty-two First Division clubs, reduced over a couple of seasons to eighteen by relegating more clubs than were promoted. The existing twenty-two members of the First Division would simply be invited to resign from the Football League and sign up instead with the Premiership. It was unlikely that any would refuse to do so. But if up to four did, it would simply mean that the target of eighteen would be reached more quickly. If more than four decided not to join up, the Premiership would invite other League clubs to fill their places. Since the FA controlled the selection of clubs playing in UEFA competitions, there would be no problem about the winners playing in Europe. Relegation and promotion to and from the Football League might be an issue, but it would be certain that the vast majority of remaining League clubs would demand that promotion from the existing Second Division (which under the new plan was allowed to call itself, confusingly enough, the First Division) to the new Premiership remained in place.

The final part of the Premiership blueprint plan – loud and clear from the start – was the key to its finances. There was an undertaking to seek a much improved television rights contract when the existing ITV *Big Match* deal ran out in April 1992. ITV's Greg Dyke was still working closely with the Big Five and had told them midway through the term of the *Big Match* deal that ITV would be prepared to increase, perhaps considerably, the money it was willing to pay in order to underwrite the Premiership financially. At the same time all the Big Five were aware that Dyke and ITV would face a strongly competitive bid from Sky TV.

It was partly the expectation that television revenue would finally start flowing that persuaded Martin Edwards and the Manchester United board that the future was sufficiently bright to take a gamble on a stock market flotation. Manchester United PLC was ready to go to the market in April 1991, to coincide with the planned announcement of the launch of the Premiership and its TV contract ambitions.

In the event Edwards decided to delay the flotation until June. The reason was that some of Alex Ferguson's spending on players was about to bear fruit. In 1990 United had won the FA Cup, their first major trophy under his management, and, since the European ban had by then been lifted, had played in the European

Chris Horrie

Cup Winners' Cup, and the large TV income from the European matches had been included in United's accounts. United had reached the final in May 1991, where they were due to face Barcelona. If United beat Barcelona they would automatically qualify for the competition, and more TV money, merchandising and other spin-offs in the next season.

Despite his vital importance to the fortunes of the club and the new PLC, Ferguson played little role in the flotation, just as he had been kept in the dark over the sale of United to Knighton two years earlier. It was reported that he was uneasy about the move. The inevitable worry was that the new PLC board would be dominated by institutional shareholders who, rightly enough, were required by law to get the most profit out of United, just like in any other business. But the economics of football were entirely different. The big Italian and Spanish clubs Ferguson was expected to compete against tended to be either privately or co-operatively owned and were under no obligation to make a profit.

The top European clubs' superiority on the pitch was the result of the availability of money for vast transfer fees to buy the best players in the world and for paying them salaries that were at least double what United could afford at the time. As a result the likes of Real Madrid, AC Milan and Juventus were always massively in debt. But this did not matter because some local multimillionaire (sometimes with political ambitions, for example Milan's owner Silvio Berlusconi) was more than happy to carry the losses in return for the prestige. Barcelona, with its international squad of million-pound-a-year superstars, was a loss-making co-operative that paid its bills by getting its huge number of club members to put up the money for transfers. As a private limited company

United had been able to carry losses in many years in a similar way, though on a smaller scale. United PLC would not, by law, be allowed to do so.

And there was another point. Edwards and the other directors stood to make a personal fortune of millions as a result of the success Ferguson and his players were starting to achieve on the pitch. Yet the manager's remuneration was modest, and the players, although well-paid employees by anyone's standards, would not benefit from the flotation. So far Edwards had been able to hold down wages and maintain an egalitarian wages policy, partly by pointing out that United was not profitable. The danger was that if United became profitable as a PLC, and especially if the directors started walking off with millions, the players would become demoralized and the new tribe of soccer agents Ferguson was finding he had to deal with would move in for the kill. But the manager remained loyally silent about all this, only much later saying that he had 'not felt comfortable with our entry into the corporate world'.

United beat Barcelona 2–1 in the European Cup Winners' Cup final, providing the ideal financial PR launch pad for the flotation. Even so the share offer, which took place on 10 June, hardly set the City alight. Not all the £42 million worth of shares was taken up and the share price, set at £3.85 on flotation day, started to plummet at once. Part of the reason was Edwards's immediate dumping of £1.7 million of his own share entitlement. This earned him an immediate £6 million and still left him with an effectively controlling 28 per cent stake in the club. He would continue to sell packets of shares at opportune moments over the next decade, eventually bringing him a cash fortune of at least £65 million, while still maintaining a *de facto* controlling stake in the club, worth an additional £200 million by the end of the decade. The Edwards family's original investment, paid for by the sale of their school dinner meat supply business, had been £600,000.

Robert Maxwell also cashed in, immediately selling his secretly held 4.25 per cent stake in United, netting him around £2 million. He then sold Derby County, bringing him another £5 million. Maxwell took the £7 million he had got from United and Derby and used it as the basis for a £9 million takeover bid for the club he believed could become the 'Manchester United of the south' – Tottenham Hotspur PLC. It was the club where the financial revolution in football had begun and one where Maxwell already held the whip hand because of his secret loan to Irving Scholar's disintegrating board of directors.

But Maxwell had his own troubles. To the world he presented the image of one of the richest and most successful businessmen in the world. The reality was that his publishing and financial empire, based around ownership of the *Daily Mirror*, was a morass of debt and corruption which might fall apart at any moment. He desperately needed enormous new flows of cash. And he knew that as owner of Tottenham he could get them. The key was the renegotiation of the all-important contract for screening live football, due to take place within twelve months. He better than anyone else knew that his bitter rival Rupert Murdoch's Sky TV was preparing to bid vast sums, not tens but *hundreds* of millions, to capture the rights. As a Big Five chairman Maxwell would have a seat at the top table in the negotiations. And he was determined to take Murdoch for every penny he had.

8.
Knock 'em Down and Drag 'em Out

In June 1991 the biggest change in over a century in the way English football was organized took place. The legal rows which had engulfed the game ever since Graham Kelly announced his plan for a breakaway FA 'Premiership' in the spring were settled. All the clubs in the existing First Division resigned from the Football League and signed up to play in the Premiership from the start of the next season.

Kelly said that the main reason for setting up the Premiership (there was a legal tussle over the use of the word 'league', which remained the property of the denuded Football League, left with only the lower divisions' clubs) was the welfare of the England national team. By reducing the number of games to be played between the smaller number of Premiership clubs and by raising the standards that players would achieve by playing in the new league, the idea was that the quality of the England national team would improve. Amid all this optimistic talk the plan, right from the start, included the point that would be the key to the Premiership and its fortunes – a commitment that one live match would be screened every week. Negotiations for these rights were due to start almost immediately, with the deadline for a new TV deal set for April 1992.

The stakes could not have been higher. The minute Murdoch's choice to head Sky TV, Sam Chisholm, had completed a forced merger between Sky and BSB in 1990 to give Murdoch an effective monopoly on British pay-TV, the two men were determined to make sure they acquired exclusive rights to show live league football.

They felt confident they would succeed. The current owner of the rights, Greg Dyke's ITV, was paying £11 million a year, and was unlikely to want to part with much more than that. Unlike Dyke, who had to deal with the politics of a fractious ITV federation, Murdoch and Chisholm were complete masters of their own house. Their best guess was that Dyke would be able to go up to only £30 million a year, whereas they were prepared to pay as much as £50 or £60 million a year. It was a lot of money and might mean that Sky would be saddled with debts for years before coming into profit. But the alternative, as things stood in the spring and summer of 1991, was almost certain financial extinction.

Against this background Robert Maxwell's takeover bid for Tottenham – itself triggered by the green light given to the Premier League – looked extremely threatening to Murdoch. Maxwell was a close ally of ITV. If he controlled a major club like Tottenham Maxwell would do everything within his power to make life difficult for Sky. At the very least he would urge the other chairmen to drive the hardest bargain, swaying them with his expertise as a media mogul. At worst he might use his influence to block a bid from Sky altogether.

Murdoch's best hope was that a rival bid for Tottenham launched by the club's manager Terry Venables would succeed. Murdoch's *Sun* newspaper had already been loudly backing Venables. But Venables simply did not have the money. Murdoch could have bought the club himself. But there was a problem with this. As the owner of Tottenham he might be ruled out of bidding for the screening rights on grounds of conflict of interest. And so in June 1991 Murdoch rang Alan Sugar – manufacturer of Sky's dishes – urging him to back Venables' bid with some hard cash. 'Don't let that fat c*** Maxwell get Tottenham,' he told Sugar. The bearded electronics wizard had never shown much interest in football before but he lined up with Venables, bought control of the club and saw off the Maxwell threat for good.

With the threat from Maxwell out of the way Murdoch and Chisholm planned to use money as their battering ram to get the rights. But they had also taken care to study and exploit the fault lines in the politics of British football and television. For months they had been courting officials at the Football League and, crucially, the FA, playing on their resentment at the way they had been treated by the existing BBC and ITV duopoly in the past. Many of those officials were still fuming over the 1985 blackout, when ITV and BBC had offered an insultingly small sum for the screening rights, told them they should be grateful for it and then walked away from the negotiations, pulling the plugs and boasting that 'football needs television, but television does not need football'.

The existing deal with Dyke, based as it was on the extremely aggressive and arrogant threat of ITV and Dyke's Big Five allies to form an 'ITV Ten' breakaway league, leaving the rest of football to stew in its own juices, was even fresher in their memory. With Sky things seemed to be very different. Murdoch and Chisholm were charm personified and candidly admitted from the start that they needed football much more than football needed them. And a huge pot of money was already being talked about. The football authorities had the whip hand for once. They liked the feeling.

The owners of smaller but ambitious clubs such as Ken Bates of Chelsea and Ron Noades of Crystal Palace were also all ears when the men from Sky TV came to call. Bates already had advanced plans to turn Chelsea into a Super Club based on a financial plan to redevelop its Stamford Bridge stadium into a hotel and shopping complex. He had been furious when Dyke and the Big Five had left him out of the proposed ITV Ten Super League, preferring to give the London places to Arsenal, Tottenham and West Ham. Had the ITV Ten gone ahead, Chelsea, who were in the Second Division at the time, would have been locked out of the golden circle of TV money, wrecking Bates's plans for the club and himself probably for good.

Since the 1988 TV deal Bates had been extremely active in League politics, leading what amounted to a smaller club backlash against the Big Five. The main bone of contention was the secret protocol that allowed the Big Five to hog appearances on the weekly *Big Match*, vastly increasing the value of their shirt sponsorship and merchandising deals, as well as giving them the lion's share of the TV appearance money. Because of all this, Chisholm and Murdoch discovered that they had allies among the chairmen of smaller First Division clubs, who were very likely to vote for a deal with Sky, not ITV, when it came to it.

When the Premier League was formed, Sir John Quinton, former head of Barclays Bank, was made chairman. Quinton had already been involved with football finance, as the man at Barclays who had nursed Tottenham Hotspur's £11 million overdraft, a position that had given him access to the financial affairs of Tottenham and a good grasp of the economics of football overall. Quinton and the newly installed Premier League chief executive, Rick Parry, were convinced that a big TV rights deal was the key to the future finances of the Premiership and its clubs. From the start they were less inclined than the big clubs to do a deal with ITV. Like many of the small club chairmen they feared the power of an alliance between the Big Five and ITV which might push the Premiership as an organization to the financial sidelines.

At first Quinton and Parry looked at the possibility of setting up their own broadcasting company, as a subsidiary. They talked over the idea of creating a subscription Premiership Channel with Chris Akers, later in the 1990s the financial power at Leeds United, but then at the Swiss Banking Corporation. One possibility was to broadcast on the Astra Channel, using empty channels owned by the ITV company Thames TV. The advantage was that the Premiership would get all the money fans were prepared to pay, rather than sharing it with a pay-TV operator like Sky. Importantly, it would establish the Premiership as the TV property, reducing the importance of individual clubs. This was naturally appealing to Quinton and Parry. The logical extension was that the clubs would become, in effect, franchises of the Premiership, even overmighty clubs such as Manchester United – as was the case in the American NFL.

In the end the Premiership Channel plan came to nothing, though the idea would be revived periodically in the 1990s, especially at times when offers made directly to clubs by broadcasters threatened to undermine the new league's central power and importance. At the time the venture looked risky – the collapse of BSB's sports channels in a morass of debt was still fresh in everyone's minds. Also, it would require a great deal of start-up capital and expensively bought-in programme-making expertise.

But there was an alternative. The Premiership could avoid reliance on ITV by talking to Sky, where Sam Chisholm was already shouting from the rooftops that he would pay a huge sum for the rights to the Premiership.

Chris Horrie

The problem for Sky was the larger clubs, especially the original Big Five, who were closest to ITV. The idea of a switch from ITV to Sky held little appeal for them, even if the money on offer was greater. At the time Sky had only a few hundred thousand subscribers against the audiences of 10 million or more clubs attracted for their appearances on ITV's *Big Match*. It was these massive audiences that had boosted clubs' income from shirt sponsorship, pitch-side advertising and merchandising. This might dry up if live games disappeared into Sky's subscription service.

In February 1992 Rupert Murdoch and Sam Chisholm had lunch with Sir John Quinton and found him cagey. He encouraged them to get involved and later said that his main aim was to make sure there was competition for the rights and not the simple renewal of the *Big Match* contract that ITV seemed to expect. But one important point was established. Quinton had no objection to Sky getting the rights, so long as the price was right. Chisholm asked him how the auction would be organized; he wanted to know what rules would be applied. 'There are no rules,' Quinton reportedly said. 'There is a knock 'em down and drag 'em out negotiation, and the last man standing is the one who wins.' That suited Sam Chisholm just fine.

The Sky team then concentrated on making sure that they would get enough votes when it came to the knock 'em down session, set for May 1992. 'We dealt with Parry,' Chisholm later told a journalist. 'He was the man we put our money on.' ITV, Chisholm said, made the mistake of 'putting their money on the old guys who knew them from before – guys like David Dein of Arsenal – and they worked through them'.

In the run-up to the May meeting Sky put a lot of

time into finding out the likely size of the ITV bid and lobbying club chairmen. They used a chat show on Sky called *Footballers' Football* to bring in the chairmen one by one, interviewing them for the programme and lobbying them or pumping them for information about ITV in the hospitality suite, finding out who their allies were. Quinton and Parry were entertained at Sky subscription centre in Livingstone, Scotland, shown the call centre where the money would be collected and the capabilities of even more lucrative pay-per-view technology that might come into play in the future.

As the TV negotiations began to draw closer the politics of football became clearer: it was going to be ITV and the Big Five versus Sky and the smaller clubs. Sky's plan was to gain a majority of votes by guaranteeing more money to the small clubs than ITV could ever afford. But first they had taken care to make sure that Maxwell did not take charge at Tottenham. His arrival might unstitch all the careful planning at a stroke.

In September 1990 Irving Scholar, in many ways the originator of the developments which led to the age of the Premiership, resigned from the board of his creation, Tottenham Hotspur PLC, though he stayed on as chairman of the club.

Things had not gone well for Tottenham or Scholar since the club's flotation in October 1983. The main problem had been a hectic diversification plan to make the PLC a ramified leisure group, which had not worked out. The PLC had bought a sportswear manufacturer, Hummel, which made football kit. Scholar had hoped to cash in on the replica shirt business – not only for Tottenham but for other clubs as well. But the market was so profitable that the existing firms used all their power with the shops to keep out Hummel, which was soon making a thumping loss. Similar ventures in computerized ticket sales and publishing also failed to prosper. Then, less than two years after the flotation, income slipped badly because of the hooligan problem and the loss of television exposure. Above all the vast increase in revenue from TV predicted by Scholar's advisers at Saatchi & Saatchi had failed to materialize.

With this lynchpin missing the financial structure at Tottenham started to fall apart. The share price dropped to 52p, half the offer price at flotation, and the board of directors were soon at each other's throats. Not helped by Scholar's determination that the club should compete as hard as any other in the transfer market, the debts mounted and the banks were soon knocking on the door demanding to know how Tottenham proposed to pay off the £12 million debt it had accumulated. They urged the Tottenham board to sell Paul Gascoigne who, after his performance in the 1990 World Cup, was valued by some at up to £15 million. The problem for Scholar was that he had nailed his colours to the mast – there would be no sale of Gascoigne. There had already been an outcry when Chris Waddle had been sold to Bernard Tapie's Olympique Marseille for a record £4.2 million the previous year. For Scholar it was a matter of honour. By 1990 he was looking for a way out.

Scholar had always been friendly with Robert Maxwell, supporting the tycoon's campaign against the League authorities aimed at getting a better TV deal. The relationship became closer when Maxwell secretly lent Tottenham £1 million so that the club could complete the transfer of Gary Lineker from Barcelona. At one point cash-flow had been so tight that Tottenham could not pay an instalment of the fee to Barcelona, whose lawyers turned up at White Hart Lane threatening to 'repossess' Lineker. There was nothing illegal about Maxwell's loan, but it had to be hushed up, otherwise the banks might have objected, demanding that if there was any cash available it should be given to them and not spent on players.

In September 1990 a press leak forced Maxwell into making a formal £12 million bid for control of Spurs. There was generalized horror at the prospect that Maxwell, who had lately been villified for wrecking Derby County, selling off most of the players and generally cashing in, would take charge. Against this background, and with the enthusiastic support of a Tottenham fan power group, manager Terry Venables launched a counter-bid. For several weeks the pros and cons of the rival bids were fought out on the back pages of the tabloids, with Maxwell's *Daily Mirror*, unsurprisingly, rubbishing Venables and Murdoch's *Sun* getting behind 'El Tel', giving a lot of space to the fan power group and 'monstering' Maxwell as 'the enemy of football'.

The problem for Venables was that he did not have anything like enough money to match the Maxwell bid. In fact it was later shown in court that he did not even have the £3.5 million which he said was all he could afford. The money, including Venables' part of the bid, was to be supplied by Alan Sugar who, having received that panicky phone call from Murdoch, posed as Tottenham's white knight and equal partner in a takeover bid put together to counter Maxwell.

Amid much drama Scholar decided to sell out to Sugar and Venables and not to Maxwell. The reality was that, just like Venables, Maxwell did not have the money. There was a vast black hole of debt at the centre of his own financial empire which was held together with a series of mutual loans from various companies under his control, all underwritten by a non-existent pot of gold supposedly deposited in a deeply secret bank account in Liechtenstein. He had become involved with the bid only because, had he not done so, people might have asked why he did not seem to have the money. In June 1991, parading the recently won FA Cup, Sugar and Venables took control of the club, with Sugar saying, 'I'll take charge of the £11 million debt at the bank, and Terry will look after the eleven footballers on the pitch.' Five months later Robert Maxwell was dead, his financial empire in ruins and, as Murdoch and Sugar had hoped, they would only have to battle with ITV and not Maxwell as well for the Premiership rights.

After the careful lobbying of the small clubs by Chisholm and Murdoch, the twenty-two chairmen of the clubs in the newly formed Premiership gathered at the Royal Lancaster Hotel on 18 May 1992 to consider rival bids from Sky and ITV. ITV's Trevor East handed each arriving chairman a sealed envelope telling at least one of them: 'I think you'll like this.' They did. The bid amounted to £262 million, roughly £2 million a year for each club that managed to stay in the Premiership. It was far more than the figure previously leaked and speculated about in the press. Greg Dyke had authorized an increase just to make sure ITV won. East was confident that it was enough to keep *The Big Match* on the air and, just as important for his boss, Dyke, enough to deal a possibly fatal blow to the chances of satellite TV getting off the ground in the UK.

At about 9.45 a.m. the chairmen disappeared into the conference room. East was walking through the hotel lobby when he saw Alan Sugar in a state of some agitation, barking the phrase 'blow them out of the water' into a payphone. East formed the opinion that Sugar was speaking to Sky headquarters. 'You don't seem to understand what I am talking about,' Sugar was screaming. 'These are the figures . . . take them down. You'd better get something done. You'd better get somebody down here quickly.' (Sugar later said that it was nobody's business whom he had been speaking to. 'I might have been calling my girlfriend,' he said before later confirming that he was giving details of the ITV bid to Sky and telling them to up their bid.)

Inside the conference room the Premier League's chief executive, Rick Parry, delayed the start of the meeting, allowing Sky time to increase its offer. Details of the ITV bid had been leaked to Sky by a second chairman (whose identity has never been revealed) in addition to Sugar. Sky's chief, Sam Chisholm, had gone into overdrive, phoning Murdoch in what was the middle of the night New York time to get permission to increase his bid. Chisholm had also been on the phone to Parry, who agreed to delay the start of the meeting until 10 a.m. Once the talking started, there was a bitter debate between the smaller clubs led by Ron Noades and Ken Bates, who poured out accusations against ITV, saying that the network had always worked too closely with the Big Five. The Premiership was officially a 'League of Equality' and Sky, it seemed to them, would treat them all fairly, scheduling an equal number of games for all clubs.

The Big Five were backed into a corner. Most of their arguments seemed self-serving. The main problem with Sky, they said, was that even if it offered as much money as ITV, the new service had only a few hundred thousand viewers, compared with the millions who watched ITV. That meant they would lose revenue from shirt sponsor-ship and pitch-side advertising. This did not worry the smaller clubs too much – their sponsorship deals were worth far less, and they realized that they would only get small audiences on ITV unless they were playing one of the big clubs.

But Chisholm had cleverly anticipated this objection and, in one of the main dramas of the day, announced that Sky had come to an agreement with the BBC. The Corporation would revive its *Match of the Day* programme, which had been in mothballs since ITV had bought exclusive rights to the League in 1988. All the clubs would be guaranteed a weekly highlights outing on the programme, thus satisfying most of the objections about sponsorship. When the rival bids were put to the vote, the clubs split right down the middle. All the Big Five except for Alan Sugar's Spurs voted for ITV, backed vociferously by Aston Villa and Leeds United. The smaller clubs voted for Sky. As it happened, Alan Sugar of Tottenham, after declaring a vested interest, had what amounted to the casting vote. Sky won the day, getting exclusive rights to live Premiership games and sharing the highlights with the BBC.

There was an immediate legal row, with ITV's Dyke denouncing the BBC as 'Murdoch's poodle'. It was said that Sky would not have pulled off the deal without the BBC's help. ITV asked for an injunction, but got nowhere and had to adjust to life without English League football.

The Sky team was exultant, even though dish sales did not take off until the 1992–93 season, the first Premiership season, got into its stride. There was shock at first at the high price of subscription to Sky's football service – £5.99 a month. Moreover, punters could buy it only if they bought the basic Sky channels first. Only 500,000 watched Sky's first televised live game between Nottingham Forest and Liverpool in August 1992. It might have been 10 million or more on ITV. But by Christmas the money was rolling into Sky and Chisholm and Murdoch found that their strategy had been vindicated. It was plain that they were sitting on a goldmine. Chisholm later recalled going into Sky's offices and seeing big sackfuls of mail filled with cheques. 'It was absolutely unbelievable,' he said. 'It was like Christmas every day.'

Within a year Sky's £47 million a year losses turned into an operating profit of £62 million. Profits increased every year for most of the following decade. A year after Sky renewed the contract in 1996 the broadcaster had managed to sign up 6 million subscribers, had gross revenues of £1.3 billion a year (almost equivalent to the whole of the BBC) and profits of £374 million.

Murdoch, whose papers had during football's darkest hour attempted to profit from Hillsborough by accusing the victims of robbing corpses, was set to profit much more handsomely from the game in the future.

Part 2.

Boom

9.
Premiership

At first it looked as if nothing much had changed. The Premier League, due to kick off in August 1992, was really just the old First Division armed with a new pay-TV deal and relieved of the burden of sharing its income with the rest of football. As far as the fans were concerned the main change was that referees and linesmen would wear green shirts instead of the traditional police-uniform black. And that, really, was it.

There had been a move by Sky to make the refs wear radio mikes so that they could explain their decisions to the TV audience, but the Referees Association put a block on that. It was the new UEFA-imposed rule outlawing back passes from defenders to goalkeepers (except for headers) that caused the most excitement at the start of the 1992–93 season, the dawn of the Premiership Age. For a few months there was an interminable discussion about whether or not full-backs would regularly get down on their knees and head the ball along the ground and, if so, whether they should be penalized.

But behind the scenes club chairmen were starting to come to terms with the Sky money, amounting to an additional £5 million per club per year – not enormous at a time when clubs were obliged to spend heavily on rebuilding their stadiums. Every Premiership club, as a condition of playing in the league, had by 1994 to bring its stadium up to the all-seater safety standards laid down in the Taylor Report. The more forward-looking club regimes had already worked out that, once the stadium investment had been made, what had previously been concrete white elephants could be turned into profit-making merchandising and catering centres. New flows of income would be created and the Sky money, needed at first for stadium spending, would thereafter go straight on to the bottom line.

Better still, football had recovered much of its popularity in the late 1980s – well before the Premiership became a reality – and had been boosted into something of a national obsession after England's creditable performance before huge television audiences in the 1990 World Cup, crowned by Paul 'Gazza' Gascoigne's 'Tears of Turin'. The new all-seater stadiums would allow clubs to increase ticket prices, exploiting, despite Taylor's pleas to the contrary, the existing convention that seats cost more than standing on the terraces. A more middle-class type of supporter could be targeted. Rebuilding, partly paid for by the public funds of the Football Trust (with the bigger clubs claiming the greater share of this public money), allowed clubs to start more or less from scratch, putting the emphasis on corporate boxes and entertainment, catering and even in some cases hotels and associated shopping complexes.

The all-seater grounds would have a smaller capacity than the old terraces, but this was not really a problem. Economists were later to show, in evidence to the Office of Fair Trading, that while clubs might compete ferociously on the pitch, they were not really in competition as businesses. Each was a classic monopoly. It was said that while a person might get divorced, change their politics, religion, or even nationality, there was no known case of somebody changing their allegiance to a football club – David Mellor (who switched from Fulham to Chelsea) being the exception that proved the rule. Companies in competitive markets found they had to spend billions every year to persuade customers that they were a Coca-Cola person rather than a Pepsi fan; a typical Nike person rather than an Adidas type. But football business did not have to spend a penny on persuading, say, a Liverpool fan that he was not an Everton fan or vice versa. The brand loyalty, if you looked at what was previously thought of as involvement in the club from generation to generation in that way, was phenomenal. 'We'll support you ever more' they used to sing from the terraces. And they actually meant it.

The free market argument that any club which put its prices up too much would lose customers to a competitor offering cheaper tickets to their games just did not apply. Football fans were addicted consumers. In the 1990s a woman was to cite Manchester United as the co-respondent in her divorce case. Her husband, the court heard, would spend up to twenty hours a day watching videos of Manchester United, many of which he had memorized frame by frame. He would talk to her or his children only about United, mostly to tell them news about the club. In any other walk of life fanaticism and obsessive or near-obsessive behaviour was regarded as undesirable, even dangerous and sick, but when applied to football, it seemed somehow praiseworthy.

All the major clubs were to exploit the reduced capacity 'Taylor effect' to the full by vastly increasing ticket prices, well ahead of inflation, and pricing many of the poorer and more traditional supporters out of the stadiums. Some clubs, including Arsenal and West Ham, went further, devising debenture schemes whereby fans were expected to pay as much as £1,000 in advance simply for the right to buy a season ticket. Manchester United concentrated on a club membership scheme costing £10 just to be entered into a lottery with about a one in ten chance of winning the right to buy a season ticket. At almost every club only possession of a season ticket, paid for up-front and a year in advance, could guarantee entry to the best games.

The combination of Sky money, much higher admission prices and new activities such as merchandising already pioneered by the floated Manchester United PLC meant that an extra £10 million a year, and maybe much, much more, in revenues was well within reach of most Premiership clubs. For some of the more astute chairmen that opened the possibility of following Tottenham and United on to the stock market with a flotation which might make them, like United's Martin Edwards, multi-millionaires.

This rosy financial future was already attracting a new generation of money-minded businessmen into football boardrooms around the country. Alan Sugar, the man who had taken over from Scholar at Tottenham in conjunction with Terry Venables, was one example. Sugar had originally become involved with the aim of blocking a takeover by Robert Maxwell, with the Sky versus ITV television rights negotiations partly in mind. But he was now convinced that he could make Tottenham profitable and thus see the capital value of his controlling block of shares soar.

Ken Bates was the most aggressive in his approach. He had spent a decade battling with developers to obtain the freehold of the club's Stamford Bridge stadium, near the fashionable King's Road in Chelsea, finally achieving his objective just before the Premiership was inaugurated. He was soon involved in a bitter boardroom struggle for complete control of Chelsea so that he could turn it into a subsidiary of Chelsea Village, a hotel and shopping complex he planned to build on the site.

Everywhere the Premiership clubs were concentrating on the financial upside, preparing in many cases for flotation in the mid-1990s. The change was felt lower down the pecking order. Once the Premiership was up and running David Sullivan, owner of a porn mag empire, moved to take over at First Division (i.e. old Second Division) Birmingham City, a big city team and a First Division regular until the mid-1980s. Clubs like these could be bought for next to nothing and with relatively modest investment in players could look forward to promotion into the golden circle of the Premiership. Another target, slightly later in the 1990s, was Fulham, bought by Mohammed Al Fayed after a bid for joint ownership of Bates's Chelsea was rebuffed. Neither Birmingham nor Fulham made it into the Premiership in its early years (though Birmingham came close in several seasons and Fulham made it at the end of the decade).

It was a slightly different story at Newcastle United and Blackburn Rovers. Newcastle, then a club with one of the biggest fan bases in the country, had been languishing in the Second Division and almost dropped into the Third, when in 1990, after a lengthy takeover battle, Sir John Hall bought the club. In February 1992, with the plan for the Premier League in place and the TV deal with Sky imminent, Hall hired ex-Newcastle player Kevin Keegan and gave him a budget to buy players capable of getting the club into the Premiership. Newcastle did not quite make it in time for the first Premiership season, but Keegan's team, bolstered by the signing of players such as Andy Cole, became First Division champions in 1993 and thus joined the Premiership in its second season, 1993–94. The investment of about £5 million in players (less than the cost of a reserve striker within a few years) must rank as one of the most astute in recent business history. Once Newcastle were established in the Premiership, Sir John was on his way to a market flotation which would earn him a personal fortune of £100 million.

Steel millionaire Jack Walker had more immediate success with Blackburn Rovers. Blackburn was a club with a long tradition – founders of the League, five-time winners of the FA Cup in the 1880s and a major force in the First Division until the Second World War. But Blackburn had not been in the top flight since the 1960s. Like their near neighbours (and bitter rivals) Burnley, the club had done badly in the TV age, losing fan base to regional TV super teams such as Manchester United and Liverpool, just as Bob Lord had always feared.

In May 1990 Walker sold his business, Walker Steel, and started to invest part of the £330 million proceeds in Blackburn Rovers, his home town club and the team he had supported as a boy. He said that his involvement was an act of pure altruism – 'putting something back' into the town where he had grown up and started his business. By September 1991 Walker had taken control of Blackburn, making it a wholly owned subsidiary of his finance company, Rosedale (JW) Investments, based in the Channel Islands for tax reasons. His first major move was to hire Kenny Dalglish – who had lately resigned as manager of Liverpool complaining of stress in the aftermath of Hillsborough – as team manager on a reported salary of £400,000 a year. Dalglish spent almost £8 million buying top-class players capable of winning the old Second Division and getting Blackburn into the Premier League.

Dalglish's spending on players in a single year was staggering by the standards of the time. It was roughly the same as Manchester United's spending on players over the five or six years since the arrival of Alex Ferguson. Even so Dalglish needed luck. Blackburn did not earn automatic promotion to the Premiership in their first season. Instead the team went up via the play-offs, beating Derby County in one of the ugliest games of the season, which saw David Speedie, one of Dalglish's expensive signings, attacked by Derby fans. It was a close-run thing, but Walker, who had already invested around £50 million in the club's stadium, had bought a place in the Premiership at a price that was regarded as enormous at the time but within a few years would look cheap given the rewards on offer.

If there were any doubts about Walker's seriousness they evaporated in the summer of 1992 when he authorized the signing of a player who came to symbolize the new age of Premiership – the 21-year-old Southampton centre-forward, Alan Shearer.

Shearer, the son of a sheet-metal worker, had supported Newcastle United as a boy, watching from the old terraces with his mum and dad (according to what was later to become the marketing legend) when they were struggling in the Second Division. He left home at sixteen to sign on as a YTS trainee with First Division Southampton, earning £20 a week and living in digs under the watchful eye of Dave Merrington, Southampton's head of youth development. Merrington spotted Shearer's qualities at once. It was not so much his technical skill which impressed, but a type of mental toughness which was about endless physical training combined with a ruthless streak both on the pitch and in the approach to football as a profession requiring absolute dedication to coming out on top.

Within a year Shearer was an England youth international, and within two he was given a start in the

Chris Horrie

Southampton first team, aged seventeen. He scored a hat-trick against Arsenal in his first game and was immediately given a contract (though it was worth only a couple of hundred pounds a week). At once he started thinking about his financial as well as his footballing future and became well known at Southampton for seeking advice about how to get the most out of the game. Fleet Street, always on the look-out for the next junior wunderkind, hyped Shearer as the face of England's footballing future.

By the end of the last season of the old First Division in the summer of 1992 Shearer had played 105 games for Southampton, scoring twenty-three goals, and had been picked to play for England. Just as importantly he had been put on the books of Mel Stein, the lawyer and football transfer agent, who in 1988 had arranged the transfer of Paul Gascoigne from Newcastle to Tottenham for the new British record fee of £2 million. The timing could not have been better. The internal British transfer market had been primed by Walker and Dalglish's spending spree at Blackburn and just about every big club was keen to sign Shearer in time for the Premier League kick-off. And, armed with the money from Sky, they were ready and able to pay.

Leading the field was Manchester United. Alex Ferguson's team had narrowly failed to win the First Division championship in the final 1991–92 season, beaten into second place by Leeds United. The team had started the season well but by January had simply stopped scoring. Ferguson contacted Southampton, asking for permission to talk to Shearer and make a bid at the end of the season. The rule was that no manager should attempt to poach, or even talk to, a rival club's players without the permission of that club. The moment the season ended

Ferguson had contacted Shearer and outlined an offer. According to Ferguson, Shearer was interested and said they could meet and thrash out details when he returned from that summer's England international tour. Then, a few days later, Ferguson read in the papers that Shearer was having talks with Blackburn. He was furious, but not entirely surprised. He had dealt with Mel Stein four years earlier when United had tried to sign Gascoigne from Newcastle and lost out to Tottenham. Ferguson now found out that Walker at Blackburn had guaranteed to better any offer he might make to Shearer.

Ferguson later remembered his last telephone conversation with Shearer, aimed at persuading him to join United, already established as favourites to win the new Premiership, rather than lowly Blackburn, who had lately struggled to gain promotion through the Second Division play-offs. 'I found him very hard work and surly,' Ferguson said. Despite the rule outlawing poaching, Shearer complained that Ferguson had not shown any interest before the end of the season. The conversation ended with Ferguson asking Shearer to think about what Kenny Dalglish would have done, given a choice between joining contenders like United or an unknown outfit like Blackburn. 'It's not about what Kenny would have done,' Shearer reportedly snapped back. 'It's about what I want.'

The next day Shearer signed for Blackburn Rovers for a transfer fee of £3.6 million and wages said to be in the region of £500,000 a year. A few days earlier Dalglish had signed Stuart Ripley, a winger, from Middlesbrough for £1.3 million, to supply crosses. After turning down United Shearer told the press that money was not really the main consideration. He had gone to Blackburn 'to win trophies'.

Chris Horrie

1992–93 season

The first Premiership season turned out to be one of the last when any team other than United and a handful of clubs rich enough to buy players in the transfer market inflated by Blackburn and fuelled by TV money had a chance of winning the competition.

Manchester United, the eventual winners of the Premiership title, conceded the first goal in the competition – scored by Brian Deane after just five minutes on the opening Saturday – during a 2–1 defeat at the hands of Sheffield United. United lost their next game, at home to Everton, 3–0 and then drew 1–1 at home to Ipswich. After coming close to winning the First Division in its last season, Alex Ferguson was now under pressure and, for the second time in his United career, there were demands for his head. This time they were confined to the back pages of the tabloids. The team recovered and, after the arrival of Eric Cantona from Leeds in November, began a long unbeaten run. In January United scored nine goals in two games to go top of the table for the first time.

Among the earlier leaders were QPR, Coventry City and Norwich, whose attack was spearheaded by one of the season's greatest discoveries, Chris Sutton, and who looked like contenders. United effectively put an end to their hopes with a 3–1 win at Carrow Road during which Cantona and Giggs sliced up the Norwich defence at will.

Blackburn Rovers, managed by Kenny Dalglish and boasting the multi-million pound off-the-peg team paid for by Jack Walker, had also looked like serious challengers, but lost their edge when Alan Shearer broke his leg.

After that, the championship was a two-horse race with United ahead and Ron Atkinson's Aston Villa chasing until the last few games. In fact it looked as if United would again slip up during the run-in, as they had done in the previous season when they had lost out to Leeds. The turning point was an April home game against Sheffield Wednesday when United defender Steve Bruce scored two goals in injury time to win the match, eliciting an ecstatic reaction from Ferguson and his deputy, Brian Kidd, who, unable to control himself, ran on to the pitch, dived and slid forward on his knees for 10 yards. The championship was effectively over when United beat Crystal Palace 2–0 away in April. Palace's Selhurst Park was packed with an overwhelming majority of United supporters who chanted 'Are you watching big fat Ron?' aimed at the Villa manager, who had been shown the door by Martin Edwards in the summer of 1986 to make way for Alex Ferguson.

United received the Premiership trophy after beating Blackburn 3–1 in their final game of the season. United had played skilful, exciting football, blessed with the talents of Ryan Giggs and Eric Cantona, and the grit of Paul Ince and Mark Hughes. They were worthy winners of a tight, hard-fought championship.

Thanks to Shearer, Blackburn were the season's highest goal-scorers but finished only fourth in the table. Leeds, the previous season's champions, had started well enough. A hat-trick and inspired performance by Cantona (before his move to Manchester) in a 5–0 win over Spurs had pushed them towards the top of the table in September. After Cantona departed, however, the team more or less fell to pieces, failing to win a single away game all season and finishing in seventeenth place – only three points away from relegation. The relegated teams were Crystal Palace, Middlesbrough and bottom of the league Nottingham Forest.

10.
The Shoe Box

While Manchester United and Blackburn chased Alan Shearer, another ambitious club was on the lookout for a striker – Tottenham Hotspur.

Alan Sugar and Terry Venables, chairman and chief executive after their takeover battle with Robert Maxwell, were struggling to tackle the mountain of debt they had inherited from the Scholar regime. The solution was the time-honoured one of selling star players. The club's main star, Paul Gascoigne, was off-loaded to the Italian club Lazio immediately, although not without difficulty. A transfer fee of £7.5 million was agreed by Venables, but Gascoigne smashed his knee during the 1991 FA Cup final against Nottingham Forest and when the transfer eventually went ahead it was for the reduced fee of £4.2 million.

The Gascoigne sale was followed by the departure of Gary Lineker to the Japanese club Grampus 8 for over £1 million. The sale of these players, together with Sugar's refinancing of the club and the new money pouring in from Sky meant that Tottenham's debts were under control for the first time in almost a decade. Sugar told Venables that he could start looking for a striker to replace Lineker. Venables decided that he wanted Teddy Sheringham, a promising young centre-forward at Nottingham Forest.

Sheringham was a Londoner who had started his career at the relative backwater of Millwall. By the time Venables began to show an interest in him he had been playing for Forest for one season. He had done well, scoring a lot of goals, but Forest's ferocious manager,

Brian Clough, was not really taken with him. He told others at Forest that Sheringham was too slow. He was the sort of player who was good at being in the right place at the right time, not contributing much but getting other players to give him the ball so he could put it in the net and claim all the credit. Clough was soon saying that he regretted signing Sheringham and would not mind recouping Forest's money with a transfer. There was another factor. Sheringham was a direct competitor with Clough's own son, Nigel, whom Clough senior thought was a much better player. Venables' interest in Sheringham was thus a stroke of luck. In July 1992, about six weeks before the start of the first Premiership season, Clough and Forest assistant manager Ron Fenton agreed to sell Sheringham for £2 million.

The fee was enormous by the standards of pre-Premiership English football, almost matching the domestic record set four years earlier with the transfer of Gascoigne from Newcastle to Spurs. Transfer fees above £1 million had been extremely rare in the depressed 1980s. The record set by Ron Atkinson when he brought Bryan Robson from West Brom to Manchester United in October 1981 had lasted for almost a decade. But Jack Walker's decision to bankroll Kenny Dalglish's spending spree at Blackburn had kick-started a bout of transfer fee inflation.

The Shearer deal set off transfer frenzy in the weeks before the start of the first Premier League season. Club transfer records were falling everywhere and the first foreign imports were starting to arrive. George Graham at Arsenal was spending heavily, buying the Danish midfielder John Jensen from the Danish club Brondby for £1.1 million. Later in the season Arsenal paid a further £2 million to Everton for defender Martin Keown.

Chris Horrie

Graeme Souness, who had taken over at Liverpool after the departure of Dalglish to Blackburn, spent £2.3 million on the far from impressive striker Paul Stewart. Chelsea bought the Norwich striker Robert Fleck for £1.3 million and Manchester City had bought Wimbledon full-back Terry Phelan for £1.3 million, breaking the British transfer record for a full-back.

Against this background the £2 million price tag for Sheringham was now nothing out of the ordinary. In order to get the best possible deal for himself, Sheringham, advised by his agents First Wave Management, played hard to get. Talks between him and Venables collapsed when the player could not get the terms he wanted. Then Brian Clough told Venables he had changed his mind about Sheringham and wanted to keep him.

The transfer was still up in the air by the time the season started in August. Events on the pitch were not going well for Venables and Tottenham. During the takeover battle expectations had been raised by all the talk aimed at the fans about new signings, a firm commitment to compete with Manchester United and Arsenal for the championship and predictions of the club's great future under the new regime. The reality was different. Spurs drew their first game 0–0 with humble Southampton, the perennial relegation tip, now lacking the services of Shearer. This humiliation was followed by a 2–0 home defeat by Coventry, a home draw with Crystal Palace and a catastrophic 5–0 defeat away to Leeds United. Venables came under intense pressure. Television and the tabloids played their part. Sheringham had scored a wonder goal in Forest's opening game of the season, televised live on Sky. The tabloids, ever eager to hype transfer news, kept up the pressure, implying that Sheringham was ready to come to Spurs' rescue, but that Venables and Sugar were holding out to try to force down the price. Having had to pay a huge increase in season ticket prices, innocently believing that the money had been earmarked to buy new players, with Sheringham at the top of the list, the Spurs fans were again in uproar.

At about this time Sugar asked Venables why it was proving so difficult to get Clough to agree to the transfer. Although both Clough and Venables vehemently denied it, Sugar later claimed during a court case that Venables had told him in a board meeting that 'Cloughie likes a bung' – meaning that if Spurs wanted Sheringham they would have to make an under-the-table cash payment to Clough. Sugar said that Venables had first told him about the use of bungs in transfers some months before, when Sugar was new to football. At a dinner with their wives, Sugar said, Venables had told him that Clough was a 'notorious' bung-taker and what 'usually happened' was that people would meet Clough 'in a motorway service station somewhere and Clough would be handed a bag full of money'. Sugar was horrified by the suggestion, saying that any sort of bung payment was out of the question.

On 27 August, two days after Tottenham's defeat at Leeds, Sheringham and his First Wave agent, Frank McLintock, met Venables at Spurs' training ground to reopen transfer talks. The agreed transfer fee was put up by £100,000 to £2.1 million in order, it was later alleged, to cover the extra money needed for 'Cloughie's bung'. McLintock walked away from the meeting with a contract in his pocket and, amazingly, a large cardboard shoe box containing £58,750 in cash. This was his fee for arranging the transfer – £50,000 plus VAT.

On their way back to Nottingham, McLintock and Sheringham stopped off at a hotel near the M1 at

Dunstable where they met Ron Fenton, Clough's assistant manager. There was later a great deal of discussion about what happened at this meeting. Both Fenton and McLintock said that all they did during it was deal with some paperwork needed to finalize the transfer. Sheringham said that he stayed in the car. McLintock said that no money changed hands. The shoe box full of cash remained in the boot of his car. Later, McLintock said, he took it home and hid it in the loft for safekeeping; then, some time later, he split the cash 50/50 with his business partner, Graham Smith, and the two of them spent all of it, or paid it into their own bank accounts. Graham Smith said he used the money to build an extension on his house. When investigations began much later both men flatly denied that any cash had been passed on to Fenton or Clough. But it was alleged by Sugar and others that all or some of it was handed over to Fenton, who then dished out the bung money to Clough as a reward for allowing the Sheringham transfer to go ahead.

Robert Reid QC, heading an FA inquiry into the matter, agreed with Sugar. After sifting through a vast quantity of evidence, much of it in the form of sworn statements taken from those involved, Reid pronounced himself satisfied that at the hotel meeting McLintock had handed over 'at least a substantial part, if not all, of the £50,000 which he had received earlier that day from Tottenham and that Mr Fenton returned to Nottingham with the money'. Reid added: 'We are satisfied that cash payments were made from the £50,000 to members of staff at Forest.' The inquiry thought it was likely that Fenton had received quite a large cut, and that he had probably used this money to pay for his daughter's wedding in September 1992. Much of the evidence given by McLintock and Smith, he said, was simply 'not credible'.

Venables was fingered in the report as having authorized the bungs he had described to Sugar. But the inquiry decided that while Venables's activities 'cannot be justified', he had not gained personally and had acted within the law and in what he thought were the best interests of Tottenham. 'He regarded the obtaining of Mr Sheringham's services as being essential for the good of the Tottenham team,' Reid said, adding: 'He regarded the payment as being an essential prerequisite of obtaining Mr Sheringham's transfer and therefore something which could properly be done on behalf of the club.'

The Sheringham 'bung' might never have come to light – opening the way, as it did, to the exposure of 'bung culture' on a large scale at Forest and other clubs – had Venables and Sugar not fallen out over the running of Tottenham. The matter came to light in October 1993 only as a side issue in a bitter legal battle between Sugar and Venables over control of the club. Six months earlier, at the end of the first Premiership season, Sugar had summarily sacked Venables as chief executive of Tottenham, booting him out of the boardroom. Sugar's anger over the bung episode was part of the reason for his action. Just as important was the financial failure of Venables's private business empire, centred on a string of pubs and a Kensington restaurant and nightclub called Scribes West. Venables was deeply in debt and, Sugar felt, was an embarrassment and liability as a business partner.

Looked at in another way Venables had outlived his usefulness to Sugar. Forming a team with 'El Tel' had been essential for Sugar in 1991 when, at the behest of

Chris Horrie

Rupert Murdoch, he was fighting off Maxwell for control of Tottenham in the run-up to the Sky TV deal and launch of the Premiership. Sugar had no track record and little knowledge of football and it was unlikely that the outgoing chairman, Irving Scholar, would have sold the club to him alone. The fans were an issue as well. Tottenham had some of the most articulate and middle-class supporters in the country, well organized into fan power pressure groups with almost unrivalled contacts in the media. By teaming up with Venables, Sugar had managed to get the fans on-side in the anti-Maxwell cause.

The reality was that Sugar had been the effective sole owner of the club from the minute Scholar sold out in June 1991. Venables had borrowed the money for his half share from Sugar. In the months that followed, Venables had struggled to keep up with the debt and interest repayments and now, two years later, Sugar was effectively foreclosing. Sugar, in any case, had been able to get a grip on the club and now understood much more about the football business. Maxwell was long gone and fan power was a busted flush now that revenue from television and merchandising made the club far less dependent on turnstile receipts. Sugar no longer needed Venables. And so he simply dumped him.

Venables, a fighter if nothing else, went to the courts in an attempt to preserve his job as chief executive and his place on the board. But the hearings, combined with the screening of no fewer than three major TV 'socumentary' programmes digging into Venables's ramshackle financial dealings, turned into a disaster for him – and for many old-style football operators right across the game. Sugar's revelations about Venables's toleration of Cloughie and his alleged bungs – all the talk about brown paper bags and shoes boxes full of cash – hit the headlines and prompted the FA, which had turned a blind eye for almost a century, to systematically investigate the transfer system, looking for signs of irregularity and, possibly, corruption.

The FA started with Clough and Nottingham Forest and soon found that the Sheringham episode was not the only transfer likely to have been subject to a bung. Within a few months they were on the trail of dozens of dodgy transfers.

The man found to be at the centre of the bung culture at Nottingham was an obscure Norwegian businessman based in the Channel Islands. Few outside the tightly organized and secretive world of football managers, agents and scouts had heard of him. But in the first few seasons of the Premiership he had become one of the most important men in English football – pulling the strings at half a dozen clubs, hyping transfer fees through the roof and unleashing a tidal wave of foreign imports.

His name was Rune Hauge.

Brian Clough

Throughout the entire first Premiership season, people said that a Forest team managed by Brian Clough and featuring players such as Roy Keane, Stuart Pearce and Clough's son Nigel was 'too good to go down'. They were relegated nevertheless, although Forest won their first match of the season – the first live Sunday game shown on Sky TV – 1–0, beating Liverpool with a goal from Teddy Sheringham. The striker moved to Tottenham shortly afterwards, and after that the

Chris Horrie

team seemed to be cursed. They won only two games before the New Year, climbed out of the relegation zone after a rally in the spring, but fell back to the bottom after losing six games in a row. Brian Clough was due to retire at the end of the season and it looked likely that one of the greatest careers in English football management would finish on the lowest of notes. Forest were relegated, their place taken by Sir John Hall's multi-million Newcastle United team, managed by Kevin Keegan.

For many the relegation of Forest and the departure of Clough signalled the end of one era and the start of a new one. Rarely had a manager inspired such loyalty from fans and players, nor shown such bravery in standing up to the grey men who ran football. 'Football hooligans?' Clough had once rhetorically asked. 'Well there's ninety-two club chairmen for a start.' His own method of dealing with the problem was to get on the Tannoy and say, 'Now, now . . . let's not have any of that nonsense,' and 10,000 grown men would fall silent. Once, when this did not work and some over-excited Forest fans ran on to the pitch at the end of a game, he came out from the tunnel and thumped them. Years before, when he walked out of Derby County because the directors did not like his outspoken approach, the team went on strike and there were mass demonstrations in the town. He combined a hatred of pomposity with a smouldering bitter streak. His own career as a gifted player in the early 1960s had been cut short when his club, Sunderland, preferred to collect a £40,000 insurance pay-out rather than let him make a sustained come-back after injury. The experience left him bitter, according to some, or with a realistic understanding that players were disposable as far as club managements were concerned and ought, therefore, not to get too big for their boots. At the same time he was determined, by his own modest standards, to do well out of the game.

Many wondered how Clough had managed to move into a sizeable house and drive a fancy Mercedes on his modest managerial salary. 'Money just seems to stick to me,' he would say. 'I've been very careful with my own money.' It turned out that some of his assistants, according to an official FA inquiry, had been siphoning off money from transfers.

But the sums were small in comparison with the millions club directors would earn through flotations within a couple of years of his retirement. Clough, a latter-day Robin Hood, did not see why all the cash should go to directors, agents and a handful of players. The 'culture of dishonesty' which an FA inquiry later said had grown up under Clough at Nottingham Forest extended to small packets of cash being redirected to cleaners and other low-paid workers at the club. Clough had twice taken lowly and run-down clubs – Derby and Nottingham Forest – by the scruff of the neck and made them champions. He had twice won the European Cup with Nottingham Forest. He insisted on doing all transfer business himself and broke the transfer record several times. His style was to do the deal, sign a contract, then phone the chairman saying: 'I've signed a very good player. But I'm afraid you are bankrupt.' He was a withering critic of the FA, especially its coaching wing, which he blamed for the introduction of the boring long-ball game. He valued skill in players over athleticism and trusted them to get on with their job, rather than endlessly drilling tactics. Mostly, he looked for players who just liked playing football and who would be loyal to him, to the fans and to each other. Prima donnas did not last long. 'Young man – get your hair cut,' he would say, if any of them started to look as if he fancied himself.

Managers would one day employ psychologists, motivational experts, scientific management methods and even faith-healers. Clough simply walked into the dressing room a few minutes before a game, held up the match ball and said, 'Now, gentlemen. This is a football. Kindly use it properly,' and then pointed towards the tunnel. He took players rejected *as too old or unfit, or written off as mediocre and turned them into international stars.*

But the age of the Premiership was to have no place for Brian Clough.

The end came when Forest lost 2–0 at home to Sheffield United. A quarter of an hour before the end of the game, when it looked certain that Forest were relegated, both sets of fans rose in unison to sing 'You'll Never Walk Alone'. And when the final whistle went, the crowd, again both sets of supporters, chanted over and over: 'There's only one Brian Clough.'

11.
Gifted Managers

By December 1993, midway through the second Premiership season, Manchester United, the reigning champions, had built up a crushing ten-point lead in the campaign. After years of underachievement United were cruising towards their second Premiership title and, in addition, the rare achievement of the league and FA Cup double.

The main opposition came from Blackburn, the multi-million team led by Alan Shearer, assembled by Kenny Dalglish and paid for by Jack Walker. Tottenham and Arsenal – the original London Big Five teams tipped to do well, even dominate, in the age of the Premiership – both struggled, at least in relative terms. Spurs finished in fifteenth place, only three points above the relegation zone, after managing just four home wins all season. Arsenal did better, finishing in fourth place, twenty-one points behind United, after drawing more games than anyone else and rarely scoring more than one goal in a match. Arsenal fans adopted the chant '1–0 to the Arsenal' – the team's trademark result (when it was not, just as typically, 0–0). Rival fans, more often than not, replied with a mournful chorus of 'Boring, boring Arsenal!'

Arsenal's disappointing and boring form was a mystery. The broadsheet football writers, churning out the analytical think pieces for the middle classes which were now a standard part of the media's approach to the national game, wondered if it was all due to manager George Graham's dour personality. The *Daily Telegraph* pondered the problem of why Graham had failed to sign exciting and talented players such as Peter Schmeichel, Andrei Kanchelskis and Roy Keane who all went to Manchester United despite rumours that they were interested in signing for Arsenal.

Graham had arrived at Arsenal in 1986 from Millwall, taking over as manager from caretaker Steve Burtenshaw, who became assistant manager. He had spent heavily on players in the early 1990s, dishing out a total of around £10 million on a series of generally lacklustre players, with the exceptions of goalkeeper David Seaman and striker Ian Wright, signings.

'Graham, who should be shopping at Harrods,' the *Telegraph* opined, 'has had to make do instead with corner-shop players like Jimmy Carter, John Jensen, Pal Lydersen, Martin Keown, Eddie McGoldrick and Chris Kiwomya'. Graham's policy in buying players was a mystery. It made no sense. What was going on?

Then, one day in December, an incident at the Arsenal training ground provided a clue. Graham was conducting a training session with his first team squad. The usual gaggle of newspaper hacks and TV reporters was hanging around. Graham tried to ignore them and get on with his job, but a Danish TV reporter called Henrik Madsen managed to get within earshot of the manager.

'Mr Graham!' he shouted. 'Mr Graham! . . . Do you know Rune Hauge? Have you ever taken any money from him?' The camera was running. Graham froze in horror, frowned, allowed Madsen and his cameraman to approach and gave the Dane his full attention.

Graham snorted, a stifled laugh of contempt. 'Those are very serious allegations,' he replied. But he did not deny contact with Rune Hauge. And he said nothing about the money. Then he bustled away.

*   *   *

Rune Hauge, the Norwegian football agent about whom George Graham was being so cagey, was born in 1955, the son of a chimneysweep, in Voss, a small town at the head of the fjord above Bergen. He grew up watching English football on television and became an Arsenal fan.

In 1974 Hauge moved to Nuremberg in Germany to study accountancy. By the end of the decade he became involved with the local Bundesliga club Nuremberg FC partly, he claimed, as a result of playing bridge with members of the club's board. By this point Hauge had formed Proman Sport, the first of his two main football-related companies. Proman's specialized in selling pitch-side advertising hoardings, first at Nuremberg and then throughout Germany. Business prospered as football appeared more and more on TV and the value of the hoardings increased.

In 1981 Hauge started to involve himself in the even more lucrative activity of brokering player transfers. At the time German football was booming and demand for players outstripped local supply, as it was later to do in the Premiership. German clubs, following the example of those in Italy and Spain, started importing foreign players on a large scale. Naturally they looked to the stars already playing in the big, well-established leagues of Italy, Spain and England. In 1977 Hamburg had bought Kevin Keegan for £500,000 – making him England's first half-million-pound player. Nuremberg were never in the big time, but Hauge persuaded them that there were plenty of useful players in Norway who might fill the gap. None of them was really world class, held back by the fact that the Norwegian league was small, competition was far from fierce and even the leading clubs were amateur or semi-professional. But

Chris Horrie

Norwegian players did have one enormous advantage at the time. They were extremely cheap.

Hauge's first attempted transfer as a players' agent involved Pal Jacobsen of Vålerengens, a Norwegian international and top scorer in the Norwegian league in 1982. Hauge met the player and proposed a move to a German club, but did not manage to pull off the deal because, he said, Jacobsen did not want to move to Germany. He had better luck with Kai Erik Herlovsen, whose transfer from Norway to Borussia Mönchengladbach of the German league he organized in the same year. Hauge moved back to Norway, taking a job as head of marketing at the small football club Bryne, so that he could both develop his pitch-side advertising business and at the same time scout promising Norwegian league players for possible sale to bigger European clubs.

Over the next few years Hauge organized several transfers between small Norwegian clubs and Nuremberg, where he was already part of the management set-up. One player, Anders Giske, moved to Nuremberg in 1983, then on to Bayern Leverkusen the following year and back to Nuremberg again within months. Two years later Giske went to FC Cologne, where he finished his playing career. Hauge's way of operating was slightly different from that of many other football agents. Instead of taking a straightforward percentage of whatever fee was obtained, he worked more like a property dealer. He would make a valuation of a player and buy his registration from the selling club, sometimes even before a buying club was in the frame. He would then sell the player on at a higher price to a German club – usually Nuremberg to begin with – keeping the difference as his profit. The selling club would not be involved in setting the price paid by the buying club.

Between 1983 and 1985 Hauge bought two more players in addition to Giske, moving Jorn Anderson from Vålerengens to Nuremberg, and the goalkeeper Erik Thorstvedt from Viking to Borussia Mönchengladbach, the other German club he worked closely with at the time. Thorstvedt played well and Hauge was soon hawking him around Europe, trying to open up markets outside Germany. He contacted Arsenal's assistant manager, Steve Burtenshaw, and almost arranged for a transfer to the London club for a fee of around £60,000, about the going rate for a young goalkeeper at the time. The deal did not go ahead because Arsenal were not able to obtain a work permit for Thorstvedt. Before the creation of the single market in the European Union in 1992 the strict rule, heavily policed by the PFA players' union, was that no foreigner (even from an EU country) could take a job which might otherwise go to an English player, unless he was genuinely exceptional. The usual test was having been regularly picked for a national team which, at the time, Thorstvedt had not.

With Arsenal ruled out in this way Thorstvedt instead went to the Swedish champions IFK Gothenburg. The goalkeeper stayed in Sweden for one season, making his crucial international debut, before, to Burtenshaw's astonishment, being signed by Terry Venables at Tottenham for £612,000, ten times Thorstvedt's market valuation only one year earlier. Burtenshaw was suitably impressed with Hauge's grasp of the transfer business and decided to stay in touch.

In August 1988 Hauge met Burtenshaw and asked him to supply information on the British transfer market.

The Norwegian said he was ready to pay for tip-offs about clubs and managers who might be interested in signing Scandinavian players or using his expertise to sell pitch-side advertising. Burtenshaw agreed to introduce Hauge to people at Arsenal, including the new manager George Graham, and others throughout the English game. In 1989 Burtenshaw signed a contract with Hauge's Norwegian-registered company, Proman. It obliged the Arsenal deputy manager to arrange 'introductions leading to the transfer of players' with important people in English football. In return Burtenshaw was to be paid 25 per cent of any profit Hauge and Proman made on transfers resulting from the introductions.

The contract, which was later scrutinized by an FA inquiry, laid down that the 25 per cent would be calculated net of any 'paybacks' Hauge made as part of the transfers. Burtenshaw claimed that he was never really sure what the term 'paybacks' meant, but gave evidence in which he agreed, after taking legal advice, that paybacks were 'palm greasers' or, in his own words, 'payments for people doing a job ... making introductions'. The reality was, as events were to show, that 'paybacks' was Hauge's word for bungs, secret cash payments given to managers who agreed to sign Proman players at inflated prices, splitting the difference with Hauge.

Burtenshaw made introductions to at least twenty people in the English game, including managers, chief scouts and coaches. One particularly important contact was Ron Fenton, the assistant manager at Brian Clough's Nottingham Forest, who was later accused of collecting the shoe box bung from Tottenham during the Sheringham transfer in 1992. In 1990 Hauge visited the

Forest ground as guest of the club's commercial manager, Dave Pullen, on the strength of his expertise in the sale of pitch-side advertising. When he arrived Hauge asked to see Brian Clough, saying that he had players for sale. Clough said he was not interested but sent his assistant, Ron Fenton, to see him instead. The two men struck up a close relationship. They later watched matches in Norway together when Fenton was scouting for players.

Hauge never placed Fenton under contract, but the way he worked with the Forest man was similar to his relationship with Burtenshaw. Hauge would phone to say that he had players available and ask if Forest were interested and, if not, whether Fenton could arrange introductions to English managers and coaches who might be. Fenton later told an FA inquiry that he arranged for the Manchester United manager, Alex Ferguson, to take a call from Hauge.

In 1992 Souness bought Stig Inge Bjørnebye, one of Hauge's players, for £660,000. The agent had guaranteed Bjørnebye's club Rosenborg £440,000 in return for the exclusive rights to sell the player to an English or European club. Rosenborg, thinking that this was much more than they would expect to get for him, had grabbed the money, only to find that Hauge had persuaded Liverpool to pay a third as much again on top. After paying Bjørnebye £85,000 Hauge kept £135,000 for himself. (Souness would prove to be one of Hauge's most valuable English customers. Over a period of eight years he bought £3,350,000 worth of players from Hauge, several of them on a similar 'fixed fee' basis. But there was never any indication of impropriety on Souness's part. Like many experienced managers, he simply found Hauge a useful contact.)

Chris Horrie

In May 1990 Burtenshaw received his first payment from Proman – £20,284, laundered through two companies that Hauge had set up in the Channel Islands and quietly paid into a bank account Burtenshaw had opened for the purpose in Dublin. Burtenshaw later said that he had set up the Dublin account not because he wanted to keep the payment secret, but to delay the payment of tax. It was never established which particular transfer or transfers had triggered the payment. But the figure of just over £20,000, investigators later reckoned, would suggest a profit of £80,000 for Proman after paybacks from a transfer to an English club resulting from introductions made by Burtenshaw. Furthermore any such transfer would have had to have taken place between July 1989, when Burtenshaw signed his contract with Proman, and May 1990, when the first payment was made. During this time Hauge was touting a number of players around English First Division clubs. They included Jan Åge Fjørtoft, Jorn Anderson, Jostein Flo, Anders Limpar, Pal Lydersen, Gunnar Halle, Andrei Kanchelskis and Peter Schmeichel. The only transfer to go through during this period was the move of Erland Johnsen from Bayern Munich to Chelsea for £306,000, which took place at the start of December 1989.

There is no indication that any sort of bung took place in any of these transfers, though the move of Kanchelskis from Shakhtar Donetsk, resulting from Fenton's introduction of Hauge to Alex Ferguson, was later investigated by the FA. Hauge had first offered Kanchelskis to Arsenal, but Burtenshaw and Graham were not interested, apparently saying the language barrier was too great. After this set-back Hauge sent Kanchelskis's details to United, where he found that Alex Ferguson and Martin Edwards were interested.

Ferguson first met Hauge in 1984 when the Norwegian was just starting out as an agent. The occasion was a pre-season friendly between Aberdeen, the club Ferguson was managing at the time, and Nuremberg, Hauge's club. Ferguson had extensive dealings with Hauge from the early 1990s, when the Norwegian brokered the Schmeichel and Kanchelskis deals, later buying players such as Henning Berg, Ronny Johnsen, Ole Gunnar Solskjaer and the less successful Erick Nevland. In his autobiography, *Managing My Life*, Ferguson described Hauge as 'a brilliant judge of a player and a real professional when it comes to finding talent'. Which was just as well. In a period of six years Ferguson was to spend over £9 million on players represented by Rune Hauge.

The spending started in 1991, when Ferguson told Hauge that he was definitely interested in signing Kanchelskis. Ferguson and Edwards negotiated directly with Wolfgan Voge, a business partner of Hauge and the man they believed to be the official delegated representative of Shakhtar, Kanchelskis's club. A transfer fee of £650,000 was agreed in March 1991. United paid Hauge £35,000, which the club officially recorded as remuneration for 'professional services in the 90–91 and 91–92 seasons', and included help in selling the overseas rights to United's European Cup Winners' Cup and European Super Cup matches, arranging a pre-season tour of Norway and 'helping in the recruitment and negotiations through contract stage with both Andrei Kanchelskis and Peter Schmeichel'. A subsequent FA inquiry found that this was a breach of the rule that clubs should not pay agents to set up transfers but that it was absolutley clear that no bung had taken place. 'There is no evidence to suggest there was any irregularity in these payments or that any part of the payment found its way back to Manchester United,' the FA concluded.

Kanchelskis's £650,000 fee was paid into a Swiss bank account set up in the name of Shakhtar Donetsk, and United officials thought that was an end to the matter. Then, amazingly, two Russians turned up at Old Trafford claiming that they, and not Hauge and Voge, represented Shakhtar, heatedly claiming that they had received no money from the transfer, that Kanchelskis was their player and should be returned immediately. Martin Edwards called the police, but the Manchester fraud squad were unable to get to the bottom of the problem. When they went to Donetsk to take statements they found that most of the club's management had disappeared or had been murdered, apparently by the Russian mafia. The transfer negotiated between United and Voge stood unchallenged.

But that was still not quite the end of the matter. In 1994 Kanchelskis, represented by an eastern European businessman, negotiated a new contract to stay at Old Trafford on greatly improved wages and, also, the promise of one third of any transfer fee if United sold him on to another club. After the deal was done the businessman approached Ferguson and United lawyer Maurice Watkins in the Manchester United car park at one in the morning after an away game at Nottingham Forest and said that he had a 'gift' for them. Ferguson told him that he would pick it up in the morning. But after Ferguson had dropped Watkins off at a hotel, the east European phoned Ferguson and asked him to go to the Excelsior hotel at Manchester airport. He said he was leaving the country in the morning and before returning to Russia, he wanted to make sure Ferguson got his gift.

Given that Manchester airport was quite near his

Cheshire home, Ferguson went straight to the Excelsior, where he found the man standing at the front entrance. 'This is a gift for you and your wife,' he said, handing over a large and, as Ferguson put it, 'handsomely wrapped' box. The Manchester United manager later said that he thought it might be a samovar or some other typically Russian memento. When he got home he opened the box and found it contained instead 'piles of cash, bundles of the stuff', amounting to £40,000 in all.

Ferguson thought about driving straight back to the Excelsior and returning the money, but decided against it, fearing some sort of blackmail set-up, possibly involving secret cameras. Instead he took the money to Old Trafford the next morning, where Maurice Watkins told him to put it in the club safe and to swear a statement in front of two sets of solicitors describing what had happened. The money stayed in the safe until the businessman turned up again at Old Trafford a year later on transfer business, when it was handed back.

Ferguson concluded that the attempted bung was intended not so much as a cut of the money Kanchelskis had so far received from United, but as an inducement, 'an encouragement towards co-operation in the future', as he put it. Nevertheless Ferguson and United decided not to tell the fraud squad or the FA's own inquiry into agents and bungs, which had begun to take evidence in 1993. The 'samovar affair' remained under wraps until 1999 when Ferguson described it in his autobiography.

Within a year of the samovar episode Kanchelskis and his agent began telling Ferguson that the player was unhappy at United and wanted to be transfer-listed, even though he was still under contract. The manager reluctantly agreed, and a bid from Everton was

Chris Horrie

accepted. Kanchelskis's representative then turned up at Old Trafford, insisting that fully one third of the £6 million transfer fee Everton were willing to pay would have to be passed on to Shakhtar. Given that United would in that case get only £4 million for the player, the transfer was held up while Maurice Watkins went to the Ukraine to negotiate. He was met at the airport by a man who claimed to be the club's legal adviser. The United lawyer doubted whether this was the case, especially when the man got into what looked like an armour-plated Mercedes in the company of three armed body-guards. After this, with United still dragging their feet on the transfer, trying to hold on to more of the money, Martin Edwards received death threats. Eventually the transfer went ahead. A few months later Shakhtar's president, Alexander Bragin, was assassinated by means of a remote-controlled bomb.

In 1990 Hauge had used his main contact in British football, Steve Burtenshaw, to try to sell the Brondby goalkeeper Peter Schmeichel to Arsenal. Through Burtenshaw, Hauge had that summer offered Schmeichel to George Graham. The Arsenal manager turned him down, preferring to buy the QPR and future England international goalkeeper David Seaman for the record fee of £1.5 million. Graham remembered Hauge saying to him: 'If Arsenal are not interested, who would be interested?' The answer was so obvious that it was amazing that a man with Hauge's contacts had to ask. Manchester United had long made it clear that they were on the lookout for a new goalkeeper. The following year Hauge duly arranged the sale of Schmeichel to Manchester United for the much lower fee of £505,000, a third of the price paid by Graham for David Seaman, which, in view of Schmeichel's record of success, Ferguson later described as 'the deal of the century'.

Graham may have let Schmeichel slip through his fingers, but there were other Hauge players he was interested in signing. From about the summer of 1990 onwards Hauge dealt not only with Burtenshaw but more directly with Graham himself. In the run-up to the launch of the first Premiership season Graham, like many Premiership managers, had persuaded his board of directors to provide him with a large sum of money to buy star players. He decided to spend a large portion of this with Rune Hauge. Burtenshaw and Graham looked at Anders Limpar, a Swedish under-21 international, and rated him at about £1 million. Hauge set up a transfer between Limpar's Italian club, Cremonese, and Arsenal at the increased price of £1.4 million and the transfer went ahead in August 1990. Hauge was paid £400,000 by Cremonese. A couple of months later Hauge paid a further £13,474 into Burtenshaw's Dublin bank account.

Next up was Pal Lydersen, a full-back. The Arsenal manager persuaded his board to pay £600,000 for Lydersen, a huge sum for a completely unknown player. The money was paid to Hauge's Channel Island-registered company, Interclub. About half of this found its way back to Lydersen's tiny Norwegian club, IK Start. Hauge kept as much as £200,000 for himself. He changed £104,500 of the transfer fee into £50 notes, which he then packed into an executive attaché case and handed to George Graham in December 1991. Graham later said that he had been surprised to receive the cash, and thought that it was probably a Christmas present. (After details of the payment came to light at an FA inquiry, he repaid the money, together with larger sums he later received from Hauge, to Arsenal.)

Then came the transfer which was to blow the lid off Hauge's less than straightforward relationship with Arsenal and lead directly to Danish journalist Henrik Madsen's televised confrontation with George Graham at the Arsenal training ground. The player involved was John Jensen of Brondby, the club from whom Manchester United had bought Peter Schmeichel.

Early in 1992, after the success of the Limpar and Lydersen transfer deals, Hauge suggested that if Arsenal wanted to sign Jensen, a Danish international, he had the contacts at Brondby to fix it. Burtenshaw and Graham looked at Jensen and decided he was a good, but not great, player, whose market value was probably about £750,000. Jensen's stock went up during the summer 1992 European nations championships in Sweden, when he scored for Denmark in the final against Germany, delivering the championship to the Danes, to everyone's surprise. But the £1.6 million transfer fee paid to Brondby in August 1992 was around double the player's market value. From the £1.6 million the Danish club paid £749,433 straight back to Hauge, who kept £247,000 for himself. He paid Jensen's share of the fee and made a further deposit of £35,000 into Burtenshaw's Dublin account. £285,000 was given to George Graham to add to the 'Christmas present' of £104,500 he had been given the year before, making the total nearly £400,000.

Things started to go wrong for Hauge and Graham when Danish journalists, led by Madsen, began investigating why Brondby had paid Jensen's former club HSV Hamburg £392,500 in the wake of his transfer to Arsenal. It was known that Brondby had made a sell-on agreement with Hamburg when they had signed Jensen. This was a common enough arrangement, designed to persuade hard-up clubs like Hamburg to sell promising young players cheaply on the understanding that they would get a share of any later sale of the player for a big to fee to a major European club such as Arsenal. It was known to Madsen that Brondby had agreed to pass on to Hamburg a proportion of any money they obtained for Jensen. The size of the transfer fee had been announced by Arsenal and Brondby as £1.1 million, almost £500,000 less than Arsenal had actually paid. The figure of £392,500 paid to Hamburg convinced Madsen that Arsenal had paid something much more like £1.6 million and that the difference had been used by Hauge to make payments to Graham and Burtenshaw.

Which was why George Graham found himself being confronted a few months later by a Danish journalist waving a microphone and asking hard-edged questions, all the while being filmed by a camera crew. Madsen was the first to suspect that money from the Jensen deal had found its way back from Brondby to Graham. But soon other loose ends resulting from this deal were to bring the authorities down on the Arsenal manager from two directions. The first was the Inland Revenue. In 1994 the Revenue descended on Arsenal claiming to have been tipped off that Burtenshaw and Graham had been banking undeclared income 'emanating from player transfers'.

The British Inland Revenue had long correctly suspected that under-the-counter payments were being made in football. The 'culture of dishonesty' as it was later to be called, dated back to the restrictions of the maximum wage.

Long before the maximum wage was abolished in

Chris Horrie

1961, clubs had got round FA rules by topping up wages with all manner of 'expenses' payments, well paid but effectively non-existent jobs for players' relatives and other scams. In the 1940s Newcastle United had gained the services of Len Shackleton, the England centre-forward and one of the biggest stars of the pre-TV age, by paying one of his relatives hundreds of pounds to supply fictitious bales of straw, which the club claimed in its accounts were needed to protect the pitch on winter nights. These payments, designed at first to thwart the FA, did not count as official income for the player and so no tax was payable. After the maximum wage rule went, players continued to use similar methods purely to avoid paying tax.

Rumours had been circulating for years, but in the early 1990s the Revenue set up a special team of investigators specifically to look at tax avoidance at football clubs. Several clubs were immediately fingered – a common scam was to provide players with free houses in lieu of wages in order to avoid tax. Eventually, in 1997, with the Premiership acting as broker, the clubs negotiated a one-off amnesty payment to avoid prosecution. The sum was reported to be about £100 million.

At the same time the booming transfer market which came in the wake of the launch of the Premiership meant that agents were playing an ever larger role in the game. The FA rules were clear – no club should ever pay an agent. But the rule was widely and routinely ignored. The argument from the clubs was that the rule was unworkable, that it was an open secret in football that it was widely flouted and that any club that did not work with agents would lose out on getting the best players. In fact just about the only major club later found to have been scrupulous in refusing to use agents, Ipswich Town, had done very badly as a result.

The agent Eric Hall later claimed that senior figures in the FA hierarchy knew that the rules were being bent and in their capacity as club chairmen and executives even engaged in subterfuge and broke the rules themselves. Hall claimed that when he acted as agent in one transfer, a league chairman said at the end of talks: 'We haven't discussed your fee. How much do you normally charge a player for doing a deal for him?' Hall said he wanted £30,000 and the chairman told him to send an invoice stating that the money was due for 'organizing a tour to Leningrad'. Hall did so – even though he had never heard of Leningrad and could not find it on a map.

Likewise Bill Fox of Blackburn had agreed to work with Hall, even when Fox was chairman of the FA. He paid Hall £17,500 for setting up the transfer of goalkeeper Bobby Mimms from Spurs to Blackburn in the late 1980s. Fox had insisted that they should negotiate only on the phone so that he could truthfully say that he had 'never met' Hall. The agent also claimed that it was 'normal' for club officials to ask 'Where's my present?' after parting with a big transfer fee for a player. Another agent, John Smith, confirmed that these practices were widespread. He claimed that an unnamed 'club president' had once asked for the expensive gold watch Smith was wearing. The agent took it off and gave it to him on the spot.

It was therefore not surprising that the Revenue would take an interest in the money Burtenshaw was drawing from the Irish bank account he had set up to receive payments from Rune Hauge. The Revenue were not especially interested in what the money was for, but they approached the Arsenal board, demanding to know why tax was not being paid. In turn the board grilled Burtenshaw.

Burtenshaw maintained that he had no role in misusing Arsenal funds and that he had cancelled his contract with Hauge when he thought that it might lead to information being supplied that would be used by Hauge to sell to other clubs players Arsenal might want to sign. An FA inquiry later heard that Graham had called Burtenshaw 'a bloody fool' for disclosing these details.

The second source of official probing into Arsenal's affairs came, eventually, from a special FA committee of inquiry into the use of agents and the possibility of bungs and kickbacks in transfer deals. The three-man FA committee, headed by Robert Reid QC and including new Premier League chief executive Rick Parry and Steve Coppell, the Crystal Palace manager, representing the League Managers' Association, started by investigating Alan Sugar's claims that the 1991 transfer of Teddy Sheringham from Nottingham Forest to Tottenham had involved the payment of a bung to Ron Fenton, Brian Clough's assistant. The committee quickly established that there was a 'culture of dishonesty' at Forest and throughout the transfer system.

The FA report on bungs issued in 1997 was devastating. It concluded that the FA's rule which prevented the use of agents was almost entirely ignored and that practically every Premier League club used agents regularly to seek out players, negotiate and sign contracts. It was the classic black-market situation. Because agents were illegal the clubs resorted to all sorts of subterfuge to pay them for their services, the most common being the use of false invoices. Agents would put in large bills for vaguely specified 'marketing services' or 'professional advice,' which in reality were charges for setting up transfers. Rune Hauge's usual way of operating – even when (as in the case of the transfers of Schmeichel and Kanchelskis to Manchester United) there were no bungs involved – was to charge for 'professional advice' on the sale of pitch-side advertising or for his role in 'arranging pre-season friendlies'.

Terry Venables and Tottenham were castigated in the report not only for the Sheringham transfer and the alleged bung payments to Fenton, but for accepting disguised invoices from agents who set up the transfers of Vinny Samways and Andy Gray. During the Samways transfer Tottenham had paid £28,750 to Eric Hall, who also told the inquiry that he routinely planted stories in the tabloids in order to hype transfer deals or create expectations of high fees. The payment was disguised as 'retainer – marketing services'. In a similar way £10,000 had been paid to Frank McLintock, the man at the centre of the Sheringham affair, to smooth the transfer of Andy Gray. But Tottenham was not the only club fingered for accepting and paying up against fake invoices. The practice had been 'common within the major clubs of the Football League'.

In addition to proof of the Sheringham bung, the committee found 'direct evidence of a fraudulent arrangement by which Mr Clough and/or Mr Fenton acquired a substantial sum of money' from the transfers of Anthony Loughlan and Neil Lyne from the non-league club Leicester United. While Fenton admitted to this, Clough continues to deny it and the FA decided not to pursue the matter.

What Fenton had done was get extra money from Forest by paying over the odds for the registration of the players, splitting the excess with their agent.

Chris Horrie

Forest's signing of Alf Inge Haaland, arranged by Rune Hauge, was also highlighted. Forest paid £350,000 for the player, but only £150,000 ever reached the selling club, Bryne, where Hauge was marketing manager. Hauge kept £200,000 and paid £45,000 back to Fenton. Most amazing of all was a bung arranged as part of the transfer of the Icelandic player Thorvaldur Orlygsson from Akureyri Iceland to Forest. A Forest official told the inquiry that 'it was his understanding that Mr Fenton had collected £45,000 in a fishing box off a trawler in Hull'.

By this time Clough and Fenton had retired from football and so there was not much the FA could do; eventually it charged both men with 'misconduct'. The main victim of their activities was Nottingham Forest, but the board and management of the club decided to take no action against the pair. After all Clough had made a tremendous contribution to Forest by winning the League and the European Cup and he had become a legend, much loved by fans and many in the city. If it was true that Clough had siphoned a little money his way, they were not too put out. Clough was left alone. The club even named its new Taylor-style stand after him. His reputation was tarnished. But not much.

The punishment dished out to Graham and Burtenshaw hurt a little more. Both maintained that they had done nothing wrong, with Graham sticking to the story that the money from Hauge was an unsolicited gift which he repaid to Arsenal in due course. Both Arsenal and the FA accepted Burtenshaw's claims that the money he had taken from Hauge was for his work in 'setting up a European-wide scouting network' and not connected to any particular transfer to or from Arsenal. But the board said Graham and Burtenshaw had 'failed to act in the best interests of the club' and both were shown the door. The

FA banned Graham from working as a manager for one year (after which he quickly returned, to manage Leeds United). Burtenshaw went to QPR as chief scout and was later fined £7,500 for breaking FA rules (he was also charged £2,500 costs).

Rune Hauge had his licence as a FIFA-registered football agent withdrawn for two seasons and he had to give various assurances that he would not engage in 'extraordinary' payments in the future. The ban did not seem to worry him much. He continued to be as active as ever, arranging the transfer of at least one player while officially banned.

Hauge used the simple device of working with a (fully licensed) partner, Frank Mathieson. In fact he continued to run one of the most prolific and most profitable transfer agencies throughout the first decade of the Premiership. There is no indication that any of the deals Hauge did after his ban were anything but straightforward, although he was again involved in controversy in 1997 after arranging the move of Tore Andre Flo and Claus Eftevaag from the Norwegian club Brann to Everton. Manager Joe Royle wanted to sign only Flo, but Hauge, as had been the case in several of his deals, insisted that Everton had to take both players or none. Royle agreed, but he was overruled by the Everton board and resigned soon afterwards. Flo eventually signed for Chelsea instead.

Arsenal and Liverpool both issued statements saying that they would not have any further dealings with Hauge or sign any players represented by him, and called on other clubs to follow suit. None did so. Despite all this any taint on Hauge's reputation soon evaporated, as his continuing dealings with Manchester United seemed to show. He even resumed business with George Graham

Chris Horrie

when the former Arsenal manager returned to management at Leeds United after his one-year ban. One of Graham's first signings was Alf Inge Haaland, the Hauge-represented player whose move to Nottingham Forest had been subject to a bung. Then he signed another Hauge player, Gunnar Halle, from Sheffield United.

By the end of the decade Hauge had diversified. He was reported to be building a marina and leisure complex in the Channel Islands where his players could relax and call on 'one-stop shopping' for legal, contractual and marketing advice from a group of subsidiary companies Hauge had set up. His wheeler-dealing had extended to ownership of clubs. He was repeatedly linked with proposed Norwegian takeover bids for clubs including Forest, Wimbledon and Leeds United. And he was also reported to be involved on the fringes of setting up the TV rights deals, which were a thousand times bigger than any transfer deal and had become the financial driving force of football in the English Premier League and beyond.

1993–94 season

The Premiership holders, Manchester United, romped to their first League and Cup double and reached the final of the Coca-Cola Cup, where they were beaten 3–1 by Aston Villa to deny them a unique treble. With Eric Cantona in his prime, United won thirteen of their first fifteen matches and were fourteen points clear at the top of the table by Christmas. They did not lose a home game until March. In January they had drawn 3–3 against Liverpool after taking a three-goal

lead. Later the match was part of the evidenc
against Liverpool goalkeeper Bruce Grobbelaar,
accepting money to fix matches.

The most effective opposition to United came from
and newly promoted Newcastle United, both clubs having
recently spent a fortune in the transfer market. Of the other
Big Five only Arsenal finished near the top of the table.
Liverpool were mediocre by their own recent standards.
Tottenham and Everton both flirted with relegation. Everton
needed to win their last game, against Wimbledon, to stay
up. Everton were two goals down after twenty minutes, but
came back to win 3–2 and avoided the drop. At the time it
was described as one of the greatest comebacks of all time –
a prime example of what made football worth watching. The
result, which meant so much to Everton, was meaningless for
Wimbledon. Before the kick-off they were bound to finish in
sixth place regardless of whether they won or lost. It was later
alleged that Wimbledon goalkeeper Hans Segers had thrown
the game in Everton's favour although, after two trials,
he was not convicted. Sheffield United were relegated in
Everton's place.

12.
Like Christmas Every Day

In June 1996, while most football fans in the country were concentrating on the England team's performance in Euro 96, the European nations championship held in England, the men who ran the Premiership were much more interested in a tournament taking place between a clutch of rival television companies for the rights to live Premier League football, by now established as the key to the future of pay-TV in the UK.

Sky had continued to do brilliantly well out of its 1992 contract with the Premier League. It had indeed been like 'Christmas every day', in Sky chief Sam Chisholm's phrase, for the pay-TV operator. In 1994, two years after acquiring the rights, the company that had once threatened to pull down the whole Murdoch empire into a morass of debt, made annual profits of more than £300 million and achieved a stunning £4 billion market flotation, valuing it as one of the UK's three biggest companies. Chisholm and two other executives, managing director David Chance and finance director Richard Brooke, shared a bonus of £3.8 million deriving from share options in the flotation. Chisholm was put on a salary of over £2 million a year, including profit-related bonuses. Eight other managers received bonuses of more than £500,000.

Rupert Murdoch claimed in 1996 that football had been used as a 'battering ram', which had 'punched' connections to Sky pay services into millions of homes. The punters, not famed for their long memories, had forgotten about his actions after Hillsborough. Sky's own figures underlined the importance of the Premiership to the company. Nine out of ten people with dishes subscribed to the Premier League, which was shown on Sky Sports, the most expensive channel. Three quarters of all subscribers had signed up solely or mainly to watch the football. Sky's share of the total TV audience dropped by half in the summer between Premiership seasons, despite heavy investment to buy summer sports such as cricket.

Sky had put some of the superprofits it had earned from the Premiership into hoovering up the rest of British football. In 1995, in the run-up to renegotiation of the all-important Premiership contract, Sky had bought the rights to the Endsleigh League and the Football League's Coca-Cola Cup (now Worthington Cup) for £125 million. The deal worked out at £25 million a season, compared with £8 million per season previously paid by ITV. Sky had also invested heavily in the FA Cup and England national team games, giving the FA a new multi-million income which came directly from the broadcaster and had nothing to do with the Premier League.

These deals gained less attention than those for the Premier League itself. But pumping money into the FA and the enfeebled Football League was a shrewd political move. Analysts said that Sky was unlikely to see much of a profit on the deals since the number of people who could be persuaded to buy a dish to watch the Endsleigh League or a one-off event like an England international was strictly limited. But they made Sky, who also owned the rights to the Scottish league, the virtual paymaster of British football. In financial terms, the deal established football as an effective partnership with Sky. Others said that the Premiership had in effect become a subsidiary of Sky TV, in the same way that ITV owned *Coronation Street*. Importantly, it meant that if Sky were ever to get into financial trouble, the FA and the Football League, as well as the Premiership, would be very badly hit – at least in the short term. And for most people in the football industry the short term was everything.

When the rights contract came up for renegotiation in 1996, Sky started in pole position. There had been grumbles at first from some of the clubs and especially managers, who objected to Sky's American-style presentation, which at first had included dancing girls, cheerleaders and attempts to get the cameras into the dressing rooms and managers' dug-outs. That had been toned down slightly and the style had settled into a combination of non-stop hype of the wonders of the game and hysterically positive commentary assuring the paying customers that the match they were watching was marvellous, no matter how dire it was in reality.

The American-style approach was carried through in the provision of welters of statistical information on the progress of the game and about individual players, giving matches the conspicuous look of the computer games that were such a big hit with teenagers. The 'feelgood' approach was bolstered by the *Sun* and other Murdoch papers roped in to promote football as a whole. Even the BBC, in its subsidiary role of showing scraps of Sky's live broadcasts, had accepted a clause in its contract promising to present the Premiership in a 'positive light'.

All of this suited the clubs just fine. Initial fears that Sky would not be up to the challenge of presenting hundreds of hours of live football had melted away. The negotiations over the 'renewal' of the contract (as Sky always put it) would be smoother than the original 'drag 'em in and knock 'em down' session in 1992.

Chisholm, his two million a year salary at stake, had nevertheless prepared the ground for the 1996 negotiations with great care. The Premiership had this time decided to use the standard procedure of sealed envelope bids. Sky would have to bid blind for the rights. But Chisholm had cleverly inserted a 'favoured supplier' clause in the 1992 contract, giving Sky the right to match any bid from a rival, once the figures were known. It went down in history that Sky had paid £304 million to beat ITV to the rights in 1992. The reality was that this headline figure was never paid because it was dependent on Sky meeting various targets for the sale of foreign rights, which would then be passed to the Premiership. These targets were never met and Sky had, in fact, paid only about £190 million. This time they were prepared to bid £670 million for a new four-year contract, with no provisos over foreign sales. The figure was hard cash. It would all go to the clubs via the Premier League.

The drama of Sky's bid and renewal presentation itself was acted out in the quaint surroundings of the Coombe Abbey hotel near Coventry. At 5 p.m. on the dot on 6 June 1996 a pair of black Mercedes with tinted windows crunched up the Abbey's long gravel drive, sweeping past the Capability Brown gardens and coming to a smooth halt before the stone steps. The doors flew open in unison and a group of business executives leapt out and jogged determinedly up to reception, led by a stocky little cannon ball of a man with a slight wheeze, Sam Chisholm, the secretive media hard man *par excellence*. Chisholm and the boys from Sky headed straight for the Court House Conference Room, a converted real-tennis court, where the chairmen of the Premier League clubs were waiting for them.

Sky had been facing competition from a variety of companies once it was realized how fantastically favourable to the broadcaster the 1992 deal had been. The most serious threat at first seemed to come from the cable TV companies who, unlike terrestrial broadcasters such as the BBC or the ITV network, could easily put the Premier League into a pay-TV system and thus quickly get their money back by selling more subscriptions.

The vast American multinationals who owned British cable operators were furious with Chisholm and the way he had refused to share Premier League football with them. As a result, the cable system had been stillborn because customers turned down the offer of a cable subscription and instead bought dishes in order to watch the football. In 1992 the cable companies had cheered on Sky from the sidelines, hoping that people would pay to watch the Sky Sports channels, which included the Premier League, via a cable TV subscription. This was perfectly possible technically and in many ways was a better option for customers than buying a dish. The problem was that Chisholm and Murdoch in typically aggressive fashion had decided to charge such high 'wholesale' rates to the cable operators for Sky Sports that they could never hope to make a profit. This was risky for Sky, who might have needed to use the cable system to gain extra subscribers, share the profits and recoup as quickly as possible the money it had invested in acquiring the rights. But Sky was determined to keep every penny for itself, let the cable industry 'go to hell' and, as a useful fringe benefit, establish what amounted to a virtual monopoly in British pay television.

In 1994, midway through the first term of Sky's contract with the Premiership, the cable companies reacted with an extremely aggressive move of their own. They launched a cable exclusive sports channel called SportsWire, signing up the rights to important second string (in terms of pay-TV sales) sports such as cricket, tennis and boxing, each time breaking all records for the rights and out-bidding Sky in each case. Then, also in 1994, the cable industry recruited Kelvin MacKenzie, the former editor of the *Sun* and architect of the paper's coverage of Hillsborough, who had moved on to be in effect Chisholm's deputy at Sky. The plan was that MacKenzie would lead an all-out cable industry assault on Sky – with the rights to the Premier League as the main prize to be fought over. MacKenzie and other cable TV chiefs roped the *Daily Mirror* into the operation, giving the newspaper group its own cable exclusive channel called L!ve TV in return for the newspaper's promotional support. This was important because Sky had needed the constant support of the *Sun* in getting across the message to armchair fans that, yes, they did have to get a dish if they wanted to watch live football. The *Mirror*, according to the plan, would do the same for the cable industry. At one point MacKenzie even had mock editions of the *Mirror* made up, showing a builders' skip full of dishes and offering a one-stop phone line to football fans who, after the intended capture of the Premier League rights, wanted to have their dish removed and cable connection installed.

Although Sky had the right to match any rival bid, the prospect of a bidding war which might double the amount the company had to pay to hang on to its main asset was terrifying. But it was a luscious prospect for the Premier clubs themselves. An auction between two such massive financial concerns, it was soon being said, would push the money on offer towards what analysts believed was its true market value of £1 billion or more – three times what Sky had apparently paid in 1992, more than five times what they had actually paid in practice.

But once again Murdoch and Chisholm showed themselves to be brilliant tacticians, exploiting divisions within the Premier League and the cable companies. In the spring of 1996 Murdoch personally brokered a truce between the cable companies and Sky. He offered the two biggest cable companies at the time, Telewest and Nynex, guaranteed supply of Premier League games at favourable prices if Sky renewed the contract. In return the two cable companies agreed to pull out of the SportsWire cable consortium which was planning to bid against him. They agreed not to mount a rival bid and, just as importantly, undertook with certain reservations not to distribute a rival channel to Sky Sports, even if such a channel bought the rights to the Premier League. At the time Telewest and Nynex controlled more than half the cable network in the UK and so the deal meant that SportsWire and, indeed, any cable exclusive sports channel would never be able to get off the ground. Better still from Murdoch's point of view, since Sky controlled the only really effective satellite distribution and subscription system in the UK, all pay-TV rivals would effectively be knocked out of the bidding before it even started.

The 'sweetheart' deal between Sky and the two cable giants caused uproar in the television business. The clutch of smaller cable companies, who had invested in SportsWire but had been left out of the new deal, felt they had been well and truly mugged. They made threats of legal action and appealed to the Office of Fair Trading, but to no avail. The Mirror Group and its cable allies felt particularly hard done by. They had invested heavily in L!ve TV, which was intended to grow into a clutch of cable exclusive channels, including Live Sport and, Live Movies, built on the back of the all-important Premier League contract.

But, after the clever politicking in the deal with the

cable industry, Chisholm and Murdoch had been just as careful to lobby the Premiership chairmen one by one, as they had done in 1992 in order to see off ITV. Their main ally, once again, was to be Alan Sugar, the former manufacturer of Sky's dishes and a long established business partner of Murdoch. Another ally was Ken Bates, who was at the time battling for absolute control of Chelsea with his former business partner, Matthew Harding. Harding had provided Chelsea with the multi-million-pound loan the club needed to establish itself in the Premiership. In return he had taken a place on the Chelsea board. But Harding and Bates had fallen out over the direction the club was taking and in particular Bates's plan to develop the Stamford Bridge stadium site into a shopping mall and hotel complex. Now Bates wanted Harding out and he saw his share of the money from the renewed Sky deal as the means of paying him off and showing him the door. According to his autobiography Bates told Sky that he wanted a £50 million non-returnable deposit for Chelsea, saying 'that is the kind of package that will swing the deal'. After checking with Parry on how and when the television money would be delivered to the clubs, Bates went to a bank, secured a short-term loan on the strength of Sky's offer, marched up to Harding with a cheque and told his startled ex-partner, 'Here's your money, now fuck off!' The relationship between Sky, Bates and Chelsea was to remain close, with the broadcaster taking a substantial stake in the club and eventually paying millions directly to the club's holding company, Chelsea Village, through the purchase of one of its uniquely expensive executive box suites at the redeveloped Chelsea Village complex.

The most influential pro-Sky figure had once again been Premiership chief executive, Rick Parry, identified in 1992 as 'our man' by Chisholm during his battle with the alliance of the Big Five and Greg Dyke at ITV. This time round Parry was, if anything, even more well disposed to Sky. The Premiership, Parry's baby, was now being talked of as a shining financial success, the latest evidence being the influx of Italian and other foreign stars into Premiership clubs. The partnership with Sky had been crucial to all this and so Parry, like others, could see no reason to upset what appeared to be a smoothly functioning relationship.

At the hotel the Premiership chairmen heard first from the least fancied of the bids – a £1.5 billion offer from Lord Hollick's MAI finance group. Hollick, who also owned the *Daily Express* and a regional ITV company at the time, wanted a ten-year deal, which worked out at £150 million a year – more than the £130 million a year the Mirror–Carlton consortium had put on the table. But the chairmen were not keen on signing up for such a long period, especially with all sorts of new money-making possibilities such as digital TV and individual match pay-per-view subscription on the horizon.

After lunch the chairmen heard from Kelvin MacKenzie and Michael Green. Out of the wreckage of the L!ive TV project the Mirror Group's MacKenzie, allied with Michael Green, head of the ITV company Carlton, had put together a £650 million offer for the rights to show Premier League games on a similar basis to Sky. The Mirror–Carlton consortium planned to sell its 'Goals' Premier League channel via the satellite Eutelsat, and appeared to be the most serious rival to Sky. MacKenzie believed that his ace card was the sheer size of the bid, which he felt, relying partly on his experience of working at Sky and partly on his contacts in the industry, was more than his old bosses were prepared to pay, especially as they would now have to share with their new cable allies at least some of the superprofits they had previously monopolized.

MacKenzie and Green's presentation did not go well. Alan Sugar savaged the proposal to use Eutelsat, saying it was fine for telephone communications but too low down in the sky to be the best option for television. Astra, the satellite used by Sky, was much better. Sugar was the expert, the other chairmen reckoned. After all he had been the main supplier of Sky dishes for years. His technical line of attack seemed to go straight over the head of MacKenzie and Green, while their advisers started squabbling with each other. Sugar looked pleased with himself. The message was loud and clear. The club chairmen had got a ton of cash from Sky, and were about to get tons more. Why take a risk? Better the devil you know . . .

The chairmen then heard from Chisholm and his team. Chisholm seemed confident as he bantered away with 'Deadly Doug' Ellis, owner of Aston Villa. Ellis said that in addition to the screening rights money he wanted a share of the revenue Sky received from advertising during live matches. Chisholm laughed. 'This is some partnership you want, Doug, when you are taking everything from us and leaving us with nothing. Don't be so greedy!'

Chisholm then introduced the head of Sky Sports to make the main pitch. Sky offered £670 million for rights lasting for a further four years. That more or less settled it. Pro-Sky chairmen such as Sugar and Bates snapped their briefcases shut. The offer was £20 million higher than the bid made by Mirror–Carlton, and more than double the £302 million Sky were already paying. (The BBC made a separate but co-ordinated bid to continue *Match of the Day*.) David Dein of Arsenal questioned Chisholm: was that figure based on the subscription money they were already pulling in from the fans, or would they immediately put the price up to restore the company's vast profit margin? Chisholm was non-committal. Dein was the only club representative to vote against the deal.

Feeling pretty certain that the matter was sewn up, Chisholm and his boys said their goodbyes and briskly swept out of the room. 'That's the way we like it – arriving at the last minute, and leaving straight afterwards. That's Sky – you don't know what they are up to, you don't know what they are thinking,' Chisholm told a journalist. A couple of hours later the Sky team were in a nearby country pub when they heard that their bid had been accepted. The 'crown jewels' were in the bag for another four years at a price that would ensure that Sky would still make record profits. According to some estimates they had bought the rights for some £400 million – £100 million a year – less than their true worth. The Sky board were highly delighted. They more than doubled Chisholm's salary from £2 million to £4.7 million a year. David Chance, the managing director, received a £2 million performance-related bonus, based on 1.5 per cent of Sky's turnover.

MacKenzie, presenter of the failed Mirror–Carlton bid, had in contrast hung about in the hotel lobby, chatting to journalists. Had he stayed at Sky, instead of jumping ship and lining up with the cable companies, he would have shared in the multi-million bonus bonanza. (As it happened he still received a £31,000 bonus from Sky in 1996, relating to the performance of the company before he left it.) 'It's tough trying to compete against a monopoly. In the end it was the money that decided it,' MacKenzie complained, before venting his spleen on the Premiership itself. The league, he said, was a cartel which he believed would one day be broken up by the authorities, allowing the big clubs to negotiate their own deals with a variety of broadcasters game by game.

Terry Venables

Tottenham Hotspur, one of the original Big Five, were in trouble during the first seasons of the Premiership. In the 1980s the club had frequently challenged for the League title and enjoyed many trips to Wembley in cup competitions. The team boasted some of the best players in the country and had supplied the talented core of the England squad for the 1990 World Cup – Chris Waddle, Paul Gascoigne and Gary Lineker. Under the ownership of Sky's ally Alan Sugar Tottenham were destined for mediocrity in the Premiership. In the first season they managed to finish only in eighth place. The next season it was fifteenth, below all five of the league's other London clubs. Part of Spurs' problem was the failure to find a manager who would settle. Tottenham's managerial problems began with the departure of Terry Venables, who had fallen out with Alan Sugar after their joint takeover of the club.

It sometimes seemed that there were 'two' Terry Venables, the successful football coach and the disaster- and scandal-prone businessman who was for much of the 1990s a seemingly permanent fixture in the courts. Venables was regarded as a master of the art of manipulating or working with journalists – now a vital part of any football manager's job. He was loved by the soccer hacks while less media-friendly figures such as Kenny Dalglish were disliked, even hated by some.

Chris Horrie

One reason was Venables's easy manner and jack-the-lad 'Del Boy' persona that also made him a natural TV performer. Another was that he ran a drinking club called Scribes West, originally located in the basement of the Daily Mail *building, where football reporters were entertained in royal style. He was especially close to the all-important* Sun, *which had backed his original bid to become joint owner of Tottenham with Alan Sugar, in order to prevent it falling into the hands of Robert Maxwell. Unsurprisingly, the* Mirror *remained Venables's biggest critic. It was part of the growing trend for the tabloids to regard particular managers, players or agents as their property, in terms of access to vast numbers of interviews, quotes and gossip about rivals newspapers needed to keep their acres of football coverage going.* Mirror *football writer Harry Harris had broken the story of Venables's less than straightforward business dealings. Venables accused the* Mirror *of waging a vendetta against him. Eventually he would be banned from being a company director by the DTI, who brought a court case against him involving nineteen specific counts of serious mismanagement relating to his holding company Edennote, to Scribes West and to his time on the board of Tottenham Hotspur. Before that he was involved in multiple libel actions and was forced to pulp his autobiography because of remarks it contained about Sugar.*

After leaving Tottenham Venables landed the job of managing the England national team. The job had fallen vacant in 1994 when Graham Taylor, the incumbent, had failed to qualify for the World Cup. Taylor, like his more successful predecessor Bobby Robson, had been 'crucified' by the tabloids – the Sun *famously turned his head into a turnip. The 'people's choice' for the job was Kevin Keegan of Newcastle, but Keegan was not interested. Venables was a 25–1 longshot, mainly because of the furore over his business affairs. On the other hand, after the tabloid horrors of the Graham*

Taylor era, FA bureaucrats had to balance Venables's awful track-record in the boardroom with his reasonable success as a team manager and, just as importantly, his ability to handle the press. What swung the job for Venables was the intervention of his close friend George Graham, the manager of Arsenal. As he was one of the most successful club managers in England, the FA had naturally approached Graham. But like Keegan, he was more interested in staying at his club. Graham's endorsement, and his willingness to vouch that despite everything Venables was fundamentally sound, persuaded the FA to make the appointment. There was irony here. A few months later Graham himself was to appear before an FA inquiry which implicated him in the Arsenal bungs scandal.

England under Venables had their most successful spell of the 1990s, doing especially well in the Euro 96 championships in England. But Venables's contract was not renewed after that, despite popular demand that he should stay on. By 1996 the DTI investigators were closing in and there had been another round of court appearances even as the England team were playing in Euro 96. A spell as manager of the Australian national team and problem-dogged involvement at Portsmouth and Crystal Palace followed. Both clubs were virtually bankrupt when Venables left them, though – unlike at Tottenham – he had no real responsibility for their financial viability. Still an absolute master as a TV pundit, in 2001 Venables became manager of Middlesbrough, when the team was struggling under the management of ex-Manchester United captain Bryan Robson. In the meantime, after serving a ban resulting from the bungs affair, George Graham had taken Venables's old job as Tottenham manager after a spell at Leeds. Venables brought about an immediate improvement in the Middlesbrough team's performance and the Venables legend – bit of a rogue but inspired manager – was back on

Chris Horrie

track – a testament to the incestuous, almost masonic, nature of the relationship between managers, players and tabloid hacks who knew how to look after each other, arranging the wagons into a circle when necessary.

13.
Bosman

It is September 1996 and a buzz of excitement runs through the marble walkways and oak-panelled corridors of Highbury, the listed 1930s headquarters of the most traditional of English football clubs – Arsenal. In the press room sit the massed ranks of national newspaper soccer hacks. The star-writer 'No 1s' who write the big features and get picture by-lines are out in force. Lined up on the podium in front of them are members of the Arsenal board – Peter Hill-Wood, representing the old money, paternalism and solid respectability of the old order, and David Dein, the wholesale food importer and self-made millionaire who represents the new. Suddenly, after getting the nod, the board members rise respectfully to their feet and break into hearty applause. A tall, gaunt, donnish-looking figure, slightly stooped, walks into the room, bows slightly and takes his seat, centre stage.

After a brief introduction from Hill-Wood, Arsène Wenger, Arsenal's new manager, the man who has stepped into George Graham's disgraced shoes, begins to speak in flawless, if accented English. The hacks are impressed. In contrast to the terse and – frankly – sometimes hostile non-statements provided by managers such as Alex Ferguson and Kenny Dalglish, or the cliché-ridden incoherent flow of Glenn Hoddle or Kevin Keegan, Wenger talks beautifully and gives them what amounts to a half-hour seminar on football philosophy.

'I like modern football made of compact lines, of pressing, quick movements with a strong technical basis,' he says, brow furrowed with concentration and reflection. Another first – Wenger makes an apology. Arsenal had been trying to sign him for several months. He had wanted to come, but had been stuck in a tight contract as manager of the Japanese club Grampus 8. Everybody had known this was the case, even though Arsenal had refused to confirm that he was their new choice of manager. It was 'the worst kept secret in football'.

'Seeing what's been happening and hearing all the stories,' Wenger says, shyly, modestly, 'I felt so frustrated. I put the club in a difficult situation but I could not get out of my Grampus 8 contract'. He then reveals that he chose Arsenal after rejecting an offer to become technical director at the FA, a job which would have given him a big role in managing the England national team. The offer had come from Glenn Hoddle, the newly appointed England manager, who had played under Wenger at Monaco, where the Frenchman had made his name.

What attracted him to England, Wenger says, was the fact that 'the roots of the game are here. I had ten years in France, three in Japan and to go to another country and be successful would be a further step in my development.' Thoughtful, credible, sober. In the papers they said he was 'messianic', and about as different from George Graham as you could get. For a start, he had an economics degree. More importantly, he had a contact book full of foreign players who, it had long been reported, would start to arrive at Highbury just as soon as Wenger's feet were under the table.

'It has always been my dream to manage a top European club at the highest level,' Wenger says.

Arsenal, one of the original Big Five clubs that had set off the chain of events leading to the foundation of the Premiership, had not at first done well in the new competition they had been forecast to dominate.

Under George Graham the team had been lacklustre and the results disappointing. In the first Premiership season, when Graham's involvement with Rune Hauge was peaking, the team had finished tenth, trailing behind the likes of QPR, Norwich and even, horror of horrors, Tottenham. They had done better in the following season, finishing in fourth place, but they were still twenty-one points behind the runaway winners Manchester United and out-gunned by Blackburn Rovers and Newcastle, the upstart clubs of the Premiership, controlled by ambitious owners who did not mind spending millions on players to buy success.

When Graham left the club in February 1995, nothing much had changed. He was replaced by caretaker manager Stuart Houston, who steered the club to a final league table position of twelfth – Arsenal's worst performance since 1976. But given the collapse of morale and the general upheaval at the club, it was surprising that Arsenal did not do even worse. Houston tightened things up a bit, sending John Jensen, the player at the centre of the bung episode, back to Brondby on a free transfer and selling Graham's other Rune Hauge import, Anders Limpar, to Fiorentina for £1,750,000. At the end of the season Houston handed over to Bruce Rioch, the high-achieving former Bolton Wanderers manager, who had been lured to Highbury with the promise that he would be given money to 'rebuild' the team – the standard euphemism for spending on players on a scale to rival that season's Premiership winners, Blackburn.

Arsenal's management were as good as their word. In the summer of 1995 Rioch signed Dennis Bergkamp from Inter Milan for £7.5 million on wages of £35,000 a week and, within a few days, David Platt from Sampdoria. But it was not enough to win the championship, or come anywhere near it. Arsenal finished the season in fifth place. Manchester United were again champions. The three other clubs who finished higher than Arsenal had also invested heavily on players at the start of the season. Second-placed Newcastle had spent £6 million on Les Ferdinand and third-placed Liverpool had broken the British transfer record by signing Stan Collymore for £8.5 million. Fourth-placed Villa, meanwhile, had spent £14 million on players over the previous two seasons.

'Rebuilding' no longer guaranteed success or even an improved league position. Vast sums were needed just to tread water. By the start of the 1995–96 season spending on players by English clubs had increased by more than 80 per cent over the previous season. The Premiership was experiencing a second wave of transfer frenzy. The first had taken place in 1991 and 1992 as clubs chased players capable of staking a place in the new Premiership. Then most of the action had surrounded not the big glamour clubs, but the smaller ones, who were terrified of relegation, of losing their place within the golden circle of the Premiership and Sky's pay-TV money. Now there was a similar effect at the top of the league, with the bigger clubs eager to win the Premiership and thus qualify for the latest TV-generated honeypot, the UEFA Champions' League.

During the 1994–95 season the existing European Cup had been changed from a knock-out competition for the winners of UEFA-affiliated European leagues to a league system, followed by a knock-out phase in the later stages. The effect was dramatic. Instead of a precarious cup competiton where a team might be knocked out in the first round, the league guaranteed a payment of £2 million to each participating team, followed by six matches in the league phase. The prize money for each league game was £500,000 with extra home gate money being worth between £500,000 and £1 million. Winning the competition was estimated to be worth up to £15 million and ensured entry in the following season. With this prospect on offer, in the summer of 1995 a clutch of clubs had joined Arsenal, Newcastle and Liverpool in splashing out on transfers. Between them the Premier League clubs spent £88 million, with thirty-eight players changing clubs for more than £1 million.

Against this background Rioch's signing of Bergkamp represented only modest spending. The Arsenal management realized that they would have to compete much more aggressively in the transfer market if they were going to get anywhere. The problem was that with all the rich clubs chasing a limited supply, the price of English players was going through the roof. Arsenal's experience with Bergkamp showed that, while top foreign players cost a lot of money, they provided much better value. Rioch was an experienced manager but it was doubtful that he had the contacts in a European transfer market swarming with agents like Rune Hauge to bring the sort of players the club needed to Arsenal. Then, a few months after Rioch's appointment, and at the end of the frenzied buying spree of summer 1996, the transfer market was turned upside down by what was to become known as 'the Bosman ruling'.

'Bosman' was an adjudication by the European Court on the case of Jean-Marc Bosman, a footballer who played for RFC Liège in Belgium. When his contract with Liège came to an end, Bosman was not offered a new one. Usually this would have meant enforced retirement from professional football since Belgian footballers, like footballers throughout the world (including

England), did not own the all-important 'registration' which enabled them to play in a professional league.

Ownership of player registrations by football clubs had been the core of the transfer system ever since professional football was established in England and then copied throughout Europe and the world. An individual player assigned his right to play in the league to a single club. It meant that he could play only for them and not for any other club – a bedrock, obviously, of the whole league system. In return for assigning his right to play, the player received a contract of employment. If he did well, another club might want to sign him, meaning that they would buy his registration.

What had always been controversial was the fact that when the contract of employment was up the club still kept the registration. It meant that a player who found himself out of contract could not play for another club even if his contract was not renewed. The effect was to enable the club to make him sign a new contract on worse terms, or retire from football. And this is what Liège had done to Bosman, refusing to allow him to move to another club, Dunkirk, that was interested in renewing his contract.

The system had been challenged many times and had produced some terrible injustices. Brian Clough's loathing of football club chairmen and his contempt for the way the game was run was based partly on his own experience as a player for Sunderland in the 1950s. After scoring thirty goals in a single season, he suffered a serious leg injury. It took him more than a year to recover after which he attempted a comeback. But, Clough bitterly concluded, Sunderland wanted to force him into retirement so they could collect £40,000 on an insurance policy. To qualify for the money the club ruled that he could never play again. Clough asked for a transfer but Sunderland would not agree as it would mean that the insurance money would not be paid. And so he was forced into what he regarded as premature retirement with, at the time, no job prospects and only a £1,000 share of the insurance money to support him.

Bill Shankly, the legendary Liverpool manager, had also suffered. At the end of his playing years, after giving good service to Preston North End, he dropped down the leagues to start his managerial career at Carlisle United. He asked Preston to transfer his registration to Carlisle so that he could act as player-manager and carry on playing for a couple more seasons. The club refused and he never kicked a football as a professional player again. Hundreds of others found that if they were not getting into the first team and requested a transfer to another club they were stuck. The club could set an unrealistically high transfer fee or simply refuse to allow a move.

This hard line had been maintained in Europe right up until September 1996 when Bosman launched his court case. In England the system had already been reformed slightly in the players' favour. In 1978 what was called contract freedom was introduced into the English transfer system. Despite the name the reform did not mean that players were free to sign with any club they wanted. Players still could not force their clubs to reassign their registrations to a new club of their choice. Instead contract freedom was a compromise. When a player's contract of employment was up, the club was required to do one of three things: they could offer him a new contract on the same or better conditions as before; if, in effect, they wanted to sack him, they could assign his registration on a 'free transfer' to any club who was interested in signing him; or, if he was still valuable or in demand, they could ask for a transfer fee. But if the fee was too high and there were no offers, a new Football League Arbitration Committee composed of representatives of the players' union, club chairmen and managers would fix a fair fee in order to allow a transfer to go ahead.

The main effect of the 1978 contract freedom reforms in England was to put up players' wages. Players approaching the end of their contracts could threaten to move to other clubs unless their wages were bumped up and could force through the threat by demanding an arbitrated transfer fee. The value of transfer fees was affected too. Bigger clubs had always been prepared to pay handsomely for the transfer of registrations of star players under contract at smaller clubs. Players subject to transfer bids received 10 per cent of the fee, which was what provided their incentive to go along with the move. But now that the star players in particular were getting much higher wages as a result of contract freedom, the amount that had to be offered as a transfer fee to make a move worth their while also had to increase.

In the first few years after contract freedom was introduced, transfer fees leapt ahead even faster than wages. In 1977, the year before the reform, the record transfer fee was the £440,000 paid by Liverpool for Kenny Dalglish. Two years later the record more than trebled when Aston Villa signed Andy Gray for £1.4 million. Fees would probably have continued to escalate if not for the deep economic recession of the late 1970s and 1980s which meant that clubs simply could not afford the fees. Transfer values started to rise steeply again only in the late 1980s and early 1990s, when the economy recovered and the big clubs began preparing for the Premiership. After 1992, when the first pay-TV deal was done with Sky, and then in the mid-1990s, when the big clubs had much greater gate receipts from their new all-seater stadiums, transfers rocketed.

The European Court set off another massive inflation in players' wages when they ruled that Jean-Marc Bosman was indeed free to move from Liège to Dunkirk. Liège's ownership of Bosman's registration, in effect his licence to play, was deemed to be illegal. It meant that Bosman was free to play for any team who wanted him once he was out of contract and that he was free to negotiate the wages, conditions or signing fee as he wished.

The repercussions of 'Bosman' were felt immediately throughout world football. The first and most dramatic effect to be seen in the Premiership was a massive influx of players born in EU countries since all restrictions on movement of players between clubs in EU countries was abolished, as part of the Bosman ruling. The fact was that there were far fewer English-born world-class players than Italians, Dutch and Frenchmen – as the dismal performance of the England national team showed. English star players were scarce and could therefore charge high wages. Relatively speaking, top-quality European players were cheaper, and the price advantage went all the way down the line to average squad players and even reserve goalkeepers.

Bosman meant that European stars, especially older ones who were coming to the end of their contracts and careers, could be signed on free transfers. A good player could wait until his contract ended and then offer himself without a transfer fee to a big club. At 1995 prices the transfer fee for a top player might already be £10 million. He could offer himself to an interested club, who could afford to pay him fantastic wages by using the £10 million it had saved in not having to pay a transfer fee.

Chris Horrie

The foreign invasion in the wake of Bosman was pioneered in the Premiership above all by Arsenal and by Ken Bates of Chelsea. In July 1995 Chelsea manager Glenn Hoddle established the pattern by signing Ruud Gullit from Sampdoria on a free transfer. Gullit then became the perfect man to lure bargain stars from Italy and Holland and was appointed to replace Hoddle as manager of Chelsea at the end of the season when Hoddle left to take over from Terry Venables as England manager. Gullit immediately signed the Juventus European Cup-winning captain Gianluca Vialli on a Bosman free. Only four years earlier Juventus had paid £12 million for his services. There was no transfer fee, but Vialli's wages were said to be £1.5 million a year. West Ham followed, signing AC Milan's Paulo Futre on a Bosman free, paying him wages put at more than £1 million a year. Two years later Chelsea signed Brian Laudrup on a Bosman free but had to pay out wages of £50,000 per week.

Later, after Gullit fell out with Ken Bates over his own demands for a managerial salary of £1 million a year, Vialli became manager and continued the process, signing twenty-two foreign players in two years. Under Vialli Chelsea fielded the first ever Premiership team composed entirely of foreigners.

The effect of Bosman at Arsenal, and especially at Manchester United, was very different. Instead of presenting them with the opportunity to sign players on free contracts, the danger was that their own stars would move to Europe on Bosman transfers at the end of their contracts. To keep players such as David Beckham, Ryan Giggs and Roy Keane in place the United management found that they had to offer vast new salary packages in return for long Bosman-proof contracts. Post-Bosman contract negotiations meant that

United's salary bill was to almost double, reaching more than £20 million as contracts came up for renegotiation. After talk of moving to play in Italy, Roy Keane broke the record set by Laudrup at Chelsea and finished the decade on wages of £52,000 a week. There was a similar story at Arsenal, where the club's wage bill leapt from £8.7 million to £13.3 million in the first year after Bosman.

By the time Wenger arrived at Highbury in September 1996 he had already arranged for Patrick Vieira, the midfielder who was to be the key to his new playing regime, to arrive from AC Milan for a fee of £3.5 million. Vieira was soon followed by the striker Nicolas Anelka from Paris St-Germain for £500,000. Wenger cleared out almost all the players he inherited from the Graham era, keeping only the defence (Graham's strong suit as a manager) built around goalkeeper David Seaman and England centre-back Tony Adams. The midfield centred on Vieira was good enough and in Bergkamp and Anelka he had forwards who, in theory, were the equal of any in Europe. But it was still not enough. Newcastle United had spent £15 million on one player, Alan Shearer, and another £6.7 million on Faustino Asprilla, and even lowly Middlesbrough had been able to find the £7 million needed to import the 'White Feather', Fabrizio Ravanelli, from Juventus. At the end of Wenger's first season Arsenal finished third, behind champions Manchester United and high-spending Newcastle. It was Arsenal's best performance in the Premiership, closing the gap on Manchester United to only seven points, and they would have been second if not for the fact that Newcastle had a better goal difference.

In the summer 1997 close season Wenger brought in another clutch of French players, the most important being the pony-tailed international midfielder Emmanuel

Chris Horrie

Petit, signed from Monaco for £2.5 million, and the Dutch international Marc Overmars, for £7 million. Altogether in his first two years in the job Wenger recruited eighteen players, all but one of them foreign. During the same period he sold seventeen players, and all but four were English. Bringing these players in alongside Vieira at last gave Arsenal a midfield to match the essentially home-grown combination of Beckham, Giggs and Scholes at Manchester United. Wenger's team was probably worth £100 million if each player was sold off, one by one, but Wenger had been able to assemble it for £20 million by using his contacts. In 1997–98 Arsenal won the Premiership by a single point from United, who significantly had spent far less on new players in that particular season.

The run-in to the championship had been strangely anti-climactic in a way. Since the spring only Arsenal and United had been in the running and the third-placed team, Liverpool, trailed more than ten points behind at the finish. Part of the reason for this was that there had been further changes in the organization of the Champions League which meant that both the Premiership champions and the runners-up would qualify for the European competition. Naturally winning the championship was still important to clubs – and even more so to their fans – but the loss of the unique honour of playing in Europe awarded to the champions seemed to take the edge off the competition.

Sometimes Arsenal and Manchester United gave the impression that they were no longer all that interested in playing in the Premiership, seeing it as merely a lengthy prelude to another season playing in Europe. United already seemed to have pulled out of the Worthington Cup run by the rump Football League, by fielding only a reserve side and regarding it as really more trouble than it was worth.

From 1998 onwards it was increasingly being said that the Premiership, the competition officially set up as 'a league of equality', was now in reality three leagues in one. First, there was the competition for the two Champions' League places. In practice only a maximum of four or five teams could realistically see themselves as in with a chance and, as the seasons passed, this seemed to be whittled down to just two, United and Arsenal, the new Big Two, who might entertain the idea of breaking away from the Premiership to play for additional tens of millions in a European Super League, much in the same way that the original Big Five had plotted to break away from the Football League.

The second league within a league involved a more varied group of about ten middling clubs, who had a chance of finishing in the top six and thus qualifying for the less prestigious European competition, the UEFA Cup. Thirdly, for another ten or so clubs there was the humiliating, but nevertheless exciting, annual struggle to avoid relegation or, if recently promoted, to stay in the Premier League in the Micawber-like hope that things would look up.

How long Manchester United and Arsenal would put up with playing the likes of Coventry City and Wimbledon in the Premier League when they could be playing Barcelona and Juventus, was anyone's guess. The main problem seemed to be that leaving the Premiership, or even downgrading it in some way, would be a risky venture, just as the original breakaway from the Football League to form the Premiership had been.

If a European Super League was ever to get off the ground it would need a massive amount of seed capital to underwrite the potential loss of the clubs' 'bread and butter' income from playing in the Premiership, a team of high-powered lawyers to deal with the inevitable legal wrangles, good political contacts throughout the continent and most importantly the prospects of a pay-TV deal so luscious that it would put even the Premiership deal with Sky TV into the shade. In the autumn of 1998 a group of Italian businessmen swooped on the Premiership offering all of these things and trying to sign up Manchester United, Arsenal and Liverpool. The move led to the bitterest battles within English football yet seen, and for a year or more seemed to threaten the very existence of the Premiership.

1994–95 season

A two-horse race: Blackburn, the eventual winners by the margin of a single goal and a single point, and Manchester United went out ahead early in the season and stayed there. Newcastle had again been contenders, until they sold leading goalscorer Andy Cole to Manchester United half-way through the season, believing that the player had a long-term injury from which he might never recover. Alan Shearer, in his best season, stayed free of serious injury for the first time since joining Blackburn, and was joined by Chris Sutton – the 'SAS' strike force. This was enough to give them the edge, especially after Eric Cantona was banned in January for more than a year for attacking a Crystal Palace fan with his infamous kung fu kick at Crystal Palace. At a press conference afterwards all Cantona would say was: 'When the seagulls follow the trawler, it is because they think sardines will be thrown in the sea'. Cantona's departure destabilized United. But even so they managed to beat Ipswich 9–0 at Old Trafford. The championship was not decided until the last eight minutes of the last games of the season. To win the Premiership for the third time United needed Blackburn to lose or draw their away game against Liverpool and win themselves away to West Ham. Blackburn seemed to have things sewn up when they went 1–0 up. But Liverpool equalized and then, with eight minutes to go, Jamie Redknapp scored to win the game for Liverpool. At the time United were drawing. If they could score they would win the championship. They failed to do so, with Andy Cole missing several easy chances. United also lost the FA Cup final, 1–0 to Everton.

14.
Welcome to Hell

The European dimension of the Premiership age began in unglamorous surroundings with Manchester United playing the semi-professional Hungarian champions Kispet Honved in a dilapidated stadium in front of a crowd of 9,000 people.

United, the first Premiership champions, had won the right to play in the 1993–94 European Cup. But since they had not appeared in the European Cup since 1969 (when they were knocked out by AC Milan after qualifying as the previous year's winners), they were officially rated as a minor team, and had to suffer the indignity of appearing in a qualification round designed to thin out the champions of countries such as Malta and Albania before the big teams from Italy, France, Germany, Spain and Holland joined the fray. For the record, United won the game 3–2. The subsequent home match against Honved in the two-legged tie was played in front of 34,000 in the half-built shell of the redeveloped Old Trafford. United won 2–1 to go through by five goals to three to the first round proper, another two-legged affair also against unfancied opposition, the Turkish champions Galatasaray, played in September 1993.

United slipped up in the home leg of the Galatasaray tie, surrendering a two-goal lead and going behind 2–3 before a late goal by Eric Cantona drew the match. It was a great result for the Turkish champions. Under the away goals rule it meant they would go through to the next round if they could draw their home leg. Either way the arithmetic was simple. Whatever else happened, if

United did not score a goal in Istanbul they would lose the tie and Galatasaray would be through.

The Turkish fans, some of the most fanatical in Europe, sensed the possibility of a rare victory over one of the most famous clubs in the world. They started gathering around the ground early on the day of the match, beating drums, letting off fireworks and generally whipping themselves into a frenzy. A huge crowd had gathered at the airport, ready to meet the United team with a wall of abuse. Alex Ferguson later said that the scene at the airport had 'the atmosphere of a bear pit – the most harassment and hostility I have ever experienced in football'. One group of fans carried a huge banner with the message 'WELCOME TO HELL' crudely drawn in giant letters. The team coach was pelted with rotten fruit as it made its way to the ground. Inside the stadium, amid the smoke bombs and continuous booing, some of the United players experienced the Turkish crowd as 'a wall of hatred', barely restrained by great phalanxes of riot police who, Ferguson later said, 'were even more frightening than the fans'. After the game many of the handful of United fans who had flown to Turkey for the match were arrested and held overnight in the cells, according to club officials 'for no other reason than that they were supporters of Manchester United'.

The Galatasaray team's tactics for the game itself were simple. All they had to do was stop United scoring and so, reasonably enough, they defended in depth for the entire ninety minutes. The problem for United was that every time their players ran into any sort of threatening position the referee would blow up and give Galatasaray a free kick. Either that or the Turkish defenders would foul the United players with apparent impunity, and the referee, Kurt Rothlisberger would wave play on.

Chris Horrie

Cantona, famously short-tempered, started arguing with Rothlisberger but managed to contain himself until the final whistle went. Then he walked up to the ref and roundly abused him. Even though the match was over, Rothlisberger gave him a red card. As Cantona walked back into the players' tunnel he was hit on the head with a truncheon by one of the riot police. Blood streaming from his head, Cantona started swearing, blurted something unprintable into a French TV's microphone and added, speaking in French, that the Swiss referee had been so biased that he must have taken a bung. For that Cantona was charged by UEFA with bringing the game into disrepute, received a four-match European ban and was heavily fined.

Subsequent events seemed to show that Eric Cantona had been justified in his suspicions. Three years later Rothlisberger was caught soliciting a £45,000 bribe from the Swiss club Grasshopper Zürich in return for which he offered to persuade a Belarussian referee to fix a forthcoming Champions' League tie with Auxerre. At the time Rothlisberger was suspended from refereeing duties because, bizarrely, he had stood for the Swiss parliament as a member of the National Council Party, using the FIFA logo and pictures of himself in his referee's kit. This was against FIFA's rules. In May 1993 Rothlisberger was the referee in the European Cup final between Marseille and AC Milan. There was no evidence that he took a bribe, but within days of the match a big corruption scandal broke in France during which it was proved in court that Marseille chairman Bernard Tapie had systematically bribed or attempted to bribe referees in the French league all season. During the 1994 World Cup in the USA, Rothlisberger was sent home by FIFA after he was unable to explain why he failed to award Belgium a blatantly undeserved penalty in their 3–2 second-round defeat by Germany. In 1997 FIFA banned Rothlisberger from refereeing anywhere in the world and then ordered investigations into allegations of bribery in World Cup qualifying matches involving Switzerland, Turkey and Norway.

None of this should have come as a complete surprise. The fact was that the European competition, on which all the top Premiership clubs were now focusing their attention and ambition, had been riddled with match-fixing and bribery for at least twenty years. The European Cup had always been dominated by clubs from Spain, Italy, Portugal, Russia and other countries where corruption in public life was commonplace. Milan, the leading club of the 1980s and early 1990s, and its owner Silvio Berlusconi were by the 1990s caught up in a mass of allegations of fraud in the overlapping worlds of banking, property dealing, and politics. Long before he became a cocaine addict, Diego Maradona had gone on the record to say that his Italian club, Napoli, was 'in the hands of organized crime'.

There were similar problems in Spain. In the year 2000 the president of one of its leading clubs, Jesus Gil of Atlético Madrid, was jailed after it was found that he had laundered $3.2 million stolen from the city of Marbella through the accounts of the club, disguising the fraud as payment for shirt advertising. Other charges included tax evasion on a massive scale, fraud involving the signing of street derelicts as squad players on vast kickback contracts, the use of double contracts for genuine star players and embezzlement of club funds. A major Spanish club, meanwhile, were allowed to run up debts of £160 million with impunity and were accused during a corruption trial in France of having attempted to bribe referees in 'every

Chris Horrie

game' they played in European competitions.

The Romanian league admitted that match-fixing was 'endemic', and the country's greatest modern player, Gheorghe Hagi, went even further, saying that the Romanian league was 'entirely fixed'. He claimed that the chairmen of two of the country's club sides 'meet in a restaurant and write on pieces of paper; that one will get the title, that one will be relegated'. Ten years earlier the neighbouring Yugoslav league found that match-fixing was so widespread that it took the extraordinary step of nullifying an entire season's results. Then one of Yugoslavia's leading clubs ended up in the hands of 'Arkan', the paramilitary terrorist implicated in war crimes who was subsequently murdered. It was discovered that in 1984 the Belgian club Anderlecht had bribed a referee in order to beat Nottingham Forest in the semi-final of the UEFA Cup. Through the mid-1990s individual or multiple instances of bribery and thrown games came to light in Cyprus, Georgia, Belgium, Switzerland, Germany, Russia, Greece, Malta and Ukraine, where in 1995 Dynamo Kiev were banned for two seasons after being found guilty of attempting to bribe the Spanish referee in a Champions' League game against Panathinaikos.

In 1996 UEFA at last took action, setting up a committee to investigate corruption in the European competitions. The spur was an apparent attempt by Dynamo Kiev to bribe a referee in a home Champions' League match. The following year a newspaper reported UEFA official Rene Eberle as saying that they were not getting very far. 'We are still pursuing a number of active cases,' he said, 'but in a lot of cases we run into dead ends and we get furious.' One recommendation from the committee was that referees for Champions' League matches should not be selected until twenty-four hours before the game and that they should then be accompanied by a UEFA minder at all times until the match was over.

The UEFA inquiry eventually came to centre on Portugal, where clubs were linked through transfer activity to the criminalized mess of Brazilian and South American football. The chairmen of two top clubs, Porto and Sporting Lisbon, admitted that they had regularly bribed referees. Jorge Gonçalves, a former chairman of Sporting who had fled to Angola to avoid tax evasion charges, said that he had fixed 'dozens' of games and that bribery was 'widespread' among leading clubs in Portugal and Europe. Other club directors in Portugal were placed under investigation for arranging holidays in Brazil for referees, paid for by the club. UEFA found that Porto had bribed a Romanian referee to fix a 1984 Cup Winners' Cup semi-final against Aberdeen.

In addition to the UEFA inquiry the French law courts began to tease out the details of systematic match-fixing in the European Cup involving French clubs. In 1996 former Olympique Marseille chairman Bernard Tapie was jailed over football-related bribery and fraud stretching back to 1993. The club was stripped of its 1993 European Cup win and relegated from the French First Division. This was followed by another sensational case which saw directors and officials of Bordeaux in the dock on fraud and corruption charges.

Former Bordeaux manager Didier Couecou was given a four-month sentence for using Yugoslav agent Ljubomir Barin to hand out bribes on a grand scale to referees in charge of the club's European games. The fixing dated back to Bordeaux's 1–0 defeat by Hamburg in a 1981

Chris Horrie

UEFA Cup game. Hamburg had won by means of a disputed penalty and the Bordeaux management were convinced that the referee had been bribed. Barin told the court that he remembered telling the Bordeaux chairman that if he wanted his club to achieve European status he would 'have to act like the rest of them'. Barin said that after word got around that Bordeaux were willing to hand out cash and take care to cover it up, 'referees scrambled over each other to come here'. In addition to cash, referees of European matches were treated to gourmet meals, luxury hotel rooms and call girls costing up to £2,000 a night. 'Sometimes we needed to hire three or four women and when the referees were greedy they insisted on two nights,' Barin told the court. 'We also had to think of the referees' wives. Officials went home with suitcases full of watches and fur coats.' According to Barin, after one UEFA Cup game against Naples in 1988 the three German match officials were given £35,000 between them. All this was done, Barin said, merely to give Bordeaux a chance of competing with other clubs. Real Madrid, he claimed, used to bribe referees with £4,000 Rolex watches.

Over a period of several years Bordeaux spent £5 million on bribes. The money came from a slush fund created from kickbacks on player transfers. Four club officials were found guilty of avoiding tax on £4 million received from the sale of six players in 1996, £600,000 of which was diverted into the slush fund. Another case was that of the transfer of the former Manchester United player Jesper Olsen. Bordeaux's accounts recorded a payment of £890,000 made for the player. But only the agreed fee of £850,000 went to United, who were entirely unaware that £40,000 had been paid into Bordeaux's slush fund. According to Barin, dozens of other transfers throughout Europe were done in this way.

Most match-fixing had taken place in order to win competitions and gain the relatively small rewards, given the risks involved, of prize money and gate receipts. But from the early 1990s a new threat emerged – the rigging of games shown on TV in the Far East for the benefit of syndicates of criminal bookmakers. The problem was that betting in countries like Singapore and Malaysia was extremely popular but illegal. Betting had always been in the hands of criminals and they had systematically corrupted most sports in their own countries, including football. In 1995 the Malaysian authorities finally acted, announcing that fifty-eight games in a single season had been fixed and arresting 150 players. Long before this the punters had realized that the games were rigged and not worth betting on. In contrast the World Cup and European games, including Premier League matches, now available for the first time on satellite TV, had the reputation of being clean and began to attract massive numbers of bets.

The criminal syndicates followed the money. The head of the Asian Football Federation, Peter Velappan, claimed that the syndicates had targeted the 1994 World Cup in the USA and had offered bribes to players and officials, especially in the later stage games, which drew vast audiences in the Far East. A Malaysian book-maker called Rajendran Kurusamy was jailed for six months after it was found that he had made a profit of £8.4 million in three months from betting on World Cup games, some of which were likely to have been fixed. US national squad members Roy Wegerle and John Harkes told the British press that they had been approached by representatives of Far Eastern syndicates offering bribes to throw a World Cup qualifier against

El Salvador. They reported the matter to the US soccer authorities.

In 1997 match-fixing came closer to home when two Premiership goalkeepers, Bruce Grobbelaar of Liverpool and Hans Segers of Wimbledon, stood trial twice on charges of accepting money from a Malaysian business-man to throw games. A third player, John Fashanu, was accused of acting as a go-between. Grobbelaar was charged with taking a £40,000 bribe in 1993 to let in goals during a game against Newcastle, which Liverpool lost 3–0, and of collecting £125,000 for letting in three goals in a game against Manchester United, ensuring that the game ended in a 3–3 draw. At the time, the Liverpool–United game had been raved about as one of the most exciting in history. United had gone three goals up in the first few minutes before Liverpool scored three in the last part of the game. Schmeichel later revealed that after the match manager Alex Ferguson 'wasn't just livid, he was absolutely hysterical' and 'heaped derision' on his performance, at one point threatening to throw a cup of tea in the goalkeeper's face. Schmeichel phoned his agent Rune Hauge the next day and asked him to look for a new club. But the row blew over and Schmeichel continued to play for Manchester United.

Segers, meanwhile, was accused but not convicted of taking money to produce draws in more than one Wimbledon match, including a crucial 1994 bottom-of-the-table game against Everton. Wimbledon had been in front 2–0 before Segers let in three goals to give Everton the points and save them from relegation. The source of the cash was Heng Suan Lim, a London-based business man with links to Far Eastern betting syndicates.

The evidence had started to mount up after 1994, when a former Malaysian match-fixer turned supergrass and became a key police witness in a number of bribery cases. The trail of corruption led to the World Cup and the Premiership. The leading Malaysian journalist Johnson Fernandez, covering the story for the Malaysian *Daily Mail*, claimed that he had seen the names of six top players in the English Premiership on a list of players the syndicates planned to bribe around the world.

During the two goalkeepers' first trial the prosecution alleged that twenty-five matches involving Liverpool, Wimbledon and Southampton – Grobbelaar's club after his transfer from Liverpool – might have been fixed. The *Sun* had obtained a video of Grobbelaar appearing to take cash from businessman, Christoper Vincent, and undertaking to throw games in return. During the trial Segers admitted taking £45,000 from Lim, who claimed that he had also made payments to Grobbelaar. There was evidence of extensive mobile phone contact between Lim, Grobbelaar, Segers and Fashanu, apparently related to the placing of large bets on particular games.

Lim said that he was acting mainly for an Indonesian 'benefactor' called Johannes Josef, who would bet up to £50,000 a week on Premiership games. Segers claimed that he took the money in return for innocently 'forecasting' (predicting results) and that he was being paid for his football expertise and not to actually influence the outcome of games. Forecasting itself was a breach of FA rules, because of the obvious danger of players taking steps to make the predictions for which they were being paid come true. Segers and Grobbelaar both denied throwing games. Fashanu exercised his right to stay silent and said nothing.

After thirty-four days the first trial ended with the jury unable to reach a verdict. The re-trial was, if anything, more dramatic than the first, lasting twelve weeks and costing more than £12 million. The key defence witness was Bob Wilson, the former Arsenal goalkeeper turned broadcaster, who impressed the jury by examining a number of goals on video explaining how Grobbelaar and Segers had done all they could to stop the goals or had simply made honest mistakes. Even after Wilson's *tour de force* the jury could not reach a verdict that the crime had taken place 'beyond reasonable doubt'. In order to avoid a third trial the judge, Mr Justice McCullough, formally entered a verdict of Not Guilty. In September the FA charged Grobbelaar and Segers with breaking the FA's rules on betting. Grobbelaar sued the *Sun* for libel and won damages. The case dragged on to appeal, until in January 2001 a High Court judge reversed the verdict in the libel case finding, in effect, that Grobbelaar may indeed have been guilty of taking bribes.

But even after Grobbelaar's and Segers's court appearances attempts to affect the outcome of games in order to defraud bookmakers continued. The method used exploited the fact that for betting purposes results stood even when games had to be abandoned, so long as at least one minute in the second half had been played. The scam involved sabotaging the floodlights, causing matches to be abandoned in the second half once the required score was achieved. In a game between West Ham and Crystal Palace at Upton Park in November 1997 the floodlights failed seconds after Frank Lampard had scored for West Ham in the sixty-fifth minute, bringing the score to 2–2. In retrospect much about the game seemed odd. In the first half Palace went ahead by two goals, both scored by out-of-form striker Neil Shipperley, who had scored only once in the whole of the previous season. The widely quoted odds on Shipperley scoring the first goal were 8–1 and on him getting two goals in the game probably more than 20–1. And, as it happened, both goals were flukes.

The first came when a West Ham defender took a throw-in half-way inside his own half. Most of the West Ham players were well up the pitch, but the defender unexpectedly lobbed the ball backwards towards his goalkeeper, Craig Forrest. The goalkeeper kicked the ball weakly, straight towards Palace player Simon Rodger. With the West Ham defence up the field, the ball was passed to Shipperley, who kicked it into the net from 20 yards. Minutes later Rodger and Shipperley combined again. Rodger took a corner and Shipperley, left entirely unmarked, headed the ball straight at Forrest. The ball bounced off the goalkeeper and went over the bar. Shipperley had better luck in the final minute of the first half when he got the ball in the six-yard box. His West Ham marker fell over, allowing him to side-foot the ball into the net past a stranded Craig Forrest.

In the second half Shipperley was again involved in goals, this time for West Ham. In the fifty-third minute he fouled West Ham's David Unsworth, providing the home side with a free kick in a dangerous position, from which they scored. Lampard scored for West Ham ten minutes later making it 2–2. Then the lights went off. There was never any suggestion that the match was fixed or that Shipperley was involved, though it was later shown in court that the floodlights had been sabotaged so they could be turned off by remote control if a 2–2 scoreline was achieved. After the game West Ham manager Harry Redknapp had nevertheless quipped that he wished he had put a 'monkey' (betting slang for £500)

Chris Horrie

on the result, adding that he was 'only joking'. He had recently criticized stricter FA rules aimed at banning from gambling managers and others in the game with potential power over results. Doubtless, in retrospect, Redknapp would have thought his innocent joke unwise.

Earlier in the season a match between Derby County and Wimbledon had been abandoned when the floodlights failed after fifty-one minutes, freezing the result at 2–1 to Derby. It was only after the third Premiership floodlight failure of the season, with the score at 0–0 one minute into the second half of a game between Arsenal and Wimbledon at Wimbledon's ground, Selhurst Park, on 22 December that the police started to take an interest. It was later shown that 'devices of darkness' had been inserted into the Selhurst Park floodlight substation, enabling criminals to switch off the floodlights at will using a gadget similar to a TV remote control, once the desired result had been achieved.

In 1999 Scotland Yard detectives discovered that bets of up to £30 million a time were being placed on matches where floodlights failed. They found that since the English Premiership began to be shown on satellite TV in the Far East, the Malaysian, Hong Kong and Singapore betting syndicates who had been the source of money paid to Segers and Grobbelaar had targeted it. It was estimated that the syndicates could make profits of up to £30 million on a single Premiership game, which meant that they had plenty of money to bribe whoever it took to achieve the rigged result.

They also had no difficulty in finding London-based criminals willing to sabotage the floodlights at West Ham, Wimbledon and Crystal Palace, the three proven cases. The courts heard how Chee Kew Org, a London-based Malaysian gambler and car dealer, had bribed a security guard at Charlton's ground to allow him and an electronics engineer into the floodlight control room, where they inserted the ingenious remote control device. When they remotely switched the power off the lights would go out. They would then switch the power back on a few seconds later. This did not restore the light, because floodlights take fifteen minutes to warm up, but when engineers investigated the power would be flowing normally. The remote would be used to switch the lights quickly on and off until the match was abandoned, leaving everyone mystified.

The police evidence was that Chee Kew Org was being paid by Wai Yuen Liu, a Hong Kong-born gambler and convicted credit-card fraudster, who was wanted by the Hong Kong police in connection with illegal betting and attempted bribery during the 1994 World Cup. The problem of corruption in Chinese football, emanating from gambling-crazy Hong Kong, was so severe that in 1998 five international players were jailed for systematically fixing league games and World Cup qualifying matches. An official government newspaper announced an anti-corruption campaign, claiming that every club in the Chinese national league had been involved in match-rigging. The problem was, if anything, worse in Malaysia and Singapore, where over 100 players were arrested during one anti-fraud operation. Wai Yuen Liu, the organizer of the Chinese–Malaysian floodlight gang in London, was described in court as the 'fixer' for the Far Eastern syndicates. The scam was uncovered when Chee Kew Org offered £20,000 to a security guard at Charlton Athletic to allow his electricians into the ground ahead of the game between Charlton and Liverpool. The guard told the police who made arrests.

Chris Horrie

Before the arrests Mike Saunders, the managing director of Victor Chandler, the biggest offshore betting organization in Europe, had told the British press that match-fixing was 'rife' in Europe and they were taking extra care before accepting very large bets on individual games in the Premiership or Champions' League.

Following revelations about attempted match fixing during the 1994 World Cup in the USA, a promised FIFA crackdown on match-fixing in the World Cup did seem to be entirely successful. In the run-up to the 1998 World Cup in France it was estimated by bookmakers that £3 billion would be bet on the competition, with most of the money coming from the Far East and being wagered on the early rounds featuring teams from notoriously corrupt football associations in Africa, South America and Eastern Europe. A large bookmaking firm traced back to Malaysia a £15 million bet placed (using a great number of 'cut out' agents to buy the actual stakes) on a match between Paraguay and Cameroon. Cameroon had recorded some extraordinary results over the years, including a 1–0 victory over Diego Maradona's Argentina, then reigning world champions, in the opening match of the Italia 90 World Cup.

Then there was the new sensation of 'spread betting', which expanded the possibilities for corruption enormously. In a spread bet it was no longer necessary to predict the result or final score. Punters could bet on any aspect of the game – for example, the time of the first throw-in or the number of yellow cards. And they no longer had to get even these details absolutely right to make a killing.

Spread betting originated among commodity brokers in the City of London and was modelled on the way financial traders bought and sold 'positions' based on their predictions of the way stock and commodity prices would move. It works best with sports such as cricket, where there are a lot of variables. A bookie might offer fixed odds on a particular number of runs being scored in a match, but getting this right is so improbable that the bet is hardly worth it, no matter how astronomical the odds. Spread betting allows the bookie to offer a range ('spread') of results – for example, between 200 and 300 runs being scored in a cricket match. If the punter thinks that more than 300 runs will be scored he can 'buy' runs over 300, the upper limit of this particular spread, for a fixed amount of money per run, say £10. If the actual score is much higher than the top of the spread he will make a fortune. A score of 400 would make him 100 x £10, amounting to £1,000. On the other hand, he will lose £10 for every run under 300. So if the team scores only 100 runs he will lose 200 x £10, amounting to £2,000. Alternatively, if the punter thinks that the team will do worse than the lower end of the spread, he can 'sell', gaining £10 for every run under 200 and losing £10 for every run scored over 200. One attraction is that there is no limit to the amount of money that can be won (or lost) by placing a spread bet. It is an extremely exciting – and, for some, addictive – pursuit, described in the industry as 'the crack cocaine of betting'.

Spread betting offered immediate and obvious opportunities for corrupting sport in ways which would be easier than ever to pull off, very hard to detect and need not involve a player in throwing or losing a game. This is exactly what happened on a massive scale in cricket when Hansie Cronje took to fixing exceptionally high or low scores that did not necessarily affect the outcome of a match. In football it meant that it was no longer necessary to predict an exact result in order to win a lot of money. A spread could be offered on the total number of goals – much easier for would-be match-fixers to control – rather than a win, loss or draw. It also meant that trivial aspects of a game could be fixed without affecting the result.

At first spread bets were taken, for example, on the time of the first throw-in. The spread betting specialists IG Index offered a spread of around two to three minutes and allowed punters to buy or sell positions based on seconds. They stopped taking bets on throw-ins when they lost a lot of money on a Premiership game in 1998. The game kicked off and the ball was knocked straight into touch. But spread betting was still available on such things as the number of yellow cards, the amount of injury time added to a game, the number and time of substitutions – all matters that could be influenced by players, referees or managers without seriously affecting the course of the game.

One of the official reasons for the establishment of the Premiership had been that it would provide the top clubs with the money they said they needed to compete effectively in Europe. By the late 1990s that goal had become a reality. But in Europe cases of match-fixing and bribery were uncovered so frequently that they had even started to lose their ability to shock.

Kenny Dalglish

For many, Blackburn's championship win had a strange air of artificiality about it. It was not the first time that a team had come up from the Second Division to win the championship, or come close, in the following season. In fact in the pre-Premiership age it happened fairly often. Brian Clough had done it twice with Derby County and Nottingham Forest. But never before had a rich businessman like Jack Walker arrived at a club, buried the past within a matter of months, hired a manager like Kenny Dalglish who had already won the championship both as a player and as a manager, bought a team of international stars off the peg and provided them with a brand-new stadium in which to play. The presence of Dalglish, a figure completely identified in the public mind with Liverpool, at the centre of the drama also had a weird, unbelievable air to it.

Dalglish was the last of a long production line of hard-bitten Scottish players and managers who had dominated English football for much of the century. As a teenager he played for Cumbernauld United and Celtic, where he once played in midfield in a reserves game against Alex Ferguson, then Glasgow Rangers' reserve centre-forward. Ferguson retired and Dalglish graduated to become Celtic's centre-forward before following the well-worn path from Glasgow to Liverpool during the Merseyside club's heyday. The Liverpool teams of the 1970s and 1980s which had dominated English football contained many talented and skilled players, but above all they were physically strong, disciplined, aggressive and drilled with military precision by tough-minded Scottish managers tinged with fanaticism.

This was football as warfare. While their great rivals Manchester United went for skilled individualists and enter-tainers, Liverpool were a solid phalanx. They would run twice as far, tackle twice as hard and watch each other's backs. Often the latest set of talented dilettantes at United would beat Liverpool in League matches. But Liverpool would go on to grind out results, winning trophy after trophy. Dalglish fitted the mould. 'I was such a competitive player,' he once said, looking back, 'that I have punched players. I didn't regard myself as a dirty player. Simply one prepared to look after himself. Battling against defenders can be a violent business.' In the Liverpool team his greatest friends were fellow 'jocks' Alan Hansen and, above all, Graeme Souness, a player who Dalglish said 'had everything' but who was best known for his 'courage' (meaning ferocious tackling) and iron determination to win.

That was Liverpool: backs to the wall, courage and determination above all else, underdogs against the world, building the team from the defence forward, strikers expected to tackle back. 'Intimidation is part and parcel of a defender's game,' Dalglish said. 'Their job is to find a striker's Achilles heel, sometimes literally, to put him off his stride, to get him off the pitch.' It got results. Liverpool, a city that carried both a massive chip on its shoulders and the scars of Irish religious sectarianism, was the perpetual loser of the English social scene. But Liverpool FC won everything.

'This is Anfield', it said above the players' tunnel leading to the inferno of a pitch surrounded by what in the pre-Premiership age was a wall of noise – 'abandon all hope ye who enter here' seemed to be the implication. It was designed to intimidate visiting teams. More than one said that it used to scare the pants off them even before they saw the likes of Graeme Souness steaming towards them. Football as war.

Liverpool's team spirit was such that they liked to promote people to managerial positions from within the club itself – ex-players went to the boot room – or from within a pool created by the Liverpool–Glasgow axis. Dalglish followed this pattern: blooded in the team and then groomed to take over as manager. He became manager just after the Heysel disaster which ended the club's long series of European Cup runs and wins. He was manager at the time of Hillsborough, fearing at first that his own son had been killed in the disaster.

He attended the long series of funerals and church services afterwards and then felt physically ill when he took his team to play at Hillsborough in the following season. By 1990 Dalglish was suffering such emotional stress that he started coming out in rashes. Then he almost killed himself in a bizarre gardening accident. He was electrocuted by an incorrectly wired garden strimmer and would have died if his wife had not rushed out to pull the cable from the plug. One of the pins burnt a deep hole in his thumb. The strimmer accident, the rashes and the fact that he often found himself unable to concentrate or make decisions led Dalglish to decide he needed a break from football. He resigned as manager in 1991 and was replaced by his old pal Graeme Souness.

Apart from Hillsborough and the pressures of football management, there had been another factor in Dalglish's unhappiness at Liverpool. When the board had wanted to extend his contract in 1990 Dalglish had asked to be included in a share option scheme, giving him a stake in the company. Like many he had worked out that the formation of the Premier League, and the TV deal that was then in the offing, might make clubs like Liverpool worth a great deal more. At Tottenham Terry Venables was already starting to prepare to move out of the manager's dug-out, where wages were still measured in tens of thousands a year, and into the boardroom, where hundreds of thousands might be available if stock values increased. In fact if Dalglish had been given a 5 per cent block of shares, it would have been worth around £25 million less than a decade later. Dalglish later said that his motive had been merely sentimental. The stake-holding would give him 'a continuing attachment to the club I loved' if he had to leave. His motive had not been financial because 'football shares were not seen as a good investment at the time'. There was no reason why Dalglish should have read the Financial Times, *but if he had he would have found that the paper was predicting that a 'tidal wave of cash' was about to hit big clubs like Liverpool. Manchester United was already preparing for market flotation. Throughout football, businessmen as shrewd as Robert Maxwell, Alan Sugar and Sir John Hall were buying into clubs in the hope of huge capital gains.*

The Liverpool board refused to give him any shares but Dalglish claimed that played no part in his decision to leave 'the club he loved'. He resigned blaming 'pressures of the job' and said he had no job to go to and just wanted a rest.

Dalglish recovered remarkably quickly. A simple annual family holiday in Florida relieved his angst so effectively that within weeks he was sitting in a hotel in Geneva, speaking to the deeply corrupt figure of Bernard Tapie, the owner of the French club Marseille, about taking over as manager on wages that would have dwarfed his Liverpool salary. At the time Marseille was already under investigation for tax avoidance but Dalglish had no idea that Tapie was also involved in systematic match-fixing in the French league, and no blame attached to him. Dalglish was ready to go and Tapie planned to announce his arrival after the French Cup final in May 1991. But before that could happen Dalglish was phoned in Monaco by Bill Fox, the chairman of Blackburn, who offered him the manager's job at Rovers. The call led to a meeting with Blackburn's benefactor, Jack Walker, who arranged a big salary for Dalglish – undisclosed but reported to be £400,000 – and promised him a multi-million-pound budget for buying players.

Dalglish took the job and started spending money like water, his transfer shopping spree culminating in the signing of Alan Shearer, a player very much in his own mould. Dalglish went for players who were physically strong, who would slug it out in the battling, backs-against-the-wall style he had learned as a player and manager at Liverpool. This approach was personified by Colin Hendry, the ferocious central defender, and David Batty, a little terrier of a midfielder. Shearer, a granite-chinned, diet-obsessed super-athlete (who endorsed or advertised fast-food McDonald's and Coca-Cola to the nation's youth), specializing in blasting the ball at the net from a great distance, could dish it out as well. Blackburn were promoted into the Premiership at Dalglish's first attempt in 1992, and came fourth (two places above Souness's Liverpool) in the Premiership in 1993. In the close season which followed, Jack Walker got out his chequebook again, spending a further £10 million on players such as Graeme Le Saux, Kevin Gallacher, Paul Warhurst, David Batty and Tim Flowers. It was not enough to win the title, though, and the championship went once again to United, with Blackburn in second position. But the big signing, in July 1994 – shattering the British transfer record set by the Shearer signing – was Chris Sutton, the Norwich striker. Walker and Dalglish again outbid Ferguson and Manchester United, paying the staggering sum of £5 million and offering wages believed to match Shearer's reported £500,000 a year. At the time Sutton was only twenty-one, was not an international and had played only ninety senior league games. In 1994–95 Blackburn finally won the championship, beating United by a single point and in effect a single goal. Jack Walker had bought the title, establishing what was to become the golden rule of the Premiership – success in the league depended on buying players.

Sutton's signing was later described as the 'quantum leap' in English transfer fees and player salaries. It signalled that English clubs were now ready to part with the sort of money previously only on offer from the big loss-making Italian and Spanish clubs which, like Blackburn, could rely on super-rich benefactors to bail them out.

Almost immediately Dalglish again began to suffer the

effects of pressure. Blackburn had qualified for the European Cup, but he was not very interested. 'Europe wasn't an attraction for me at that time,' he later said. 'I had had enough of the daily grind. I didn't want that any more. I just couldn't be bothered.' He stepped down as day-to-day manager and took the position of 'Director of Football' on wages of £300,000 a year. After that the Blackburn team slowly began to fall apart. Shearer was sold to Newcastle for £15 million amid much hype, yielding Jack Walker a £12 million profit. In 1997 Dalglish followed Shearer to Newcastle, taking over the manager's job from fellow stress victim Kevin Keegan Dalglish with his string of managerial honours – a record of success far better than Keegan's – was in place in time for Newcastle's flotation as a PLC. Under Keegan Newcastle had won nothing, but they had run Manchester United close in a couple of seasons and at least had played exciting, flowing football very much reflecting Keegan's personality – boyish enthusiasm, a little naive but given a bit of steel by the old Liverpool formula. Keegan, whom Dalglish had replaced as Liverpool centre-forward in 1977, was a typical chip off the Anfield production-line block – a player blessed with only average skills, more than compensated for by a willingness to run himself into the ground, defend from the front and never, ever give in no matter how hopeless the cause.

Shearer and Dalglish played an important role impressing investors about the club's ambition and the Newcastle board made a fortune from the club's flotation. But on the pitch the team failed to prosper. They dropped down the table and played unattractive, boring and defensive football. Dalglish was soon on his way again, leaving behind what his managerial successor Ruud Gullit was to call 'a relegation team'. Dalglish had left the dug-out apparently for good. His next move was to put together a takeover consortium for a major club, using money salted away from the huge salaries he had been paid at Blackburn and Newcastle. He was not much liked by the Liverpool, Blackburn and Newcastle fans he had walked out on. But he was much nearer to realizing the ambition he had first nurtured at Liverpool a decade earlier, to become one of the owners of the football industry and not a mere employee. Dalglish was looking to pile up some of those football shares, which only a few years before he had assumed to be the ultimate bad investment and of sentimental value only.

15.
The Snake

England was not the only footballing nation where the new forces of pay-TV, sponsorship, transfer agents and feuding bureaucrats were working a revolution in the sport.

England may have been the birthplace of football, but it was South America, and Brazil in particular, which made it the world's number one sport. Brazil was the symbol of everything that was good about football – 'the beautiful game' in the phrase of one of the game's greatest exponent, Pelé. But by the 1990s, according to Pelé himself, the game had been corrupted from top to bottom. Appointed by the Brazilian government as a special sports minister and international goodwill ambassador, Pelé had slowly turned from an inoffensive national mascot and figurehead into the scourge of the football authorities in Brazil and FIFA, football's Brazilian-dominated world governing body and organizers of the biggest TV event on earth – the World Cup.

For those who took an interest the first, mystifying clue that everything was far from well in Brazil came when Pelé was banned from attending the draw for the 1994 USA World Cup by the aged FIFA president for life, João Havelange. Pelé's crime had been to accuse the Brazilian equivalent of the FA, the CBF, of being 'a corrupt organization'. At the time the CBF was run by Havelange's brother-in-law, Ricardo Teixeira. Pelé, meanwhile, was in the process of drawing up an anti-corruption law, 'the Pelé law', and starting the arduous task of getting political support from the Brazilian senate.

It was a surprisingly modest measure, merely requiring Brazilian clubs to keep properly audited accounts, appoint directors according to company law and pay their taxes within two years. The most far-reaching proposal was to grant players European-style contract freedom. At the time most Brazilian players were signed on minuscule wages in return for life-long contracts which made them virtual slaves of the clubs.

The law passed on to the statute book in March 1996. But it managed to scratch only the surface of what appeared to be a mountain of corruption in the Brazilian game, judging by the scale of opposition to Pelé's campaign. In the weeks before the act became law, he was first smeared by the CBF and then linked by the media to the pay-TV company Globo, which had come to dominate Brazilian football even more completely than Sky dominated the English game. In 1995 Globo did a Sky-style deal with the Brazilian league worth £3.9 million a year to show live and exclusive games. The broadcaster demanded that selected matches kicked off at 7 p.m. on Sunday evenings, the ideal time in its ratings wars with rival networks. The deal was blamed for a drastic reduction in the numbers attending grounds. In the first season after the deal, attendances at major club matches dropped to one or two thousand when games were televised. One newspaper commentator complained that Brazilian football had been reduced to 'clinical displays by athletes in deserted superbowls'. Later some clubs refused to turn up for televised games at all after squabbles over the amount of money paid and the way it was shared between clubs. Globo was to pay $460 million to FIFA for the rights to show the 2002 and 2006 World Cups. They said it was Pelé and not the CBF who was corrupt, accusing him of taking rake-offs from TV rights deals for Brazil's international matches. Pelé maintained he was entirely innocent, but the accusations kept coming. Havelange joined in the campaign of intimidation, appealing directly to the Brazilian Senate and people and threatening to throw Brazil out of the World Cup if the law came into force.

Once the law was in place it had little effect. By the end of the decade Pelé had managed to persuade the government to set up a committee of inquiry, the Sporting Justice Commission, to sift through the bank accounts of the CBF and individual clubs, investigating claims of massive bungs on transfers, tax evasion, match-fixing, bribery, racism, money laundering, counterfeiting of passports and the influence of drug dealers and organized crime on the game.

The multi-million transfer fees being paid by European clubs, including some in the English Premiership, were having a devastating effect on the Brazilian game. 'The administration is terrible,' Pelé said. 'Clubs say they sold a player for $10 million and the player says it was $5 million, then the manager says it was $12 million.' By the end of the decade the problem of counterfeit passports was a major worry. The practice resulted from restrictions in European leagues, including the Premiership, limiting the number of non-EU players in any side to three. When Arsenal tried to sign the Brazilian midfielder Edu in 2000, part of the attraction, and the reason why Arsène Wenger was prepared to pay £6 million for the player, was that Edu claimed dual Brazilian and Portuguese nationality. This meant that he could play alongside non-EU Arsenal players such as Kanu (Nigeria), Silvinho (Brazil), Lauren (Cameroon) and Vivas (Argentina). Without Portuguese nationality he might be able to play only in half of Arsenal's matches and would, therefore, be unlikely to justify the transfer fee. As it happened Edu was held by immigration officers at Heathrow who found that his Portuguese passport was a fake.

Edu was not the only example. All over Europe there were dozens of South American and East European players under investigation for suspected forgery of passports and nationality papers. In 2001 the French club St Etienne were docked seven league points and heavily fined for colluding in fake passport scams involving two players, Brazilian striker Alex and goalkeeper Maxim Levitsky. Alex claimed that the club forced him to sign a forged Portuguese passport so they could play him in league games. Levitsky, who had played as both a Russian and a Ukrainian international, held a fake Greek passport which, he admitted in court, he had produced on his own initiative.

Alongside the forged passport scandal, transfer agents in Brazil were accused of making payments to the Brazil national coach Wanderley Luxemburgo to field their players in the national team, even if sometimes only for a few minutes as a substitute. The idea was to boost their value in the transfer market, not only because of the prestige of being a Brazilian international but also because of the restriction that overseas players were granted a work permit to play in the Premiership and some other European leagues only if they were 'of international class'. Otherwise, the players' union, the PFA, argued unscrupulous or cash-strapped clubs in the lower divisions might simply replace their squads with players imported from the Third World, who were no more talented than local professionals but who were prepared to accept much lower wages.

During the corruption investigations in Brazil Renata

Chris Horrie

Alves, the former private secretary to Wanderley Luxem-burgo, claimed that in 1993 and 1994 he used to leave weekly business meetings with agents with bundles of cash stuffed into his briefcase, payment for select-ing players for the squad and entitling them to work permits.

In other parts of the world, including some European countries, the work permit and nationality problems did not exist. By the turn of the century there were some 10,000 Brazilians playing professional football outside their homeland in what was described as a 'new slave trade'. In countries such as Japan, Korea, Saudi Arabia and the Gulf States there were club sides composed entirely of imported Brazilians on very low wages which were nevertheless much more than they could expect to earn trying to make a living in the slums of Rio or São Paulo. The system was underpinned by the lack of contract freedom at Brazilian clubs. Clubs gave life-long contracts to dozens of young prospects on poverty wages, hoping that one of them would turn out to be the next Ronaldo. If that happened, they would collect millions on the transfer fee to a rich European club.

In Belgium an investigation into the influx of Brazilian and African players uncovered some harrowing tales. There was the case of the player Fabio who was part of a gang of Brazilian youths 'bought' by agents who paid £2,000 per head to their parents. They were supplied with crudely forged Portuguese passports and hawked around lower division clubs in Europe. Fabio stayed in Belgium for eight months. As an illegal immigrant he had to put up with being kept in a cramped flat shared with other 'football slaves', he was paid no money and only given food which he had to cook himself from time to time. When the immigration authorities closed in the agent disappeared and left the youths to be deported.

The fate of players from African countries was in many cases even worse. There were stories of teenagers from Nigeria, Angola and Ghana being smuggled into Europe in the boots of cars and then offered around lower league clubs in Spain, Portugal and Italy. Investigations into corruption at Atlético Madrid, one of the largest clubs in Spain, found that president Jesus Gil had signed an Angolan asylum-seeker and an unemployed Senegalese refugee on poverty wages, pocketing their huge transfer fees himself.

Closer to home Premiership Southampton were briefly and innocently caught up in the Third World trade when manager Graeme Souness signed the Senegalese player Ali Dia in September 1996. Dia's agent had told Souness that the player was a relative of AC Milan's George Weah and a Senegalese international who had played for Bologna and Paris St-Germain. Souness signed him for an undisclosed fee. Dia came on as a substitute for Matthew Le Tissier in a match against Leeds United, but was so obviously an amateur standard player that he was taken off again in the eighty-fifth minute amid huge derision. Souness claimed that Dia had 'conned' him by claiming to be a top-level player. But Dia remembered things differently. He had paid his agent £1,000 for setting up the deal and had never spoken to Souness before he had his trial. Dia was transferred to non-league Gateshead where, at the right level for him, he played with great success.

In April 1998 Pelé took time off from his crusade in order to visit England and at the request of his old friend Bobby Charlton open Manchester United's new £4 million club museum, the central attraction in what was becoming the theme park dimension of United's Old Trafford ground. During the trip Pelé asked United PLC's deputy chief executive Peter Kenyon if he would attend a conference Pelé had organized in São Paulo to discuss the problems in Brazilian football and advise on the possible reorganization of clubs and the Brazilian league. Kenyon accepted the invitation. But the main result was to have little to do with curbing South American corruption. As it turned out, Kenyon spent much of the conference talking to two Italian businessmen, Paolo Taveggia and Andrea Locatelli, about the details of a breakaway Super League, the brainchild of Silvio Berlusconi, the right-wing Italian prime minister, property dealer and media magnate, who owned AC Milan and was reputed to be the richest man in Italy.

As Kenyon was meeting the Italians quietly under cover of the anti-corruption conference, Rupert Murdoch and Berlusconi were having talks about jointly establishing a pan-European pay-TV channel which would feature the proposed league and be the key to its financial success.

There was thus a certain symmetry about the two sets of talks. Taveggia and Locatelli both worked, or had recently done so, for Berlusconi. And the way things stood in May 1998, Kenyon thought that he might soon be working for Rupert Murdoch. Back home in Manchester and London Murdoch's company Sky TV was about to have a secret offer to buy United from Martin Edwards accepted in principle. At the level of the billionaires, Berlusconi and Murdoch were working to put together a European Super Channel. At the level of the actual and would-be millionaires, Edwards, Kenyon, Taveggia and Locatelli were working to create the European Super League – essential viewing for tens, maybe hundreds, of millions of subscribers from Portugal to Poland, from Scandinavia to Sicily. If everything worked out it would be just like the Premiership deal with Sky all over again. Those involved stood to unlock yet more astounding riches from the beautiful game.

Silvio Berlusconi was born in Milan in 1936. Soon after graduating from the University of Milan in the late 1950s he became a property dealer and developer in the city and made his first millions from developing a large plot of derelict land near Milan airport. A key political contact from the start of Berlusconi's financial career was Bettino Craxi, who built up Italy's Socialist Party on a wide network of political patronage and bribery that not only financed the party but also feathered Craxi's own nest. In 1993 Milan prosecutors found that at least $6 million had been moved over a period of years from various Berlusconi companies to bank accounts in Tunisia controlled personally by Craxi.

By the mid-1970s Craxi was on his way to government and Berlusconi had become a dollar multi-millionaire and one of the richest men in the country, expanding his political influence and adding supermarkets, cinemas, publishing companies and department stores to his empire, creating a holding company called Fininvest which, by the 1990s, grew to be the second biggest company in Italy (Fiat was the biggest), controlling about 150 subsidiaries.

In 1974 Berlusconi made his first move into television, setting up the cable pay-TV which by 1980 was to grow into Canale 5, the first private-sector broadcaster in a

Chris Horrie

country with a highly regulated and politicized television system. With the addition of two new channels, Rete 4 and Italia 1, grouped together in the holding company Mediaset, Berlusconi came to control 90 per cent of TV advertising revenue in the country, and 45 per cent of the audience.

In 1980 Berlusconi bought AC Milan, which had along with Lazio just been relegated into Serie B (the Italian second division) as punishment for their involvement in systematic match-fixing. Once in control, the ever flamboyant Berlusconi took to arriving at home games in Milan's San Siro stadium in his helicopter, landing on the centre spot while the PA system blasted out 'The Ride of the Valkyries'.

Through the 1980s Berlusconi ran the club at a vast loss, spending enormous sums buying players such as Donadoni, Paolo Maldini and the Dutch trio of Marco Van Basten, Frank Rijkaard and Ruud Gullit. Milan won the Italian championship in 1988 beating Napoli, featuring Diego Maradona, by three points. Although Milan were never accused of doing anything wrong, two years later Napoli were deemed to have thrown the championship, gaining only one point from their last five matches after leading all season. The Italian league announced an investigation into eighty unnamed Serie A games where match-fixing was suspected during Milan's championship season. Twelve clubs, including Napoli, Bari and Udinese were indicted for 'sporting fraud' as a result.

Controversy was never far away from AC Milan. The club's last match of the 1992–93 season produced one of the most extraordinary moments in European football. Milan needed only one point from their last game at home to Brescia to secure the title. The match, captured for posterity by the TV cameras, was one of the most boring in history. The two sides seemed strangely content with 0–0 (there was nothing at stake for Brescia) and was so uncompetitive that the twenty-two players might as well have sat in the centre circle for the ninety minutes. Then with the score still at 0–0 and five minutes to go Demetrio Albertini kicked the ball towards the Brescia goal. It deflected off a defender and sailed into the net. The home crowd went wild, but all the Milan players looked crestfallen and one started berating Albertini. Brescia scored straight from the kick-off, with the Milan players more or less allowing Brescia to walk the ball into the net, restoring the drawn scoreline. Nothing was ever proved, but it was widely believed in the betting world that the match was a fix.

In 1992 Berlusconi broke the world transfer record by paying £13 million for the Torino striker Lentini. It was later discovered that the figure included a £2.5 million bung. Then, in 1993, Milan lost the European Cup final 1–0 to Olympique Marseille. The match was proved to have been fixed and Marseille's owner, Bernard Tapie, eventually went to jail.

In the same year a series of corruption scandals swept some of Berlusconi's political allies, including Craxi, out of power, and a new 'clean' government set up a wide-ranging corruption inquiry and moved to break up Berlusconi's politically protected monopoly on commercial TV. Berlusconi moved in two ways to see off the threat. First he paid $8 million to Oscar Mammi, the minister in charge of drawing up the new television laws, to ensure that they did not affect him too adversely. Berlusconi later claimed that the money had been paid as a 'consultancy fee'. Magistrates maintained that it was a 'bribe'.

Chris Horrie

Then, in January 1994, he set up his own political party with the aim of becoming prime minister and thus controlling the Communications and anti-corruption Justice ministries which threatened him. The party took as its title 'Forza Italia', which was the chant of fans of the Italian national football team. Soon Berlusconi was installed as prime minister of Italy, his popularity boosted by AC Milan's 4–0 win over Barcelona in the European Cup final which took place during the election campaign. While Berlusconi is prime minister, the case against him is unlikely to come to court.

In 1996 Berlusconi began talks with Rupert Murdoch aimed at setting up a pan-European pay-TV channel. Up until that point Murdoch had always steered clear of involvement in the media of continental Europe, preferring to concentrate his activities in the more familiar English-speaking world of the UK, Australia and the US. He worried that he did not really understand the highly regulated European markets, and he detested the idea of European integration in principle, seeming to share the view of his old ally Margaret Thatcher that 'everything good' came from the English-speaking world and 'everything bad' came from continental Europe. But having increasingly come up against limits to his domination of the media scene in the UK and to a lesser extent America, he decided to put his toe in the water.

Working in partnership with Berlusconi seemed to make sense for Murdoch. The Italian understood both pay television and the proven key to its success – football. He had political contacts. His Forza party had MPs and officials working at the European parliament and so could keep an eye on the Europe-wide media regulators. Murdoch was as aware as anyone that the European

Commission, which would inevitably become involved with the pan-European TV idea at some point, was riddled with corruption, and so it made sense to ally himself to somebody who knew how it all worked.

Berlusconi had already laid the foundations of a Europe-wide TV operation by making a series of investments in television companies in Spain and Germany which cleverly got round one of the banes of Murdoch's life – the regulators' insistence that TV companies should not be owned by foreigners like himself. Berlusconi had taken a large stake in the Kirch pay-TV network in Germany, circumventing the foreign-ownership rules by giving Kirch a similar stake in his Italian TV holding company Mediaset, rather than buying control outright. Mediaset and Kirch had then set up a pay-TV station called Telecinco in Spain. Spanish law limited Berlusconi's holding as a foreigner to 30 per cent but he got round this by using a number of 'dummy' investors, whom he controlled, giving him in effect an 80 per cent stake in Telecinco.

Berlusconi thus had a base in Italy, Germany and Spain and Murdoch brought England into the frame, giving them four of the six main European markets – only France and Scandinavia remained to be conquered. Both men's experience had convinced them that exclusive live football was essential to their venture. They might have considered a simple, direct bid to show the existing Champions' League, preparing the way and making an offer just as Murdoch had done with stunning success in winning the rights to the Premier League in England. A UEFA subsidiary auctioned the rights, but the problem was that UEFA had a policy of ensuring that the competitions were available to the general public on free to air TV channels such as ITV in the UK.

This was no good at all for Murdoch and Berlusconi.

Chris Horrie

If the financial success of Sky was to be repeated on a European scale, they needed to use football to sell subscriptions to a pay-TV system. Berlusconi had a separate complaint about UEFA. After being so dominant in the early 1990s, AC Milan had slipped down Serie A, falling behind Juventus, Lazio and Inter Milan. Even with the change allowing second-placed teams into the Champions' League, a place in the competition was no longer guaranteed. The scale of spending on transfer fees and post-Bosman wages necessary to be sure of qualifying was daunting. For these reasons Berlusconi needed a new Super League, with a place guaranteed for AC Milan as one of the founder clubs, which would get round the need for qualification as champions or runners-up in national competitions and, also, confound UEFA's ban on matches being shown on the new pay-TV channel only.

The details of a proposed new rival to UEFA, simply called the Super League, were worked out by Paolo Taveggia and Andrea Locatelli, the two men Manchester United's Peter Kenyon had met during Pelé's conference in Brazil. Taveggia was a former general manager of AC Milan under Berlusconi in the early 1990s at the time of the £2.5 million bung on the Lentini transfer. He had left in 1993, the day after AC Milan lost the European Cup final against the match-fixers of Marseille, and had gone to help Havelange organize the 1994 World Cup, the competition marked by Pelé's accusations of corruption, which had led to his ban from the ceremony of the draw.

Taveggia returned to Milan to run the financial affairs not of AC Milan but of the rival Inter, where in 1997 he organized the payment of £18 million to Barcelona for the transfer of Ronaldo. Kenyon knew Taveggia slightly because he had made an offer to buy Eric Cantona at the time of the United star's suspension for kung fu kicking a fan.

Andrea Locatelli was another of Berlusconi's lieutenants, and had been head of TV sports rights acquisition at Mediaset, Berlusconi's TV company, as well as head of AC Milan's own cable TV channel. Taveggia and Locatelli were working with Rudolfo Hecht, another former Berlusconi adviser, who ran a Milanese sports rights consortium called Media Partners. Previously Hecht had been head of strategic management at Berlusconi's Fininvest and in addition head of sport at the Italian pay-TV company Telepiu, in which Berlusconi had a 10 per cent stake. The company had introduced the first pay-per-view operation in Europe, approved by the Italian league in 1997. It had produced astronomical profits and so it was not surprising that Berlusconi and Murdoch wanted to repeat the same thing on an even bigger pan-European scale. Back-of-envelope calculations indicated that top pay-per-view Super League matches might generate gross income amounting to as much as £5 million per game. Hecht was to be the public face of the Super League proposal, which was referred to in the British press as 'The Media Partners' plan'. Care was taken to keep Berlusconi out of the spotlight.

Kenyon was impressed with the outline proposal Taveggia and Locatelli had shown him and organized another, more formal meeting at the offices of Slaughter and May, the blue chip London law firm Media Partners were using in London. Hecht made a presentation explaining that the plan was based on the American NFL, in which a few big clubs criss-crossed the country to play each other. The existing UEFA Champions' League was 'an underperforming asset' – the amount of money

Chris Horrie

which could be charged for the TV rights was far greater than what UEFA raked in – mainly because of its ban on pay-TV. United's representatives were reminded of the tidal wave of money which had hit them when English football moved from selling its rights to the free-to-air ITV to selling them to a pay-TV system. The Super League would do the same.

In their prospectus Media Partners offered participating clubs 'three major advantages' over the existing Champions' League. Firstly, there was 'permanent membership', which, the group said, would allow clubs to forecast their income accurately, instead of relying on whether or not they qualified and then how far they progressed in the competition. These things, after all, were still subject to those great bug-bears of all financial planning – luck and sporting chance. Permanent membership was immediately appealing. The reigning European Cup winners at the time, Real Madrid, had earned £8.5 million extra income from their participation in the competition. United, who had been knocked out in the quarter finals, had earned £5.37 million. United had just lost the championship, by a single point, to Arsenal. That meant they would have been excluded from the competition had it not been for UEFA's decision to allow second-placed clubs in the Champions' League. The fear was that the club might have one bad season, fail to qualify and, weighed down by the massive wage costs which had come in the wake of Bosman, find themselves facing a loss-making year.

In contrast the Berlusconi team was offering £20 million to each participating club guaranteed for at least three seasons. All they had to do was withdraw from UEFA's competitions and sort out any resulting problems with their domestic league. The money looked rock solid.

It would come at first from a $2 billion on-call loan Media Partners could demonstrate they had set up with the US merchant bank J.P. Morgan. After that the money would come from a pay-TV deal. Officially, Media Partners said they had no idea which broadcaster would want to buy the rights, but it was obvious to those in the know that Berlusconi and Murdoch would be on the inside track.

The second advantage on offer was a reduction in the overall number of games in the European competition. The way UEFA had organized things in the early stages of the Champions' League, glamour teams such as United, Barcelona and the Milan clubs found themselves playing against obscure and unfashionable sides from Eastern Europe as part of UEFA's obligation to treat the champions of all affiliated leagues – Slovenia and Iceland as well as Italy and Spain – equally. These games had little appeal and clogged up the fixture list. In the Berlusconi plan only glamour clubs would be involved and so every game would be a ratings-grabber and ground-filler.

The third advantage was the related and more technical one of 'key country membership'. It meant that teams chosen to play in the Super League would have to come from countries with 'significant TV markets'. This was to avoid the problem of playing games against clubs from countries like those in Eastern Europe where the home audience would be tiny and, therefore, not very profitable. The offer was a straightforward financial package – essentially a scaled-up version of the thinking that had led to the establishment of the Premiership – and it was refreshingly free from all the guff about equality between clubs and the need to help promote and protect the beautiful game.

There was a hard-sell purity about the Media Partners

proposal, which extended even to the way clubs were expected to apply for membership. The launch date for the new European Football League was set as the autumn of 2000. Any club signing up for the scheme before March 1998 would receive a £3 million cash bonus. They did not even have to resign from their national leagues yet. Clubs signing up between March and September would get no bonus, but those seeking to join after September would have to pay a £3 million financial penalty and any club which had not signed by December 1998 would have to consider themselves 'dis-invited' and not allowed to join.

Anticipating opposition from national leagues about to lose the teams which supplied most of their TV audience, Media Partners offered the prospect of a revived knock-out European Cup to run alongside the proposed Super League. That would be open to large numbers of clubs in the existing leagues, offering them the chance of extra TV money. If they won the Cup and had the good fortune to come from a country with 'a significant TV market', they might be allowed to join the Super League and share some of the untold riches.

United executives were by now enthusiastic, but wanted their interest to be kept secret. Kenyon started playing a role in shaping the detail of the new competition and Maurice Watkins joined Media Partners' finance subcommittee, working closely with the finance directors of AC Milan, Marseille and Bayern Munich. The main danger from United's point of view was that not enough clubs would sign up to make the project viable. So the attitude of other clubs was crucial. Media Partners already had the two Milan clubs lined up and claimed to have interested top clubs in Germany as well as Ajax of Holland. But at the very least United wanted to know what the two other English clubs Berlusconi was keen to recruit, Arsenal and Liverpool, thought about the scheme.

At this stage the concern was not the potentially destructive effect that a breakaway might have on their domestic leagues, and certainly not the reaction of the existing fans, but what the new competition might mean in terms of players' already phenomenal wages. It was feared that if clubs resigned from UEFA and were expelled from their domestic leagues, players who were registered with their national versions of the FA and with UEFA would be out of contract and could demand huge pay rises before they assigned their registrations, which they now controlled, to the new Super League. This was a particular worry for United as a PLC because there was constant pressure to keep wages down. Berlusconi at AC Milan did not have the same problem. He owned the club outright and could pay whatever he saw fit.

A second secret, formal presentation took place in July 1998, this time attended by representatives of Arsenal and Liverpool as well as United, and from Ajax, Marseille, Paris St-Germain, Borussia Dortmund and Bayern Munich. Clubs from Greece, Portugal, Turkey and Spain were reportedly interested and were likely to join in later. It turned out that the Arsenal board had split over the plan. Most were in favour of exploring the detail, but deputy chairman David Dein was dead against. Dein, the main financial force at the club, was at the time the FA's representative on the UEFA subcommittee that ran the existing Champions' League and so he was less than keen on a plan which would wreck the existing competition. Rick Parry, the former Premier League chief executive, who was representing his new employer, Liverpool, also had reservations, partly because Liverpool had gone through a long bad spell, were not the force they once were and might struggle in a Super League. As it happened Liverpool did not attend any more meetings, saying they would 'await developments' once news of the breakaway plan finally became public. Kenyon, by now emerging as the most enthusiastic and reliable advocate of the breakaway, later accused Liverpool of 'letting others do the dirty work, arriving late and then drinking all the champagne'.

After the July meeting news of the plan leaked to the British press. Peter Leaver, chief executive of the Premier League, said that he had first heard about it from David Dein, who in the ensuing crisis phoned him 'every day' about developments. The original report in the *Sunday Telegraph* was remarkably accurate. The new league, the paper revealed, would involve sixteen clubs, led in England by Manchester United, and was due to launch within two years. United issued a statement denying any involvement. 'There is no truth in this at all,' the club said. 'It's pure speculation. We are getting fed up with stories linking us with a European Super League.'

But the cat was out of the bag and Media Partners prepared for a public relations battle. They hired the most influential financial PR company in the UK, Brunswick, with a brief to downplay the fact that Berlusconi was the driving force, emphasizing instead the role of Media Partners' chairman Rudolfo Hecht. A number of ano- dyne profiles of Hecht duly appeared in the broadsheet newspapers, where he described the Super League as 'a hobby' he had dreamed up because he was 'just an ordinary football fan'. Further burying the involvement and interest of Berlusconi and Murdoch, Hecht said he had 'an open mind' about who might buy the rights to show the new Super League games. The official line was that they would set up the competition first, using the $2 billion loan from J. P. Morgan to pay the guaranteed £20 million a year to participating clubs, and look for a TV deal later. These details were pushed to the background as Hecht emphasized a commitment to provide a proportion of the new Super League's total income for investment in amateur, school and youth football and then published an opinion poll claiming that 70 per cent of fans were in favour of a Super League. The reality was that a fairly small sample of members of the general public had been told that the Super League would mean 'more English clubs playing in Europe' and 'millions more for youth football'. More than one commentator noted that it was surprising that they had not got a 100 per cent approval rating for loaded questions such as those.

Meanwhile, Peter Leaver went berserk. There had been tension between Manchester United and the Premiership authorities right from the new league's foundation, based on a simple divergence of commercial interests. As United pulled away from the other clubs in terms of popularity and success, they began increasingly to act as though the football industry belonged to them and not to the Premiership. But the formal position was that United was in a subsidiary position. In the model of the American NFL pushed by many who set up the Premiership, they would be a mere 'franchise' of the larger Premiership 'product'. But United were operating on an exact reversal of that power relationship. The argument was that they brought the money into football and therefore should keep more and more of it. Things had come to a head in 1996 with the bitter row over Sky's pay-per-view plan which meant that most of the new money from television would go straight to the televised clubs (i.e. mainly to United) with only a token sum going to the Premier League to be shared out between the other clubs. United had found themselves outvoted and Sky's plans were left in tatters.

The breakaway of Manchester United and the other big clubs to form the Premiership had forced the old Football League into receivership within weeks. The same fate might befall the Premiership if United and possibly Arsenal and Liverpool as well left, since most of the value of the Premiership TV rights contract involved these teams' matches.

Now United had decided to go off on their own, Leaver was determined to stop them at all costs. His first act was to issue a High Court writ to United at the end of July 1998, demanding written undertakings that they would not join any new Super League without first obtaining the permission of the Premiership and, further, demanding that they hand over to him any documents setting out their plans. The writ was basically ignored though a week later United admitted they had been involved in talks. The admission looked very threatening to Leaver and the Premiership. It came on the day that Real Madrid, Marseille, Bayern Munich, Galatasaray and Panathinaikos confirmed that they were ready to sign up to the Super League. With the two Milan clubs already on board, the new Super League, including United, had at least eight clubs, probably enough to be viable and attract a stampede of others, including the divided Arsenal and the undecided Liverpool, fearful of being left out. Sir John Hall, owner of the recently stock market floated Newcastle United PLC, was reportedly 'putting out feelers' for a fourth English place in the new set-up if it went ahead.

The battle lines were thus drawn within English football for the second time in a decade. On one side were the Premier League and UEFA fighting for their lives, supported by the small clubs and claiming the backing of the fans, the regulators and public opinion. On the other was an alliance of Manchester United, Media Partners, J. P. Morgan and their $2 billion seed money, lined up with the pay-TV operators, especially Sky.

What nobody knew during the Media Partners crisis in the summer of 1998 was exactly how close the alliance between Manchester United and Sky was about to become if Murdoch got his way.

1995–96 season

After winning the championship in the previous season Blackburn Rovers immediately fell apart. Dalglish effectively retired, taking the part-time job of Director of Football, signalling the start of the sell-off of star players. The club had a rollercoaster season, flirting with relegation at one point and eventually finishing in seventh place. It looked as if it might be the season when Manchester United's run of success would come to an end. Alex Ferguson had a clearout of players: Ince went to Inter Milan, Kanchelskis to Everton and Mark Hughes to Chelsea. Cantona was suspended and talking about leaving English football, and could not return to the team until October even if he stayed. Ferguson promoted members of the youth team to the senior squad, including David Beckham, Paul Scholes and the Neville brothers, Gary and Phil. Beckham scored the 'goal of the season' in the first match against Wimbledon, launching the ball into the net from the halfway line. But the team stumbled in some of its early games, prompting Alan Hansen's famous prediction that 'you don't win anything with kids'.

Chris Horrie

Newcastle were widely tipped to win the title after sign-ing a clutch of expensive players, including manager Kevin Keegan's answer to Cantona, the flamboyant French star David Ginola. The purchase of David Batty from Blackburn half-way through the season took Keegan's spending on players to £44 million in four years. But to the growing amusement of everyone else, he had still not won a major trophy. At first it seemed that Liverpool, who spent more than £8 million buying Stan Collymore from Nottingham Forest, would make it a three-way race with Newcastle and United. In fact they remained inconsistent. For much of the season Newcastle were way ahead in the table – twelve points clear by January. But then they started dropping a lot of points away from home. In February they gained only four points from a possible eighteen – relegation form. A revival started after a 4–3 defeat away to Liverpool reckoned to have been one of best games of the century.

Manchester United were massively boosted by the return of Cantona and won a second league and Cup double, beating Liverpool in the FA Cup final and taking the championship ahead of Newcastle by the relatively small margin of four points, with Liverpool finishing third, eleven points behind. Nobody else came close. Slip-ups for United were rare, but in April they were stunned to find themselves 3–0 down at half-time in an away game against Southampton. The players complained that they could not see each other in the latest of United's many shirt changes. This one was an insipid grey and Ferguson told them to change into brighter, blue shirts at half-time.

In many ways the 1995–96 Premiership season would be seen as a high point. The game was more popular than ever, the new influx of money was starting to attract some top European players – Bergkamp, Cantona, Ginola and Gullit – and the season ended with the success of Euro 96, held in

England – almost hooligan-free and remembered for the new chant 'football's coming home'. Shearer and Gascoigne played well for the England national team and Terry Venables, the England manager, was widely praised.

But the main news was that Manchester United had managed to bounce back after losing out to Blackburn in the previous season, breaking the usual pattern of rise and fall, and putting together a second championship-winning team which was even better than the first. To a great extent this was the personal achievement of one of the most influential figures of the Premiership age, one who was often uncomfortable with the direction football was taking – Alex Ferguson.

16.
Takeover

The new age of the Premiership, the alliance between media and football, had led to a vast increase in the amount of space newspapers dedicated to the sport. There were entire new newspapers-within-newspapers devoted to the subject, led by *GOALS*, the *Sun*'s Monday supplement, which exploited its access to Sky, part of the same media empire. The *Mirror* had responded with the lacklustre *MANIA*. The broadsheets had piled in with endless analysis and artsy features devoted to the beautiful game and its psychological, literary and cultural ramifications, leaving no sociological stone unturned.

So there was high excitement in newsrooms in the run-up to the 1999 August bank holiday. Word was that there was an 'enormous' Manchester United story about to break. The rumours ran from Alex Ferguson's imminent Keegan-style resignation attributed to 'pressure', through speculation that one or more of United's household name teen-stars was about to come out as gay, or confess, like Paul Merson had when at Arsenal, to drug addiction – or both. The trouble was nobody could make anything stand up. United had gone very quiet. Calls were not returned, leads ran into the sand, contacts became shy and, all-embracing 'no comment' statements were being issued. All of this merely confirmed to the hacks the absolute certainty that something big was about to break.

Then, on bank holiday Sunday, the *News of the World* landed what most people assumed to be the big story that United did not want to discuss, a classic tabloid sex scandal involving the club's latest star signing, centre-forward Dwight Yorke, signed just a few weeks before from Aston Villa. The news arrived on the nation's breakfast tables in a banner headline:

ORGY VIDEO SHAME OF £12 MILLION YORKE

'Soccer star Dwight Yorke made a shameful secret video of a drunken orgy at his home,' the paper said. 'The goal ace, who has just joined Manchester United for £12.6 million, filmed the hour-long romp with a hidden camera. It shows him, his former Aston Villa team-mate Mark Bosnich and a third man, dressed in women's clothes and frolicking with four girls.'

Pictures of the girls in bed with Bosnich were splashed over an inside double-page spread. Readers were also treated to the news that the girls had 'spanked Bosnich with leather belts'.

Martin Edwards must have read the story with mixed feelings. It was bad publicity, of course, but not that extraordinary by the standards of tabloid reporting of footballers' private lives. Edwards had himself been 'rolled' some years before by the *News of the World*'s rival, the *Sunday People*, which exposed his adulterous affair with an Estée Lauder cosmetics salesgirl eighteen years his junior. The boozing, womanizing, drug-abusing, wife-beating and car-smashing antics of soccer stars had become a tabloid staple.

The upside, as far as Edwards was concerned, was that the story distracted attention from the real news involving United that weekend – that in conditions of strict and absolute secrecy, Martin Edwards and the Manchester United PLC board had accepted an offer from Sky which would give the pay-TV company control of the club.

*　　*　　*

Chris Horrie

The question of buying an English football club had long been debated at the top level within Sky and Rupert Murdoch's media empire. Sky had the money to buy any one of its choosing, at least at the capital values being quoted on the stock exchange. But Sam Chisholm, the head of Sky, had always been against it. By the time of the 1996 renewal of the company's exclusive ownership of Premiership television rights, Chisholm had gained an expert understanding of the internal politics of the Premiership. He was convinced that Sky would face a dangerous backlash if they moved too close to any particular club. Even the relationship with Alan Sugar could be tricky at times. Until he disposed of Amstrad and his Sky-dish manufacturing operation, he had always been forced to declare an interest when voting on TV rights matters, offering to surrender his vote because of the clash of interests. It would be much worse for Sky if they actually owned a club. And if it was United there was a chance that the rest of the football industry would turn against them.

But in August 1997 Chisholm left Sky, citing pressure of work and deteriorating health, to be replaced by a Murdoch-groomed American called Mark Booth, who, as he was later to confess, knew next to nothing about English football and its piranha-pool corporate politics. Booth had two big issues on his agenda when he arrived at Sky. The first was the introduction of digital technology which would give Sky the ability to broadcast hundreds of new channels (if the company could find anything profitable to put on them). The second was the related development of pay-per-view television, the plan to charge subscribers extra money to watch particular films or football matches with the introduction of an electronic 'box office' or, in the case of football, 'turnstile'.

Booth made an immediate splash by announcing that by 1999, if the clubs wanted it, Sky would be able to broadcast simultaneously every single Premiership and, possibly, Endsleigh game live on Saturdays, each one appearing on a different channel. Sky would also be able to have several camera crews at each match, with the output shown simultaneously on different channels, enabling viewers to switch between the camera behind the goal to one on the half-way line or yet another trained on a particular player.

Most of the clubs did not like the sound of this at all. The ancient argument that they would lose paying customers at the grounds if fans could stay at home and watch the game was revived. More important was the immediate realization that the big club matches would attract much higher viewing figures than the small clubs, thus replicating the inequality in attendances and gate money. The offer was immediately turned down.

Next up was the thorny issue of pay-per-view. Chisholm had inserted a clause into the 1996 deal which specified talks about the development over the next few years, with money to be paid to the Premier League on top of the sum for the basic rights deal. Booth was very keen to introduce the system. Sky had tried it out by charging subscribers who had already paid for Sky Sports £15 to watch a boxing match between Frank Bruno and Mike Tyson, which had been a great financial success. At the same subscription rate a top Premiership game, such as Manchester United–Arsenal, might generate as much as £8 million, compared with the £500,000 to £1 million taken at the turnstiles. But a match such as Coventry versus Wimbledon, both of whom were in the Premiership at the time, was likely to bring in only a fraction of that sum. Further, there would be a strong and probably legally enforceable argument that clubs should get TV money related to pay-per-view audience and sales. Whereas the pot of money given by Sky to the Premiership under existing arrangements was shared fairly evenly by the twenty clubs, the introduction of pay-per-view would mean the well-supported clubs would get much more; and the smaller clubs could end up eventually getting far less.

Sky's plans to introduce pay-per-view did not get off to a good start. Leaver, the Premier League chief executive who had replaced Sky's great ally Rick Parry after Parry's move to Liverpool, was not particularly well disposed to help Sky bring in a pay-per-view system which would strengthen Sky's stranglehold on the finances of the game. It would also provide the likes of Manchester United with a vast new stream of income which would further boost their independence and financial might when dealing with the league or with other clubs. In fact he was keen to avoid anything that might entangle Sky any more closely in the finances of individual clubs, as the provision of club pay-per-view channels certainly would. One reason was the need to hold the Premier League together, preserving the remnants of the 'league of equality' idea at a time when the league was under threat of being broken up as a TV wholesaling cartel by the competition authorities.

Another reason for Leaver's hostility was his interest in setting up the Premier League as a broadcaster in its own right, using one or more of the hundreds of soon-to-be-available digital channels to carry a Premiership channel, owned by the league and the FA itself. If that could be set up the super profits that up to then had gone to Sky would stay inside the game, and coincidentally make Leaver one of the most powerful and important business-men and media operators in the world. A Premier League channel would inherit Sky Sports' audience and much of its £1 billion annual subscription income overnight. Such a financial powerhouse would provide the perfect base for another venture he was beginning to explore, a new European league or cup competition to rival both the existing UEFA set-up and the (still secret) Berlusconi Super League, which would be run by a consortium of domestic league organizations with the Premiership playing the leading role. To help him explore these avenues and show the worlds of media and finance that he was deadly serious, Leaver hired Chisholm himself, on the New Zealander's customary multi-million-pound salary, along with Chisholm's deputy, David Chance.

Leaver allowed Sky to put its proposals for pay-per-view to a June 1998 meeting of club chairmen. Peter Kenyon, attending as Manchester United's representa-tive, while secretly talking to Berlusconi's people at Media Partners about joining the proposed breakaway Super League, was extremely keen on the idea. But, with the exception of Aston Villa, where Doug Ellis had been persuaded of the system's merits, all the other clubs were against, many of the smaller ones very strongly so.

Some club chairmen were later reported to have been 'insulted' by the small sum, £15 million, or less than £1 million per club, per season, which Sky and Booth were offering as compensation for the introduction of the system. Others objected to Sky's demands that as many as half of each Saturday's Premiership fixtures should be switched to Sunday so as to make them more marketable as pay-per-view games. Still others were starting to question the relationship between Sky and football. Since the 1992 deal, Manchester United's capital value had increased vastly and the club was on track to be worth £800 million within the next year, but Sky had grown from being worthless to reaching an £8 billion valuation – ten times more. One anonymous chairman was reported as saying at the time: 'Look at those valuations and then tell me who has done well out of the Sky football deal. The clubs are waking up to how much Sky are making and realizing what they could make by holding on to their own screening rights.'

The proposals were voted down – a great humiliation for Sky and Booth personally. And it was after this that Booth decided to go ahead with the plan to buy Manchester United. The first offer was made at a meeting with United executives at Sky's London headquarters originally arranged to discuss progress on pay-per-view. After an initial encouraging response, a series of further meetings took place in great secrecy, increasingly concentrating on the price that Sky would pay.

At the time important figures inside the club were feeling gloomy, or at least uncertain, about United's prospects. In the season just ended, 1997–98, Arsenal had won the league and Cup double, while United had been knocked out in the quarter finals of the European Cup by humble Monaco and had won nothing. There was a feeling in the boardroom that this might have signalled the end of United's good run under Alex Ferguson and that the baton might now pass to Arsenal. There were those who believed that eventually one or more of the London clubs would get their act together and put United in the shade. They had all the advantages of location and a much richer London and south-eastern base of supporters to aim at. This was the historic pattern. Until 1990 Tottenham Hotspur had enjoyed a higher turnover than United, and even once the Premiership was under way, the London clubs found they could charge far higher prices for tickets and get much more for the hire of catering facilities.

Now United were under sustained pressure from Arsenal and there was a fear that they might quickly catch up and take over. In the age of Premiership either you were number one or you were nowhere. To a far greater extent than in the old Football League, it was now a matter of 'winner takes all'. At the very least United would have to spend millions to compete with and stay ahead of Arsenal in the transfer and players' wages stakes. The Bosman effect on wages was really starting to cause problems. United's wage bill was already around £20 million and it looked set to double over the next few years when the contracts of the club's stars came up for renewal. As a PLC, Manchester United was under pressure from the board to keep wages down in response to City grumbles that football PLCs were paying far too high a proportion of their income in the form of wages – way above the average for the 'hotels and leisure' section as a whole.

Meanwhile, the board was facing demands from Alex Ferguson that they should spend phenomenal sums on buying in players in order to see off the Arsenal threat and to have a better chance of winning the Champions' League. In June 1998, just as Sky was making its first approach to buy the club, Ferguson rejected a transfer budget of £14 million offered to him at a meeting with Martin Edwards, saying it was entirely insufficient. Ten million pounds had already been earmarked for the purchase of Jaap Stam, and the recruitment of Swedish winger Jesper Blomqvist was in the pipeline at a cost of £4 million. On top of this Ferguson wanted at least another

£20 million so that he could buy the striker Dwight Yorke and other players, possibly including another world-class striker.

After some acrimony Ferguson mostly got his way. Yorke was signed from Aston Villa in August 1998, with the cost being pushed forward into the next financial year. But the continuing increase in United's spending on players at this sort of rate was bound to hit profits and eventually cause the share price to plunge. And if Arsenal continued to do well, beating United to all the top prizes, the club would face the well-known syndrome of falling income and rising costs as the manager and fans demanded more transfer spending to put things right. If that happened, United would quickly turn into a financial disaster as spectacular as the financial miracle of the 1990s. Of course this was not certain, but the threat was realistic enough to make Roland Smith, United's chief executive, think that now might be a good time to sell the club, cashing in on the high share price, and pass the risks and responsibilities on to somebody else. Martin Edwards had been trying to do it for years anyway.

After haggling, a price of 217.5p per share was agreed between the United and Sky boards, thus valuing Martin Edwards's 14 per cent stake at about £80 million. He had been dipping in and out of United shares since the flotation and had made £35 million during the 1990s, so a sale to Sky would see him gain well over £200 million pounds from his involvement with Manchester United. Throughout the dramas that followed, all the members of the United board were keen to sell out to Sky, except for Greg Dyke, the former head of ITV, who had been brought on to the Old Trafford board to advise on television matters. Dyke, who had previously led ITV's efforts to capture the Premiership in competition was not inclined to do a deal with his old foe Murdoch under any circumstances. But by company law he could not prevent an offer being put to the shareholders – and it looked likely that they would accept it. If the deal was going to go ahead, however, Dyke was determined that Sky would have to pay a much higher price than it was offering. Apart from anything else, at the time the club was secretly being promised £20 million a year to play in Berlusconi's Super League. Sky's bid was based on United's value on the stock exchange plus a premium. But the share price and stock market valuation would doubtless have been much higher if investors had known about the Berlusconi plan. Beyond this Dyke was convinced that it would only be a matter of time before United was able to sell its own TV rights or put live Premiership and European games on the club's own MUTV channel, which he had been brought in to help set up, which would also vastly increase the profitability and value of the club.

It was essential, in the meantime, that talks between Sky and the United board be kept secret. The danger was the inevitable backlash from the other clubs, the fans and the rest of the media. Almost every aspect of Sky's activities closely skirted the rules on media regulation and fair competition and the last thing it needed was a prolonged controversy which might prompt the regulators and government to get involved. Ideally, both sides wanted to present the takeover as a done-deal and get on with business with as little fuss as possible.

With Dyke delaying things by haggling over the price and details of the takeover, the people at Sky began to map out a defensive PR strategy. It was decided from the outset that it would be essential to have both Alex Ferguson and Bobby Charlton 'on side' as they put it. Edwards was not trusted by the fans, or at least by the vocal, well-organized, media-savvy and politically connected minority who took an interest in the club's business affairs. A group called the Independent Manchester United Supporters' Association was already active, complaining about the commercialization of the club and above all the sterile atmosphere which had developed at Old Trafford in the wake of the ground's redevelopment and transformation into what was, in effect, a giant, heavily policed open-air TV studio where supporters were expected to behave as though they were an invited studio audience.

For the organized fans Ferguson was a totemic figure. As they saw things, Edwards had presided over the long years when United failed to win the league. He had led the club to the brink of disaster before it had been rescued, more or less by accident, with the arrival of Ferguson. When Edwards featured in the papers it was usually because he was rejecting demands for United to buy yet more expensive players or was involved in yet another distasteful commercial venture. The organized fans had their own version of history, which was that the club had been created by Matt Busby and that the Edwards family had usurped it and then cashed in. Links with the Busby era were now largely symbolic and were personified in the venerable figure of ex-Busby team captain Bobby Charlton, a man suffused with the almost religious authority of being a Munich survivor, who functioned as a sort of constitutional monarch of Manchester United, with little formal power but immense moral authority. It had been Charlton's disapproval that had delivered the fatal blow to Edwards's last attempt to sell United, the aborted 1989 proposed sale to property developer Michael Knighton. For the organized fans

Edwards represented the alien PLC and everything that was wrong with the club and football in general, and Ferguson and Charlton were the symbols of the Busby legend, the football club, the team and everything that was right.

Sky was keen that Ferguson should come out in favour of the takeover on the grounds that a 'partnership' with Sky would give him more money to spend on players. At the very least they wanted to make sure that he would not side with the opposition. There were some real indicators that this might happen. Like many managers, he had no reason to be enamoured of Sky or the Murdoch organization. Sky brought in money but it was a nuisance, forever demanding post-match interviews and even access to the changing room. The tabloids, led by Murdoch's *Sun* and the *News of the World*, were even worse – hyping transfer news, working with agents to promote transfers he could not afford, siding with players who were demanding higher wages, selectively quoting him, probing into players' personal lives and generally making his life a nightmare.

But when Sky proposed that Ferguson should be told about the deal, be 'brought into the loop', as they put it, Edwards was dead against. The football and business journalist Mihir Bose, in a meticulously researched and well-sourced book about United, later reported that Edwards had warned Sky that Ferguson should be kept in the dark at all costs. 'He has got very close to New Labour and to Number 10,' Edwards reportedly told Mark Booth and other executives at Sky. 'He is very friendly with Alastair Campbell. He is a socialist, you know. Very strange. All this friendship with New Labour and Campbell I do not understand.' During another meeting, after Sky had suggested that Ferguson's approval of the deal, or at least his silence, should be obtained, Edwards reportedly reacted by saying: 'Don't give him money, for Christ's sake. The man's useless.'

In the event Ferguson first heard about the deal in September 1998 when a friend phoned him at home with the news that the sale of United to Sky was all over the front page of the *Sunday Telegraph*. Bobby Charlton, who as a member of the board of the football club, rather than the PLC, first heard about the plan on the radio in Thailand, where he had stopped off on his way to the Commonwealth Games in Malaysia. The *Sunday Telegraph* revelations, which had been a leak, were followed the next day by a story on the front page of Murdoch's *Sun*, hailing the deal as 'good for United and good for football . . . from top to bottom'. The headline in the Sun was 'GOLD TRAFFORD' and took the PR line that Sky had hoped could be sold to Ferguson, that Sky would somehow provide lots of money for him to buy new players. Sky had wanted to name Ronaldo as the player United would now be able to buy, but had been warned off by lawyers. Instead the more plausible rumour was circulated that Ferguson would now be able to buy the Juventus star Patrick Kluivert, who it was well known he had been considering signing for a while.

The line that Sky would somehow boost United into a position of untouchable and permanent domination of English football was of course essential if United's supporters were to be won over. But the organized fans, who included investigative journalist Michael Crick and economics professor Jonathan Michie among their leaders, were not convinced. The opposite was true, they plausibly argued. Sky had just spent £625 million on Premiership rights and was now proposing to spend another £625 million on buying United. As an organization, Sky was just about as far away from a charity as you could get. It was also a PLC like United, required by law to make a profit, and not allowed to spend money just for the fun of winning trophies. Far from pumping money into United, Sky would have to take huge sums out of the club to get a return on its investment.

The *Sun* weighed in by selectively quoting some comments about Sky TV, in which Ferguson had said that the money the company had provided to football had been useful, and by running the headline 'SKY'S GOOD FOR THE GAME – BY FERGIE' to give the impression that he approved of the takeover. Ferguson's real opinion, later expressed in an interview, was that Sky had 'sold fans down the river' and had hit hard at the old and the poor. But at the time he decided to stay out of the row, as did Charlton and most of the well-known figures associated with the club. The anti-takeover campaigners turned to the ex-United striker Brian 'Chocky' McClair, a great Old Trafford hero and close personal friend of Ferguson. But the manager himself said nothing. He did not even mention the episode in his otherwise extremely detailed autobiography, beyond making the comment that, around the time of the takeover deal, he had 'for too long allowed the PLC to overwhelm me, accepting too readily all the cityspeak about institutions and dividends and the harsh realities of the business world'. Ferguson was due to appear at an academic conference on the future of the football business organized by some of the anti-takeover campaigners, but pulled out at the last minute, though he issued a cautious statement criticizing the 'GOLD TRAFFORD' approach and simply saying 'it is in everyone's interest to maintain some degree of league balance. The Premiership is a fantastic league because there's fierce competition. On their day, anyone can beat anyone else. And that's how it should be.'

The Premier League, meanwhile, immediately declared itself officially neutral on the Sky deal. Peter Leaver went on the radio on the morning of the leak to confess, 'I don't know very much about it.' But many in the football industry were hopping mad. Not least Sky's erstwhile ally Rick Parry. His first reaction was to tell journalists that a Sky–Murdoch-owned United should be thrown out of the Premier League. Ken Bates of Chelsea reportedly said the same.

Apart from United's fans, most people in the country, among them all other nineteen club chairmen in the Premier League, did not want United to do well. To win them over Sky needed to present the deal in exactly the opposite way they had used for the consumption of United fans. They had to explain why a plan which was supposed to make United even more successful would be good for all the other clubs as well.

It was a tricky problem and soon Sky's public relations strategy was in tatters. A crucial moment in the PR battle came when Mark Booth, at the formal press conference to announce the deal, was asked who played at left-back for Manchester United. Booth said that he had no idea and that 'football is not my area of expertise'.

The day after Sky reached agreement with Edwards and Kenyon for the takeover of Manchester United, Rupert Murdoch was in Milan, talking to Silvio Berlusconi about 'Project Traviata' – a joint plan to create the new pan-European pay-TV channel based on Sky, Berlusconi's Italian and Spanish channels and Kirch, the German company which would sell subscriptions to the new European Super League.

Kirch had been pushed into the red by buying expensive German rights to Hollywood movies, the 1998 World Cup in France and other sports rights. From Berlusconi and Murdoch's point of view buying the company meant acquiring those rights which, alongside the Super League, would be extremely useful in getting the new European channel off the ground. Despite its cash-flow problems, a few weeks earlier Kirsch had bought a stake in the putative consortium by buying back from Berlusconi a one third share in his own channel for $102 million. Additional money arrived in the form of billionaire Saudi Arabian prince Al Waleed Bin Talal who was interested in acquiring a stake in the new pan-European operation.

But everything depended on getting the Super League off the ground. At first the prospects looked good. Berlusconi had AC Milan and Murdoch, expected in due course to be effectively the owner, via his de facto control of Sky, of Manchester United. At several secret meetings Berlusconi's lieutenants, working through the Media Partners group, had already gone a long way to signing up many of the other leading clubs.

When news of the plan leaked, UEFA, who ran the existing Champions' League, reacted immediately, opening up emergency negotiations with affiliated leagues and with individual clubs identified as having dealings with Media Partners. UEFA officials used a combination of threats and promises to head off the new, competitor league. The threat took the form of a warning that UEFA would force national leagues to throw breakaway clubs out of their domestic league competitions. The warning raised the stakes. Clubs, including United, might choose to join the new set-up, but they would burn their bridges. They would not be allowed to play in the Premiership or the Champions' League, if they went ahead. The promise was UEFA's undertaking to change the Champions' League, increasing the proportion of TV money that went to the clubs rather than UEFA itself and, crucially, increasing the size of the competition so that as many as five top clubs from a league like the Premiership would play in the Champions' League or other European competitions each season. The idea was to counter Media Partners' guarantee that a club like United would play in Europe every season and not miss out simply because they failed to play well enough to win the Premiership.

But there was a further complication – Peter Leaver's plan for an English Premiership-led European championship. Despite UEFA's opposition, Leaver had been working on this project since September 1997, when he had organized the first meeting of major European domestic leagues to discuss the possibility of setting up an 'inter-league' European competition to replace or run alongside UEFA's Champions' League, consisting to begin with only of clubs from the English, Italian, Spanish, Portuguese, French, Dutch and German leagues.

There was now a three-way fight on. The contenders were Berlusconi's Media Partners' Super League to be shown on the new Berlusconi–Murdoch–Kirch pan-European pay-TV channel. Then there was Leaver's less well developed plan for the inter-league championship, possibly to be featured on the Premiership's own pay-TV channel. Lastly there was the existing UEFA competition, financed on free-to-air networks such as Britain's ITV and involving not just the big clubs but all UEFA-affiliated clubs including those in Eastern Europe.

On 25 August 1998 Media Partners made a formal presentation to the UEFA inter-league committee at a meeting in Geneva, hoping to persuade them that their own plans met UEFA's objectives. The Media Partners' project had by now taken definite form. Their Super League would consist of sixteen invited 'founder members', drawn from the major leagues only. These sixteen would continue to play in their domestic leagues, their participation in the Super League replacing the games they would have played in the UEFA Champions' League. There would be a second league, consisting of teams who qualified from domestic leagues 'on merit', and the two competitions would run in tandem, with the champions and runners-up playing each other at the end of the season in a sort of European 'Super Bowl' to determine the overall champions.

The meeting was antagonistic. The Media Partners' position was that they would go ahead and set up the new competition anyway. Once it was off the ground there would be little UEFA and the domestic league authorities could do to stop clubs signing up because the money on offer would be so massive. If the existing authorities wanted to have any role in the future, they had better approve the plan. If they did, Media Partners were prepared to allow UEFA a continuing role as the overall regulator of European football, similar to the FA's role in relationship to the Premier League – looking after the rules of the game, refereeing and so on. Media Partners would also work with the existing domestic leagues, recognizing them as the qualifying competitions for the second, non-invitation league. If UEFA chose to fight, they would be left with a rival, inferior competition based on the excluded eastern European leagues. The danger was that football might well fragment into a series of rival championships with endless re-unification competitions – the fate that had befallen boxing, also as a result of the growing power of pay-TV.

The meeting broke up with nothing decided and most of the national leagues rejecting the plan out of hand. The Spanish were particularly hostile and immediately threatened to throw out of their league any club who continued to talk to Media Partners.

The Geneva meeting was followed a week later by a Media Partners presentation to all twenty chairmen of the Premier League. It was in many ways even more fraught than the Geneva gathering. Leaver had organized for Media Partners to make their pitch and then for UEFA's Gerard Aigner to make a presentation straight afterwards. The intention was to kill the project stone dead. After the knockback they had received in Geneva Media Partners had changed their plan from two leagues of sixteen teams to three of twelve, which meant that a fourth club, likely to be Chelsea or Newcastle, would have guaranteed participation. For the others there was the carrot of a new 'Pro Cup', a knock-out competition with enormous participation money. Six Premiership teams would play in the Pro Cup. Together with four guaranteed Super League places, it meant that ten Premiership clubs could join the gravy train. Given that the clubs taking part would change, almost all of the twenty could at least live in hope of getting into Europe, whereas as things stood with the present UEFA competitions, the overwhelming majority of Premiership clubs had no chance of playing in Europe more than once or twice in a lifetime.

Several chairmen immediately warmed to the idea. It meant that they would only have to finish tenth in order to get a slice of European money – put by Media Partners at over £5 million for participation in the Pro Cup. This was all new and free money; the television revenue they received from the Premiership would remain unchanged.

Gerard Aigner's presentation on behalf of UEFA followed directly. He outlined a plan to expand the Champions' League and other competitions, which would mean five or six clubs would henceforth play in Europe, with higher payments for participation. The offer was not as spectacular as the Media Partners plan, but it worked along the same lines – practically a virtual guarantee that the likes of United, Arsenal and other big clubs would play in the Champions' League every season and a greater chance that the others would be involved if they could finish in the top third of the table.

The chairmen debated the rival merits of the plans as well as the prospects for Leaver's own European project. Much of the discussion involved chairmen bitterly criticizing Manchester United for having negotiated in secret. Ken Bates allegedly said that if United wanted to join a non-UEFA approved competition they could 'piss off' and do so. More conciliatory voices thanked the parties for at least being prepared to discuss everything in the open.

The chairmen agreed that no Premiership club should join the Super League, or even continue discussions with them. They had all heard Aigner's offer to reform the Champions' League, making it more profitable for the big clubs. That was good enough. It also left open the door for Leaver's inter-league plan at some point in the future. The meeting's chairman then asked each club in turn to give an undertaking that they would cease any further contact with Media Partners.

When it came to Manchester United's turn Edwards gave the undertaking with no quibbles, much to the horror of his deputy Peter Kenyon and United's lawyer Maurice Watkins. Kenyon contacted Leaver afterwards, saying that Edwards's promise had been the result of a misunderstanding, but Leaver remained adamant. United had given the undertaking and if they went back on it now, they risked expulsion from both the Premier League and the European Champions League – thus losing all their Sky pay-TV money. Certainly Arsenal and Liverpool would not be taking part, and after the Geneva meeting the participation of Real Madrid and Barcelona was extremely unlikely. It meant that United would be out in the cold like a latter-day version of the Harlem Globe Trotters, playing meaningless exhibition games against Berlusconi's AC Milan on a little-watched European pay-TV channel.

But the fact was that, entirely unknown to Leaver, the United board had secretly agreed the sale of the club to Sky. They were still haggling over the price, and United's availability to play in the Berlusconi Super League was a vital prop underpinning the deal. Almost a year's careful planning was starting to fall to pieces. Anything could happen. Sky might now even pull out of the deal.

News that Sky had already agreed to buy the club leaked within days. If they pulled out now just because the Super League plans were on the verge of collapse, it would mean having to explain the scale of their involvement with Berlusconi. And so Sky ploughed on. The anti-takeover lobby and the clod-hopping PR response of Sky had done enough to create the political storm Booth and Edwards had always feared. On 30 October 1998, six weeks after it had been leaked to the press, the bid was referred to the Monopolies and Mergers Commission, who would investigate whether Sky's ownership of United would give them a monopolistic grip on football as a whole, as was being alleged. The commission's approval would be needed before any deal could go ahead. The deadline for a decision was set for

March 1999 and officials began organizing hearings and gathering information. It did not mean that the deal was off – far from it. Many, including the anti-takeover campaigners, expected it to be approved and were hanging on to the hope that there would be restrictions and guarantees that United would be protected in some way from direct control by the Sky board.

In the meantime, other Premiership clubs started looking for possible takeovers by media companies. Arsenal renewed their on-and-off talks with the London ITV company Carlton about a possible takeover, which would have brought the existing Arsenal board personal millions to rival those on offer to Edwards at United. Liverpool moved closer to their regional ITV company, Granada.

Most dramatically of all, the board of Newcastle United announced their intention to sell the club to the cable pay-TV operator NTL, one of Sky's deadliest rivals, if the Monopolies and Mergers Commission approved Sky's takeover of Manchester United. Newcastle, the club's owners said, had a 'bright future' as a subsidiary of the American cable company.

Alex Ferguson

Alex Ferguson was born in Govan on New Year's Eve 1941 in a grim tenement building overshadowed by the cranes of shipyards working flat out for the war effort. By all accounts he had a happy and secure childhood within a tight-knit community which existed for only one thing – work. Many years later, when football had boosted him into the millionaire bracket, he was at pains to emphasize

Chris Horrie

his roots, wax lyrical about Govan – populated, he would say, by a 'master race' of special people. He imbibed a sort of gut socialism, tinged with the puritanical streak of his father's Scottish–Irish Glaswegian Protestantism. He always claimed that he was brought up to abhor the Protestant–Catholic sectarianism that at one time inflamed Glasgow almost as much as Belfast and found its expression in football. His mother was Catholic. Rangers, the team he supported as a boy and then played for in a not especially glittering playing career, was the Protestant team; Celtic was for Catholics.

Ferguson started playing football seriously as a schoolboy, and represented Scotland at international level. Craig Brown, later the Scottish national side's manager, played in the same team and remembered Ferguson as 'fiery, bright and aggressive' but, above all, 'full of Glaswegian patter', an engaging and cheeky character whom others either intensely liked or disliked. By the time he made his Scottish league debut for Queen's Park as an amateur in 1957, he had left school to take a job as an apprentice tool-maker at the local Remington typewriter factory. In the early 1960s Ferguson took part in the notorious engineering apprentices' strike that swept Glasgow's shipyards. A contemporary later recalled how together with another apprentice, one Billy Connolly, he had 'marched up to Remington, met with Ferguson and the other apprentices and soon had them out on strike'.

Had Ferguson been born a decade or so later, a man of his abilities might have gone to university or made it into one of the white-collar professions. But in the 1950s that was still practically impossible. Instead, like many other working-class lads of his generation, he found an outlet in the twin escape routes of the Labour movement and sport. He became a shop steward and was remembered as a militant. Later, after he had started his professional career in football, he stayed in contact with trade union figures such as Jimmy Reid, strike *leader and organizer of the work-in designed to prevent the closure of the Upper Clyde shipyards which had been the focus of the Govan community.*

Ferguson did well enough as an amateur to be taken on as a part-time professional by St Johnstone in 1960, where he played centre-forward while finishing his apprenticeship. It meant that if his risky venture into football did not work out he would always have something to fall back on. He became a full-time professional in 1964 after moving to Dunfermline, finally signing for Rangers at the age of twenty-six in 1967, the year Celtic became the first British club to win the European Cup. Ferguson's time at Rangers was not a happy one. He felt that he was discriminated against, even persecuted, when it was discovered that although he was a Protestant himself, his mother was Catholic and so was his wife Cathy. After two and a half bitter years, which Ferguson later claimed had 'scarred him for life', he moved down the pecking order to play for Falkirk, his best years already behind him, before finishing his career playing for Ayr United in 1973. He was an activist in the Scottish Professional Footballers' Association, and at Falkirk as player-coach led the players out on strike when the manager docked their wages after a 6–1 defeat. He retired with just enough money to open a pub in his beloved Govan, which he described in his autobiography as a rough place which despite his efforts was forever full of petty criminals and drunks looking for a fight.

Ferguson's career in management started at East Stirlingshire – about as low as you could get on the ladder. It was a struggle to find enough players to field a team, and for a while the club played without a proper goalkeeper. His first dealings with the people who ran football, the club chairmen and directors, removed any illusions he might have harboured, especially coming on the back of his bitter experiences at

Rangers. It was a tale of stupidity, arrogance and neglect. His time at St Mirren, his next and slightly bigger club, was hardly any better. Eventually Ferguson was sacked after the board found he was siphoning money from the turnstiles into a special fund under his own control. The money was used to persuade parents of promising schoolboys and apprentice players to sign with him and not with rival clubs. In fact the accusation of poaching was to dog Ferguson throughout his career. Much later rival clubs would complain that players such as Ryan Giggs, who had been on the books at Manchester City, and David Beckham, who Alan Sugar claimed had been 'associated' with Spurs, had been 'poached' by Ferguson. In 1996 United were fined £20,000 by the FA after making an illegal approach to a seventeen-year old Oldham player, David Brown, and were officially censured after similarly talking to a teenage Arsenal defender, Matthew Wicks.

At the start of his managing career in Scotland Ferguson cleverly befriended the scouts who were paid to seek out the best young talent for Rangers and Celtic, exploiting the sectarian stupidity of the clubs. If a Rangers coach found a promising young Catholic, he knew that Rangers would never sign him, but he would nevertheless be reluctant to see him ending up playing for Celtic. Often the coaches would tip off Ferguson and he would move in, using his special fund. When the St Mirren board found out about the payments they showed him the door, even though there was no suggestion that he had acted in anything other than an honest way and in the best interest of the club. In fact, returning to type as trade unionist, he took St Mirren to an industrial tribunal on those grounds and claimed that every club did the same thing, one way or another. The tribunal, however, found that the club had been within their rights in sacking him.

After his battle with St Mirren, Ferguson landed the job that was to make his reputation. In 1978 he took over as manager of Aberdeen, where he broke the Celtic–Rangers monopoly on the Scottish championship, winning the title three times during his eight seasons with the club, as well as a clutch of other trophies. By then another key part of Ferguson's approach was in place. He was not only superb at finding young players, he also had a natural ability for training and motivating them. The key to this was ferocious discipline in private, combined with effusive praise in public. At Aberdeen he bought only seven players in eight years, spending only £100,000 at a time when players at big English clubs were changing hands for up to £500,000. He preferred teams of young players moulded by his own hand. His discipline could at times be humiliating. The story was told of how a group of young players had been showing off at Aberdeen by roaring past him on the main road in a flashy Mercedes after a training session. Ferguson caught up with them, made them get out of their car, drove them back to the ground and then forced them to walk back to town. Another time the landlady of the digs where some of his players were staying complained that they had been causing a nuisance by playing hide and seek and behaving in a childish way. Ferguson made them memorize nursery rhymes and recite them in front of the others.

By the time he pulled off the greatest achievement of his Scottish managerial career, Aberdeen's victory over Real Madrid in the 1983 European Cup Winners' Cup final, Ferguson had such complete control over his players that he could more or less map out the play from start to finish. It was a version of the Shankly method at Liverpool – underdogs against the world, drill, dedication, surrender of individual wills to the common good.

On 6 November 1986 Ferguson took over from Ron Atkinson as manager of Manchester United, after leaving Aberdeen and spending a short spell as manager of the Scottish national team. He approached the job with trepidation – the club had swallowed up numerous managers since the time of Busby and some had come close to nervous breakdowns. Indiscipline was such that United was known as 'the drinking club', an easy touch for top professionals who could earn a fortune and, given their superstar status and the massive transfer fees paid for them, could more or less blackmail the manager into fielding them regardless of their attitude or level of fitness. He was horrified to find many of the players hung-over and completely unfit after Atkinson's leaving drinks party, just two days before a league match. His first meeting with them was a brief and terse affair amounting to not much more than an instruction to turn up at the gym the next day prepared to put in some work. But from then on he saw his task as straightforward and simple. United had some of the best players in the country, the money to buy some more and the infrastructure to support his own strategy of finding and bringing on young players. All he had to do was stop them drinking and instil some discipline. Some of the more notorious boozers left immediately.

At Manchester United Ferguson spent heavily on players in order to patch things up, and then got on with building the youth team that would form the core of his championship-winning sides of the 1990s. In the meantime, however, United continued to underachieve and after three seasons without winning anything he was widely tipped for the chop. On the third anniversary of his arrival at the club a banner was unfurled at Old Trafford reading: 'Three years of excuses – ta ra Fergie' and there were chants of 'Fergie Out'. According to football folklore what saved him was an away win against Nottingham Forest in the third round of the FA Cup in January 1990. If United had been knocked out, their season would have been over and Ferguson most likely on his way. In the event the team won not only the match, but the Cup

*itself. When United won the European Cup Winners' Cup in
the following season, his position seemed secure and the rest,
to use the cliché, is history: League Cup winners and League
runners-up in 1992; the signing of Cantona and the creation
of the youth system which either produced or procured Giggs,
Beckham, Scholes, Wes Brown and the Neville brothers; the first
Premiership championship in 1993, United's first title win in
twenty-six years; the club's first League and Cup double in
1994; four more championships before the end of the decade,
including another double; the European Cup and the treble.*

*Yet against the background of all this success Ferguson
often seemed uncomfortable with the direction United and
English football were taking. He had at first dismissed the
Premiership as 'a piece of nonsense'. Sky TV, the source
of much of the new money in football, he said, was an
operation which 'sells supporters right down the river and
hits hardest at the most vulnerable part of society – the
old'. He maintained his socialist outlook even when, after
a struggle with Martin Edwards and the United board, he
signed a contract giving him a tiny share of the hundreds
of millions his talent had helped to generate. He appeared
in a European election party political broadcast for the
Labour Party after winning the European Cup and was
called upon to advise the party during a wobbly moment
in its 1997 general election campaign. 'Just keep going on
the things that matter to people,' he reportedly told Blair,
'jobs, schools, hospitals, crime – and hold your nerve'. At
the time of the great commercial changes at United he
decided it was wise to keep quiet. But after announcing
his intention to retire in 2002, he started to become more
outspoken. The sort of wages players were demanding in
the wake of the Bosman decision, he said, represented 'pure
greed' which was damaging the game. 'We are talking about
a small percentage who have let everyone down . . . let*

their profession down,' he said during a TV interview in August 1999.

'The best thing a manager can do now – and this is going to be very important – is not get involved in the money side of it, because I am sure the temptation is going to be there.'

Ferguson's grip on the playing side at United was such that the announcement that he was about to retire from management at the end of the 2001/2002 season seemed to completely de-stablize the United team. Amid rumours that he was preparing a bid to buy the club, United struggled to get results in the Premiership for the first time in a decade.

Part 3.

Cashing in

17.
The Best in the World

Freddy Shepherd, the chief executive of Newcastle United PLC and Douglas Hall, chairman of the club, are sitting in Milday's Palace, a brothel in Marbella, Spain, on Sunday 8 March, the day after Newcastle won a place in the 1998 FA Cup semi-finals. They are talking in the bar to a couple of fellow Brits, whom they assume to be business-men. In fact they are undercover reporters from the *Sunday People*, and the conversation is secretly being tape-recorded for posterity.

Well-oiled with drink, the Newcastle men begin to bray that they have come to Spain for sex because 'Newcastle girls are all dogs – England is full of them. The girls are ugly and they are dogs,' they repeat, adding: 'English girls are crazy. They do it for nothing.' Shepherd and Hall boast they can have their fill of 'the best in the world . . . We've had Penthouse pets . . . the fucking lot . . . the best in the world!' For good measure, Hall adds that he has had '600 . . . 700 mistresses'.

After this initial chit-chat, the talk turns to football and the affairs of Newcastle in particular. Alan Shearer, the striker they signed at the start of the season for a record £15 million, Shepherd and Hall say is 'boring' and money mad. 'We call him Mary Poppins. He never gets into trouble. We're not like him though,' they boast, 'we've already made our money,' says Hall. 'He needs to make £3 million a year, but we've already made our money.'

This is true. Shepherd, Hall and his father Sir John Hall had in the previous year steered Newcastle to a stock market flotation which had made them multi-millionaires.

The success of the venture was based on the exploitation of the Newcastle fans' loyalty. They were some of the most fanatical in the world, and forked out more for season tickets, replica shirts, and all the other trinkets and merchandise of the modern football PLC with unrivalled enthusiasm. Shepherd and Hall boast that they charge £50 for a replica shirt which costs only £5 to make.

Shepherd and Hall say Keegan, the departed Newcastle manager, is a mug and a wimp and they were glad to see the back of him. They add, 'He's got no vices, not like us. We used to call him Shirley Temple.' Shepherd says that they had once taken him to a brothel in Amsterdam, but he was so shy that he stayed downstairs and did not get involved. They had sacked him, they say, because Newcastle had provided £60 million to buy players and yet Keegan had 'won nothing'. His best bit of business, they add, was selling Andy Cole to Manchester United for £7 million when they knew he had a long-term injury. In fact Cole missed most of his first season for United, hampered by a serious leg muscle injury which at one point looked like ending his career. He was not fully fit for two years. After Keegan went, Shepherd and Hall say, they had tried to lure Ferguson 'but we ended up with Kenny Dalglish' who, they think, is also no good.

When an account of what they had said in the Spanish brothel was printed a few days later, Shepherd and Hall tried to brazen it out. But then the newly launched Newcastle United PLC started to take heavy hits on its share price and they resigned. A few months later they returned to the board, saying that they had been 'silly and stupid' in making their remarks, apologizing to all concerned and promising that they would not do that sort of thing again in the future.

*   *   *

Buying into and taking over a privately owned football club, even one as big and potentially valuable as Manchester United, Tottenham or Newcastle, had proved astonishingly easy before the wave of market flotations, paradoxically because it had long been thought to be impossible. Louis Edwards at Manchester United and, more spectacularly, Irving Scholar at Tottenham had shown how it could be done. But the real object lesson in buying a club by stealth, turning it around in financial terms and then achieving a stunning profit by means of a stock market flotation was provided by Sir John Hall at Newcastle United.

Hall was an ex-Coal Board property surveyor who had made a fortune developing the Metro Centre in Gateshead. In 1987 he sold his half-share in the freehold of the shopping centre site (which he had bought a few years earlier for £100,000 when it was an ex-Coal Board ash tip) for an undisclosed sum thought to have been around £30 million. He invested some of the money in creating an upmarket housing estate based around Wynard Hall, the stately home and country seat of Lord Londonderry. Then in April 1988, amid all the talk in the football world of the ten-fold increase in the amount being offered for TV rights by British Satellite Broadcasting, and a new-money rich ITV league consisting of regional superclubs, Hall announced that, Ken Bates-style, he planned to 'rescue' Newcastle United. He put in £500,000 as a loan and acquired a seat on the board.

At the time Newcastle had just dropped into the Second Division and financial problems meant they had had to sell Paul 'Gazza' Gascoigne to Tottenham Hotspur. Hall spoke of his involvement in terms of regional pride and the need to regenerate the North East. Newcastle

Chris Horrie

United was a very familiar business proposition to a man with his background – the golden opportunity of an undervalued and underdeveloped property in an underdeveloped city-centre location, which with a modest amount of investment, a bit of general sprucing up and a pinch of good luck was likely to shoot up in value. Hall followed the examples of Louis Edwards and Irving Scholar and began quietly buying packets of the club's original 2,000 ten-shilling shares issued in 1890 and, in many cases, still held within families as souvenirs. Hall offered £50 per share, which valued the club (the cost of owning it 100 per cent) at £100,000. The amazing thing, pundits were later to say, was that Hall almost got away with buying the club for this price, just one per cent of its value less than a decade later.

Hall's masterstroke was the employment of a professional researcher, local historian and genealogist to track down the relatives of the 1890 shareholders and make them an offer. Holders of the precious documents were found as far away as Australia and, as had been the case a few years earlier with Irving Scholar, many reacted as though they were punters on the *Antiques Roadshow*, amazed that this worthless-looking piece of yellowing paper was of interest to anyone, grabbing the money with great delight and banking it without asking too many questions.

But unlike Edwards and Scholar, Hall was rumbled by the existing board who, led by chairman Gordon McKeag, counter-attacked by trying to buy the shares themselves. A bitter fight for each share followed. Some of the original shareholders cashed in, bidding up the value of their small shareholdings to thousands of pounds. The battle spilled over into the papers, with Hall denouncing McKeag and the old regime for their role in presiding over the decline of the club and being remarkably successful in getting the fans on his side.

The War of the Newcastle Shares lasted for about eighteen months and ended in May 1990, when it was announced that Hall had won effective control of Newcastle United Ltd with 48 per cent of the shares, bought at an estimated cost of £2 million.

Hall followed the example set by both Martin Edwards and Irving Scholar by immediately offering new shares in the company he had bought. The money raised would help pay off some of Newcastle's debts, as a similar rights issue had done at the start of the Irving Scholar regime at Tottenham (also repeated by Alan Sugar when he bought the club from Scholar in 1991). If successful, the issue would also have the effect of massively increasing the value of Hall's stake in the club.

At Newcastle, however, there was to be a twist. Hall had worked hard to get the fans on his side during the takeover battle. His rescue consortium, the Magpie Group, was set up along the lines of new-wave fan power groups such as the Tottenham Independent Supporters' Association which had played a key role in the PR battle to ensure that Alan Sugar and not Robert Maxwell acquired control of the London club. And so the rights issue was couched as a plan to 'democratize' Newcastle United, giving the fans a chance to become shareholders and have a say on the board of directors.

It was not a success. The target of £2.5 million was ambitious in the circumstances. Many of the fans were put off by the minimum share subscription of £100 – a lot of money in the North East. City institutions were not keen either. Newcastle were in the Second Division and saddled with debt. The future appeared to be bleak. After the flop Hall denounced the fans for not being prepared to match his own financial commitment to the club and announced that he was stepping down from his high-profile role at the club. He later said, 'I was so desperately disappointed that the fans didn't buy the shares. I was so gutted that I walked away from the club.' It was later reckoned that he nevertheless got his initial investment back, through the issue itself and the temporary sale of his stake in the club. Hall maintained his power over the Newcastle board by leaving his £500,000 loan in place, and he and his son Douglas continued to pull the strings, even though Sir John dropped out of the limelight for a while.

Hall returned to the centre stage at Newcastle only in spring 1991 after the publication of Graham Kelly's and the FA's *Blueprint for the Future of Football*, the plan to set up the FA Premier League. The FA and the League continued wrangling over the details of the project until October, when Kelly's plan got the legal green light in addition to the support of the existing First Division clubs. Against this background, Hall cranked up a noisy PR campaign, exploiting the 'disgrace' that Newcastle had dropped into the Second Division and looked in danger of disappearing into the Third, while traditional rivals were setting up a Super League, as it was still widely called. Newcastle remained crippled with debt and Hall was able to persuade the 'shamed' directors who, he said, had 'failed the club' to resign and sell their stakes to him. Even Gordon McKeag, Hall's bitterest opponent, bowed to what was increasingly seen as inevitable and sold his shares. Hall ended up with 87 per cent of the shares in Newcastle United Football Club.

The Hall regime, led by Douglas Hall and Freddy Shepherd, acted quickly to improve matters on the pitch. In February 1992, half-way through the last season before the formation of the Premiership, Newcastle lost 5–2 to Oxford United and sank dangerously down the Second Division table towards the relegation zone. Shepherd and the Newcastle board gave team manager Ossie Ardiles the 'kiss of death' vote of confidence, saying that his position as manager was 'as safe as houses'. Three days later they sacked him.

After following the Edwards and Scholar textbook in achieving the takeover of the club, Shepherd and the Halls turned to another model – Jack Walker at Blackburn Rovers. They got out their chequebook and started buying a team. 'My ambition is to see this club within the next five years established,' John Hall said, 'as one of the top three in the United Kingdom and, over the next ten years, amongst the top ten in Europe.' But in order to buy players, as Walker had found, a club first needed to show it had ambition, by hiring a well-known manager who would be trusted by players and who had the contacts in the football world to sign them up.

The choice, Kevin Keegan, was inspired. Like Kenny Dalglish, the man Jack Walker had put in charge at Blackburn, Keegan was an ex-Liverpool centre-forward. But after finishing his playing career he had not gone into management, or even into media punditry. Instead he had disappeared off to Spain, where he was best known for playing golf. But he was a great hero with the Newcastle fans. After his best years with Liverpool were over Keegan had played for Newcastle in the mid-1980s, leading the team to promotion from the Second Division and a good run in the First. He was associated with the only good times within living memory of most fans and, above all, associated with the idea of promotion.

At first Keegan said his involvement might be only temporary. The 1991–92 season was half-way through and all Keegan would say is that he would do his best to save the club from relegation (and possible 'extinction', according to the hype in the press), more or less for old times' sake. As it happened Newcastle escaped relegation by beating Leicester City on the last day of the season, 2 May 1992. But Keegan was not keen to stay involved. Douglas Hall, Freddie Shepherd and Freddie Fletcher, the three men who ran Newcastle United, had to fly out to Spain and promised Keegan a lot of money to buy players. He later said that the men from Newcastle had told him, 'We are ready to go flat out, we're as ambitious to buy the best as you are. You now have a settled board of directors with the financial muscle to turn us into a great club.'

Keegan made a number of key signings in the summer: Barry Venison from Liverpool, John Beresford from Portsmouth, Scott Sellars from Leeds, Robert Lee from Charlton and Paul Bracewell from Sunderland. Keegan also tabled a bid to sign Alan Shearer in competition with Manchester United and Blackburn. Newcastle's offer of £3 million was not enough to attract Shearer, who went to Blackburn. Instead Keegan signed Andy Cole for £1.75 million from Bristol City. Keegan's off-the-peg team was by far the most expensively assembled outfit in what had become the First Division, now that the Premier League had been set up. Andy Cole was especially effective, scoring twelve goals in eleven starts in the final part of the season. He scored one goal and made the other in the 2–0 win against Grimsby that secured automatic promotion as champions to the Premier League.

Keegan's team took the Premiership by storm, with Andy Cole proving just as effective in the top league as he had been in the previous season in the First Division. People began to wonder why it was that Cole had been allowed to leave Arsenal, under George Graham, to go to Bristol City and then to Newcastle. It was put down to bad luck and poor judgement on Graham's part. Newcastle pushed Manchester United and Blackburn all season and finished in third place. Keegan had spent heavily once more, bringing the total player bill towards the £60 million later mentioned by Hall and Shepherd in the brothel in Spain. But despite this, income was booming to such an extent that the Halls and Shepherd could begin to plan a second, and this time much more successful, market flotation. Turnover had increased from £4 million when Hall first took over to £40 million by the end of the 1996 financial year. Profits were boosted further by the sensational January 1995 sale of Andy Cole to Manchester United for £6 million in return for the transfer of United's winger Keith Gillespie to Newcastle.

The Cole sale was a shock to Newcastle fans and Keegan was under pressure when Newcastle finished only sixth at the end of the 1994–95 season, their second campaign in the Premiership. But behind the scenes Keegan had already targeted Alan Shearer, the Blackburn striker he had first tried to sign two years earlier, and the Cole money had been earmarked for that purpose. In the summer of 1996, after Shearer's praiseworthy performance for England during Euro 96, the striker signed for Newcastle for £15 million. The signing itself was a public relations masterpiece. Workers at the Scottish and Newcastle brewery, Newcastle United's sponsors, were given the day off so they could see the elaborate post-signing ceremony where Shearer, The Super Geordie (or 'Mary Poppins' to Freddie Shepherd and Douglas Hall) was unveiled. The player himself emphasized his local roots by telling the story of how as a boy he had stood on the Newcastle terraces with his sheet-metal worker

Chris Horrie

dad. Sir John Hall, glorying in the limelight, declared that 'never again' would Newcastle be forced to miss out on, or sell, local talent like Shearer, the last in a long line of players, the best of their generation, starting with Bobby and Jackie Charlton, Gascoigne and Chris Waddle, who had moved south. Getting slightly carried away by the ecstatic mood of the fans, Sir John even said that he saw a time in the near future when Newcastle would field a team of eleven (super) Geordies. The Newcastle fans now had a new chant, officially sanctioned and promoted by the club: 'Shearer's coming home' – echoing the pop record anthem of Euro 96, 'Football's Coming Home'.

Newcastle started the following season in great form, neck and neck with Manchester United, threatening to win a trophy at last. But Keegan was far from happy. Despite soaring income Newcastle was carrying heavy debts, mainly because of the board's rush to rebuild its St James's Park ground, turning it into a modern conference and banqueting centre on the lines of Old Trafford. In additon, Sir John Hall wanted Newcastle United to branch out into other sports including basketball and rugby, draining yet more millions into ground- and team-building. The sale of Andy Cole for £6 million had provided part of the money needed for the Shearer signing, but Keegan had been told by the board and the club's bankers that he had to sell players to meet the rest of the £15 million bill. This proved impossible. Some players who might have attracted big fees, such as Les Ferdinand, were injured and therefore off the market. Others, such as Paul Kitson and Lee Clark, did not attract much interest from buying clubs. The problem led to a series of rows in the first half of the 1996–97 season between Keegan and the Newcastle board during which, it was later claimed, the manager resigned or threatened to resign five times.

After Newcastle lost to Blackburn on Boxing Day 1996, slipping well behind in the race for the championship, Keegan again resigned. This time the board took the threat more seriously. The reason was that Hall was putting the final touches to Newcastle's stock market flotation prospectus. Keegan later said that the reason why he was being put under so much financial pressure was that Hall needed to keep the banks on-side in the run-up to the market flotation. 'The flotation had taken over everything,' he later said, 'even the most important part, the team.'

The laws governing what can be said in documents offering shares in a company for the first time are extremely strict. It is essential for a company approaching flotation to give assurances about key staff. The acquisition of Shearer on a long contract had been fantastic from this point of view – he was the best-known footballer in the country and the City could see how by owning his registration the company could make predictable profits from replica shirt sales. It could also claim to have a good chance of unlocking extra money from the European Cup and from television by winning the Premiership. Such a claim was credible only if, in addition to Shearer, the club could prove that they had the services of Keegan, a successful and well-known manager. But this would not work if Keegan kept threatening to resign all the time.

The manager was given an ultimatum. Either he signed an iron-clad two-year contract, to see Newcastle through the all-important flotation, or he left immediately. Keegan responded by saying that he wanted to go at the end of the season. But that was no good, in terms of the flotation prospectus. It would mean uncertainty over the future, and uncertainty was the thing that the City and institutional investors liked least of all. On

Chris Horrie

14 January 1997 Kevin Keegan announced his shock resignation as manager of Newcastle United, saying that he could no longer take the stress of managing a Premiership club. The story was widely believed since, some months earlier, Keegan had made an extraordinary outburst on TV against Alex Ferguson, repeating over and over in bitter and emotional terms that he would 'love to beat Manchester United . . .' to the championship, '. . . just love it', which led commentators to suggest that he might be cracking up.

After the Newcastle board sounded out Alex Ferguson for the job – his signature might have added tens of millions to the valuation of Newcastle's prospects – and Bobby Robson, who turned them down, Kenny Dalglish followed Shearer from Blackburn where he had been in what amounted to semi-retirement. Dalglish, a multiple trophy winner, including the Premiership at Blackburn, took pride of place in the Newcastle flotation document.

Dalglish impressed the City, but he was a far from popular figure with the fans. He was a dour man with a reputation for dour football and was seen, since his resignations from Liverpool and Blackburn, as a manager with an apparent tendency to walk away at crucial moments. He did not endear himself to the Newcastle supporters when, in one of his first moves, he switched training sessions from a pitch in Durham – where the poorer fans who had no chance of getting into the all-season-ticket Newcastle stadium, St James's Park, used to congregate to watch their heroes – to a more discreet and security-guarded compound at Chester-le-Street. Under his leadership the team that had challenged Manchester United for the championship under Keegan slipped to a finishing position of thirteenth. They had struggled to avoid relegation until the penultimate game of the season and a lot of the enthusiasm slipped away, the drop in form coinciding as it did with news of the Marbella brothel outrage. According to the *Mail on Sunday*'s football writer Bob Cass, Newcastle United in the space of a year had gone from being 'the most loved to become the most hated team' in the country.

Newcastle United PLC was floated on the stock market on Wednesday 2 April 1997. The timing was perfect. In the previous year the City had welcomed Leeds, QPR, Sunderland and Ken Bates's Chelsea Village onto the stock market with successful flotations. In 1997 they were joined by Sheffield United, West Brom, Birmingham City, Charlton, Bolton, Leicester City, Aston Villa and Nottingham Forest. In the wake of the 1996 satellite TV deal, the expansion of the Champions' League, the soaring interest of middle-class supporters who had followed England's performance in Euro 96 and, above all, the astronomic increase in the share price of already floated Manchester United, football stocks were fashionable and the City could not get enough of them.

With these fair winds in its sails Newcastle United PLC achieved a market valuation of £180 million, almost ten times the value placed on the operation at the time of the failed Magpie Group flotation a few years earlier. The Hall family's share of the club, bought for an undisclosed figure thought to be about £2 million, was now worth £102 million. Other Hall allies on the board also gained millions. Freddy Shepherd's stake alone was worth £13 million.

After flotation Newcastle's share price fluctuated wildly with the Halls dipping in and out, selling and buying as the price moved. After the hype and glamour of the Keegan era Newcastle were not doing well and football shares had come to be extremely sensitive to transfer speculation, the arrival of profitable opportunities like the Media Partners' Super League and events on the field. The share price at flotation had been 135p and thousands of Newcastle fans had piled in. By the spring of 1998, after boardroom rows and the Marbella scandal, the share price dropped to 57p and they had lost thousands. Shortly afterwards, in June 1998, after many changes in the composition of the board, Sir John Hall announced that he would be retiring at the end of the year. He was sixty-five years old and said he had achieved all he had wanted to achieve with Newcastle United – even though the club had not won a major trophy during the time of his control.

Before he left Hall had begun work on his biggest financial coup of all – the proposed sale of Newcastle to the cable TV company NTL. The American-owned NTL was the third largest cable company in the UK and had the vast resources of its parent, International CableTel, to draw on, but was still far from profitable. At the time it was planning to roll out its digital TV services, starting in 1998. It knew that the Premier League was still, in Rupert Murdoch's phrase, the 'battering ram' – the only reliable way to get millions of subscribers to a pay-TV operation in a country where, thanks to the BBC, ITV and Channel Four, most people already got most of what they wanted on television most of the time (including, until 1992, live football) for free.

After the 1996 renewal of the deal between Sky and the Premier League, NTL and the other cable companies were forced to offer the Premiership on Sky Sports to their subscribers for very little profit, passing most of the money they were able to bring in straight on to Sky. But the deal had at least established some stability, and the number of cable subscribers was starting to creep up, boosted by the novelty of the Internet, which could not be delivered via Sky's dishes and worked best with a cable connection.

The danger for NTL was that the Office of Fair Trading would rule that the Premiership was a cartel, outlaw the practice of the Premier League bundling lots of Premiership games as a single product sold to one, exclusive broadcaster and allow the clubs to sell their own rights to anyone they liked. Sky were so worried by this prospect that they had decided to buy Manchester United, so that if the Premiership was broken up they had the inside track on hanging on to United's games, the most valuable part of the Premiership package. It made sense for NTL to go for their own club, to ensure that they were not left out in the cold. An NTL bid for Manchester United made no sense – the club was already very close to Sky and they had a joint venture in the form of the MUTV lifestyle channel. Arsenal and Liverpool were still not fully floated as PLCs and were not for sale, and anyway already had close links to their respective regional ITV companies, Carlton and Granada. That left Newcastle – a tempting 'dish', claiming to have a fan base second only to Manchester United's.

Takeover talks began within days of the leak of Sky's bid for Manchester United in September 1998, boosting Newcastle's share price by 10 per cent in a single day. The referral of the Sky bid to the competition commission complicated things, but in December 1998 NTL bought a 6.3 per cent stake in Newcastle from the Halls for £10 million, valuing the club at £160 million, and announced that Hall had invited them to make a full takeover bid if Manchester United bought Sky. The Halls, who had bought control of the club fifteen years earlier for less

Chris Horrie

than £3 million, stood to make £125 million if the deal went ahead.

In the event NTL pulled out of a full takeover when the government blocked Sky's purchase of Manchester United in March 1999, after reference to the Monopolies and Mergers Commission. NTL stayed involved, becoming the club's shirt sponsor and, in 1999, increasing their stake to 9.9 per cent, the maximum allowed for a media company under FA rules, giving the Halls another £6 million and providing the club with an interest-free £25 million loan which might be converted into shares if the maximum holding rule was abolished in the future. The cable company then secured exclusive rights to negotiate TV deals for the club.

A future was now being mapped out for the top clubs in the Premier League. In the decade since the ball had been set rolling with the proposed ITV Ten breakaway, the clubs had been redeveloped as prime assets ripe for sale to media companies, releasing vast amounts of capital to the handful of men who, like Martin Edwards, had been lucky enough to have inherited a club and then found money falling into their laps. Then there were those, like Hall, who had seen which way the wind was blowing and had astutely moved in.

The periodic meetings of the Premiership chairmen to bicker over pay-per-view or plans for new made-for-TV European leagues, were now gatherings of some of the richest people in the country, their total personal worth adding up to hundreds of millions. The roster of 'football fat cats', as they were sometimes called in the press, included businessmen like 'Deadly Doug' Ellis of Aston Villa (the nickname came from the frequency with which he once hired and fired team managers). Ellis bought control of Villa in 1982, the year the club won the European Cup, for a reported £500,000, after earlier spells as a major shareholder and director. He had made his money in the package holiday business. Villa was floated in May 1997, in the wake of the 1996 Sky TV deal and at the height of the City's appetite for football stocks. He sold a tranche of shares at flotation for £4 million. His remaining 33 per cent stake was worth over £40 million. By the end of the decade the value of Villa to a media company would rise to around £200 million and a sale would have given Ellis £70 million, a 1,400 per cent increase in the value of his investment over a period when the club won nothing, took no real risks and provided no innovations other than the proud boast that its stadium, in common with all the others, was no longer a potential death trap.

Another winner in the age of the Premiership was David Dein, who, after making his first fortune in the wholesale grocery business, in 1983 bought 1,161 unissued shares in Arsenal for £300,000, giving him a 16.6 per cent stake in the club. At the time Arsenal chairman Peter Hill-Wood, the former vice-chairman of Hambros Bank, said he was 'mad' to part with the money. If so, there was method in his madness. By 1991, ahead of the launch of the Premier League and the rights deal with Sky, Dein had upped his stake in the club to 42 per cent, bought for less than £10 million. If he had been able to hold on to his stake, by the time of the late 1990s' football stock mania it would have been worth around £60 million.

But in the early 1990s Dein had to cash part of his stake in order to invest more in his other businesses, selling tranches of shares to an old business associate, Danny Fiszman, a South African-born diamond dealer with an estimated personal fortune of £100 million. Fiszman then upped his stake in 1996 as the club's value again soared on the back of a renewed deal with Sky. In 1998 he sold a block of Psion shares for £14 million, using part of the cash to increase his holding in the club to 29 per cent at a time when Arsenal's Ofex-listed stock was soaring on rumours of a flotation on the main stock market. In the wake of the Sky bid for Manchester United, Arsenal formed a strategic alliance with ITV operator Carlton, which led a couple of years later to the London ITV company taking a large stake in the club and securing the right to be Arsenal's sole representative in TV rights negotiations.

Alan Sugar, then owner of Tottenham, had likewise found himself sitting on top of a goldmine. He had bought the club for £8 million in 1991 – earned back almost immediately by a rights issue – and by 2001 he was negotiating a sale to the media company ENIC for £100 million. The case of Tottenham showed that profitability and success on the pitch were not linked, at least not beyond the need to stay in the Premiership. The Tottenham fans still bought the merchandise and packed the ground almost every week, even if Spurs was not winning competitions. The business logic seemed to be that there was no sense in spending heavily on players to win competitions which, in any case were spoken for by even bigger-spending clubs such as Manchester United and Arsenal, when a cheaper, workaday team could do enough to avoid relegation. Despite far from miserly spending on players and ground improvements, under Sugar's charge Tottenham became one of the most financially efficient clubs but sank from being one of the Big Five who regularly appeared in Wembley Cup finals and often had a chance of winning the league to an outfit which sometimes appeared to aspire to mediocrity.

But if one man represented the ethos of the Premiership better than anyone else it was Ken Bates, the combative chairman of Chelsea.

1996–97 season

Newcastle United and Arsenal spent heavily pre-season in an attempt to challenge Manchester United. In the end it did not do them much good. Manchester United only looked in trouble in October when the team suddenly let in eleven goals in two games, including a 5–0 defeat by Newcastle and a 6–3 pasting by Southampton. They won the championship by a comfortable seven points. Keegan resigned and was later to complain that Newcastle had been taken over by bankers and accountants who were interested only in the club's impending flotation as a PLC. The new preoccupation with business spread to the terraces where chants now sometimes involved comments on the business affairs and transfer dealings of managers. With stories circulating that Shearer had again refused to sign for Manchester United, the chant was 'There's only one greedy bastard – that's Alan Shearer'. Later, when Shearer failed to do the business for Newcastle, performing far less well than United's Norwegian striker Ole Gunnar Solskjaer, whom Ferguson had bought for far less money, the chant was 'Ole Solskjaer – Alan Shearer was fucking dearer . . .'

Newcastle finished the season in second place, thus qualifying for the expanded Champions' League. Liverpool, who were early leaders, fell back as Manchester United got into their stride. Arsène Wenger arrived at Arsenal and George Graham returned to management from the ban imposed after the Arsenal bungs scandal to take over at Leeds United.

Chris Horrie

At the end of the season Eric Cantona announced his early retirement from the game, complaining that the merchandising department at Manchester United had tried to 'buy his soul'.

18.
Blaster Bates

Ken Bates launched himself on the business world in the 1960s, not in London but in Bob Lord's Burnley, and not in football but in the building trade. His first company, called Howarth, went bust in 1969 carrying debts of about £1 million. Bates had nevertheless been involved with football, investing and serving on the boards of Wigan and Oldham Athletic at various times.

After the collapse of Howarth, Bates moved his operations to the British Virgin Islands, where he became a property developer and ended up leasing two thirds of the largest island in the group. One attraction for Bates was the fact that the colonial administration of the Islands did not charge him any tax. In return he was obliged to provide various amenities and social services for the islanders. Eventually he gained such a grip on the local economy that the administration felt obliged to buy him out. In 1971, after what was described as 'civil unrest' on the Islands, Bates was paid $5 million (money that had been provided by the UK taxpayer as development aid) for the return of their island. It was this money that was the basis of his personal fortune.

Bates's next move was to set up a fringe bank called the Irish Trust Bank in Dublin and an investment fund called the International Trust Group, based in the Isle of Man. The affairs of these companies would prove to be troubled. The Irish Central Bank demanded that Bates should be removed as a director or shareholder of the Irish Trust Bank after discovering that he had not declared the failure of his first company, Howarth, when setting up the bank. But combative as ever, Bates sued the Irish banking regulators. They backed down and he was allowed to stay in charge of the Trust Bank.

There was more controversy in 1976 when, at age forty-three, Bates's immediate arrest was ordered by the Dublin High Court after the bank's collapse. It was alleged that Bates had illegally removed documents from the offices of the Trust Bank. After a few hours of drama the arrest order was lifted when Bates turned up at court with the missing papers. The failure of the bank, the simple matter of loans outstripping assets, was put down to the crisis of confidence that swept the whole UK and Irish banking system that year.

After the collapse of his Irish bank Bates moved to Monte Carlo where, according to some reports, he first met Brian Mears, the owner of Chelsea FC. At that time, the late 1970s, the club had overstretched itself by trying to rebuild its Stamford Bridge stadium, breaking the standard maxim in football management that a club could spend money on players or on the ground, but not on both at the same time. Unable to buy decent players, in 1979 Chelsea dropped into the Second Division and stayed down for a total of four near-disastrous seasons.

At one point it even looked as if the club might drop into the netherworld of Division Three. Chelsea crowds had dwindled to a hardcore, with a hooligan minority who compensated for their team's lack of success by kicking each other and any rival fans who fancied their chances. Egged on by the tabloids, the SCUM, as they were known, rose to the occasion with a series of pitched battles to see who were the most violently demented. The violence caused gates to collapse further in a vicious circle which was even dubbed for a while the 'Chelsea Syndrome'.

In 1982, in the middle of the 'syndrome' era, Bates

stepped in to buy control of the effectively bankrupt club for the token sum of £1 and set about the process of rescuing it. Bates underwrote the players' wages and other running costs and took on debts said to amount to £1 million. From the start Bates approached Chelsea as a business proposition. One attraction was the value of Chelsea's Stamford Bridge stadium near the King's Road, soon to become some of the most valuable land in Europe during the property development boom of the 1980s. The problem for Bates was that the old Chelsea regime had sold the lease to Stamford Bridge to a series of developers for £800,000. By the end of the decade Stamford Bridge was in the hands of Cabra Estates, a concern which also owned the lease to nearby Fulham's site and stadium. After Bates's £1 arrival there followed a bitter, decade-long struggle to win back the freehold.

By the mid-1980s Chelsea were back in the First Division and Bates was throwing his weight about within the League's management structures. He became infamous to football fans when in 1984 he installed his anti-hooligan barbed-wire-topped electrified cattle-fence in the stands at Stamford Bridge. The Greater London Council made him take it down for safety reasons.

In 1988 Bates led the revolt of smaller clubs against Greg Dyke's plan for an ITV Ten televised Super League, incensed to find that the London 'franchises' were being offered to Arsenal, Tottenham and West Ham. When the ITV Ten plan was replaced by the idea of the Premiership, Bates immediately launched a campaign to ensure that it would at first include twenty-two clubs, to increase Chelsea's chances of staying within the golden circle of TV money. After the Premiership was formed Bates played an important part in ensuring the rights to live matches went to Sky and not to his old foes at ITV.

Chris Horrie

Bates's relationship with Sky was to become closer over the years, culminating in the sale of a significant stake in Bates's creation, Chelsea Village, the holding company which owned Chelsea FC. Chelsea Village had been brought into being to develop the Stamford Bridge site. It was Chelsea Village, not Chelsea FC, which provided the key to Bates's strategy and, eventually, his vast personal fortune.

In 1988 Chelsea's lease on Stamford Bridge ran out and the club's landlord, Cabra Estates, offered Bates the site for £23 million. In a way this was a bargain. Independent surveyors put its value at between £40 and £60 million. But Cabra had financial problems and was keen to sell. Bates refused to pay and Cabra threatened to evict Chelsea. Bates ran a highly effective 'Save the Bridge' campaign, raising a fighting fund from the fans and pulling in political support from figures such as Tory cabinet ministers John Major and David Mellor. For years the residents around the ground had wanted the football stadium closed down because it blighted the area and caused traffic problems, but Bates's campaign bogged down the process of getting the planning permission any potential developer would need. Bates then launched no fewer than five separate legal actions against Cabra and also bought packets of land around the stadium, including a row of dilapidated shops, which Cabra would have to demolish if their development was to go ahead. The effect of Bates's tactics was to greatly reduce the value of the site to Cabra and, in effect, force a sale at a knock-down price to Bates.

In 1992, days after Bates had voted for the deal between the Premiership and Sky, three years of brinkmanship came to an end. By this point the property market had temporarily crashed and Cabra was carrying debts of £52 million and being pressed to sell to Bates who was, in effect, the only possible buyer. A final inducement was an offer by Bates to allow Fulham to move to Stamford Bridge and ground share. Cabra owned Fulham's even more promising Craven Cottage stadium, a luxury complex developer's dream on a leafy and prosperous bend of the Thames. Bates's offer to accept Fulham as tenants if Cabra let him have Stamford Bridge would solve a lot of problems for the developer. It never, however, came to pass.

Instead Bates stepped up his war of attrition, making life as difficult as possible for Cabra, hoping to get the freehold of the site from them as cheaply as possible. Eventually Cabra went bankrupt, having overextended themselves in the boom-and-bust London property market of the early 1990s. The bankrupt company owed millions to the Royal Bank of Scotland, who were keen to sell Stamford Bridge as quickly as possible to get some of their money back. Bates did a deal which continued Chelsea's lease, but also gave him the right to buy the freehold at the fixed price of £16.5 million any time in the following twenty years.

Bates had secured the Stamford Bridge site for less than a third of its estimated £60 million value as a site for houses or shops and did not have to pay a penny for twenty years if he chose not to do so. With this tremendous asset at its core Bates was ready to groom Chelsea Village for a market flotation, which would have been impossible so long as the company was not its own landlord.

Bates's next step was to get rid of his great rival Matthew Harding, the multi-millionaire Chelsea supporter, who had kept the club afloat with a series of loans in return for which he had been given a seat on the board.

Chris Horrie

The way Bates disposed of his former partner, Matthew Harding, is one of the most remarkable stories in recent boardroom history. The battle between the two men had become extremely bitter and was being fought out all over the pages of the tabloid press. At one point Bates opened a 'dirt file' on Harding, hiring private detectives to take pictures of the happily married Harding's pregnant mistress. Harding had assumed that his position of power in the club was secure because neither the club nor any of the other directors, Bates included, had the money to repay the loans he had made available to save the club from extinction.

But in 1995 Bates, without telling Harding anything, obtained a banker's draft for the £2.7 million the club owed him by borrowing against an expected increase in the club's revenue from Sky in advance of the 1996 TV rights renewal deal. Bates and Colin Hutchinson, the Chelsea chief executive, set out to ambush Harding during a scheduled business meeting at the Dorchester Hotel in London. The three men met and chatted, for once amiably enough, before Harding announced that he had to rush off to a meeting at the House of Lords. As he was getting up to leave, Bates reached inside his jacket and pulled out a long, thin envelope. 'Matthew,' he said. 'Here is a banker's draft for you made out for £2.7 million. Take it. We do not owe you a penny now.'

Harding protested that he had worked out a way of solving their differences, allowing them both to work together for the good of Chelsea. He began fumbling for papers setting out the arrangement.

'Too late!' Bates snapped. 'You have buggered us about for too long. We are going into the future without you.' Bates thrust the envelope towards Harding and completed his *tour de force* performance by giving his former partner twenty-eight days' notice of his intention to throw him off the Chelsea board. Harding was dumbstruck. Bates described in his autobiography how he told Harding: 'Now, Matthew, do me a great pleasure and fuck off.' His next move was to ban Harding from parts of the Stamford Bridge ground. When Harding died in a helicopter crash shortly afterwards, Bates said that he honestly could not find it in himself to feel sorry.

With Harding out of the way Bates pressed ahead with the plan which would make him a personal fortune of tens of millions, as well as providing some of the finance for the next stage in the development of Chelsea Village – joining the mid-1990s rush to float on the stock market as a football PLC. Chelsea's flotation on the Alternative Investment Market in 1996 raised the relatively modest sum of £38.2 million (compared to the £100 million raised by Newcastle United's flotation in the same year). But this was followed in 1997 by the issue of a highly unusual – or, in Bates's phrase, 'innovative' – Eurobond, raising £75 million but obliging the company to pay extraordinarily high rates of interest. Thirteen million pounds of the new money was used to exercise the option to buy the freehold of Stamford Bridge, the rest to pay for hotel building and other development at the Village.

The Eurobond meant that Chelsea was committed to pay around £15 million a year to service the loan, including a phenomenal £7 million a year interest payment, and most of this would have to come from revenue in the form of ever escalating season ticket prices and TV rights. It was vital that Chelsea should generate as much income as possible and the club's fans soon found that they were paying the highest ticket prices in the Premier League. In the 1999–2000 season a Chelsea season ticket cost £1,120. Spurs charged £796 and Manchester United £418. Bates claimed that this was the price of paying the players' wages. 'If you want five-star football it doesn't come cheap,' he told the fans. 'Somebody's got to pay and it is going to be you.' This was only partly true. Manchester United and Arsenal fielded players who were just as expensive, but their tickets were nowhere near as expensive. Bates's counter-argument was that Stamford Bridge's capacity was smaller. But, again, that was only part of the reason for high prices. Much of the cash-flow was needed to service the Eurobond and to build the shopping, apartment and hotel complex.

By the year 2000 Bates reported that Chelsea Village's share capital was worth almost £72 million and that net assets were in excess of £100 million. When in 1997 football shares experienced a peak at the height of their popularity, Chelsea's capital value reached £172 million. At the time Bates's personal stake was just under 25 per cent. It meant that he had on paper made a personal profit of over £40 million with, if all went according to his plan, much more to come. It was little wonder that he had not wanted to go into the future on an equal basis with Harding, the man who had made everything possible with the £2.7 million loan that had kept Chelsea in business.

All of this, of course, went directly against one of the key aims that the FA set out in their *Blueprint for the Future of Football*. Article 16.3.3 stated that the governing body would 'continue to encourage ground-sharing' in order to 'reduce overheads and renovation for League stadia as a whole'. The Taylor Report on Hillsborough and its aftermath had said much the same thing and had also recommended that ground rebuilding should not be used as an opportunity to put up prices. Yet in west London there were several stadiums which Chelsea might have shared. Two of them, QPR's Loftus Road and Fulham's Craven Cottage, were on the same side of town. Fulham was practically within walking distance. But Bates ploughed on, using millions of public money and revenue which might have been spent otherwise within the game to build the Chelsea Village complex.

Bates had his critics both inside the football industry and among Chelsea fans. The main worry was the £15 million a year that would have to be taken from the football club to pay Chelsea Village's debts – at least until the hotels and other businesses started making a profit. In the year 2000 that still seemed to be some way off. The new hotels were not proving as popular with tourists as Bates would have liked and had occupancy rates well below those of rival and better-established London hotels. The sharp downturn in tourism in 2001 also looked threatening. Of the seventeen super luxurious hospitality boxes Bates had built in the hope of selling them for £10 million each, all remained unsold by the end of 2000 – except for one. That had been bought by Sky TV as part of what Bates called the 'strategic alliance' between Chelsea and the broadcaster. The alliance also extended to Sky taking a nine per cent share in the club. Sky had turned to Chelsea (and several other clubs) after failing to buy Manchester United in 1998. Bates's frequently repeated promise to turn Chelsea into the 'Manchester United of the South' sounded as much like a threat as a promise.

And, finally, there was the persistent mystery of who, exactly, was the final and decisive owner of Chelsea

Chris Horrie

Village which, in turn, owned Chelsea Football Club as one of its forty operating subsidiaries. Bates had reduced his stake in Chelsea Village to about 20 per cent. The largest single block of shares was held by an entity called Swan Management, a blind trust registered in the Channel Islands. When asked who Swan Management were Bates would angrily snap that he did not know and that, anyway, it was nobody's business, though he did once say in a newspaper interview that the ultimate owners were 'the same people who helped me out in 1982 when I saved the club'.

1997–98 season

At first it looked as if Manchester United would again walk the championship, even though Cantona had departed and been replaced by Spurs striker Teddy Sheringham. By Christmas they were thirteen points clear of Arsenal and with the only other potential contenders Liverpool and Chelsea trailing. United were in such a strong position and in such devastating form that several bookmakers stopped taking bets on the championship. In the third round of the FA Cup United beat Chelsea 5–2 after being 5–0 up at half-time. The result was followed by a £13 million drop in Chelsea Village's market value as the scale of further investment in players needed to catch up with United became apparent.

The Manchester club were still well ahead in March but then started to drop a lot of points, while Arsenal put together a run of ten wins to surge past them and win the league by a single point. Much to the delight of everyone in the game and Arsenal fans in particular, United failed to win a single major trophy. They even suffered the indignity of being knocked out of the FA Cup by lowly Barnsley. In the following season *rival fans would chant: 'Oh Teddy, Teddy – You went to Man United and you won f*** all'.*

The season ended with the World Cup in France – the most commercialized so far. Some said that the competition now functioned as little more than an international trade fair for the football industry where player transfers and TV rights deals were negotiated. The gleaming new stadiums were quiet, soulless tombs, stuffed with corporate guests, whereas many of the grass-roots fans were excluded by ticket prices of up to £1,500 on the black market. The standard of play was not great – at least in comparison with top-level club football. The influence of sponsors was everywhere, leading to accusations, fiercely denied, that Nike had interfered in selecting the Brazilian team for the final against France. More plausibly, some commentators said that the final was fought out not by representatives of Brazil and France, but between Nike and Adidas (sponsors of the Brazilian and French teams, respectively); or that it was an Italian Serie A team (Brazil) defeated by what was basically a French Premiership eleven led by Arsenal and Chelsea players, many of whom in fact came from French Africa. Mike Saunders, managing director of Victor Chandler, the biggest football betting organization in Europe, told the press that match-fixing in the competition was rife. It was estimated that £3 billion was bet on the World Cup, much of it from the Far East. Bookies were worried that a £15 million Malaysian bet on a game between Cameroon and Paraguay meant it had been a bribery target.

19.
Lucky Losers

On the face of it, in December 1999 the circumstances surrounding Manchester United and Darlington FC could not have been more different. At the end of the previous season United had won the treble bringing the Premiership, FA Cup and Champions' League trophies back to Manchester, where they were greeted with mass celebrations by jubilant locals, numbering as many as half a million. In the same season Darlington's greatest triumph had been a 4–1 victory over Exeter City, watched by 3,500. United had just been proclaimed the biggest football club in the world with a capital value of over £800 million and turnover approaching £100 million a year. Darlington, of the league's Third Division, were effectively broke and would have disappeared had it not been for the big heart of sixty-four-year-old convicted safe-breaker and reformed criminal turned pillar and hero of the local community George Reynolds, who put £5 million of his own money into the club in 1999, never expecting to see it again.

What linked Darlington and Manchester United in December 1999 was the FA Cup. United had pulled out of football's oldest regular cup competition. Darlington had taken their place in the third round as 'lucky losers' from the previous round. The north-eastern club had been knocked out of the competition in the second round, losing 3–1 away to Gillingham. But their name had come out of the hat and they were back, allocated the lottery ball that would have belonged to United and drawn away against Aston Villa. George Reynolds pronounced himself 'delighted'.

Manchester United were not in the FA Cup because they were about to depart for Brazil to play in FIFA's World Club Championship instead, a tournament created by football's world governing body to feed the hunger of TV companies for more and more football.

FIFA's World Cup was already the biggest televised event on the planet, far outstripping the Olympic games. The World Cup had been significantly altered to suit television, though not as much as the companies would have liked. At one point FIFA had entertained the idea of playing USA 1994 World Cup games in four 'quarters' so that more advertisement slots could be inserted. They then contemplated ad breaks during natural breaks in play such as throw-ins. But they had settled instead for the introduction of penalty shoot-outs in the knock-out stage and the new 'golden goal' rule (first to score in extra time becomes the winner) to prevent replays, which were hard to schedule and to package in screening rights deals.

Penalty shoot-outs, which, at a time of increasing worries over match-fixing and the activities of the Far Eastern betting syndicates, and which worked as almost an open invitation to unsporting play and match-fixing, had actually proved a big ratings hit, especially for the American networks. Some executives had even wondered if they could simply cut out the preceding ninety minutes, especially given the growing number of games where both sides seemed to be playing for a 0–0 draw.

But the World Cup happened only once every four years, which was not enough for the networks, who, ideally, would have liked one every day, given the ratings they achieved. The world and continental governing bodies had responded to the mass waving of cheque-books by bumping up the profile of the continental competitions which also took place every four years, alternating with the World Cup. Thus the 1994 World Cup had been followed by the European Nations Championship, Euro 96, in England – in effect the World Cup without Brazil and Argentina – which had been followed by World Cup France 98 and Euro 2000 in Holland and Belgium.

Still the networks were not satisfied. Responding to demand, in 1997 FIFA set to work on the idea of running World Cups once every two years. The other two summers in any four-year cycle would be filled with the European Championship and a new competition, potentially the biggest money-spinner of all, the World Club Championship.

There was already a traditional one-off match between the winners of the European Champions' Cup and its South American equivalent to produce a notional 'World Champion Club'. The fixture was popular in South America where fans nursed an enormous chip on their shoulder against the richer European clubs, symbols of a colonial past, who used their wealth to lure away the best local players. But in Europe the fixture held little attraction, seen as something much more like a benefit match or a pre-season friendly. One reason was that European league football, especially the Spanish and Italian leagues, was widely followed in South America because so many Brazilian and Argentines played in Europe, whereas on the other hand South American clubs were unknown in Europe.

The only way to make the idea of a world club championship more attractive in 'major television markets', as FIFA put it, was to replace the one-off match with a ramified competition along the lines of the World Cup and featuring a larger number of recognizable clubs. FIFA's original proposal was for a massive tournament lasting through much of the summer and involving eight clubs, two each from Europe and South America and another four from Africa and other continents. FIFA announced that it planned to auction the TV rights for a price starting at £100 million and that it expected to earn another £40 million from sponsorship and merchandising. In 1997 the idea was to stage the competition in Saudi Arabia, where the royal family was reported to be interested in underwriting the whole project financially.

There were immediate objections from FIFA's European affiliate, UEFA. The fact was that while two or three South American national teams did well in the World Cup, all the world's leading clubs came from Europe. One or two South American clubs might stand comparison with a typical mid-ranking Premiership or Serie A club, but no club in Africa, North America or anywhere in Asia was much good. The winners of UEFA's Champions' League were already, in reality, the world champions, which was why everyone got so excited about the final and why the following match against the South American club champions had always been such a non-event. It was obvious to many that the proposed World Club Championship was little more than a FIFA attempt to steal the European Champions' League from UEFA, add a few non-European clubs as fodder to increase global TV appeal, stage it in the Middle East and scoop all the TV rights money.

Unsurprisingly, UEFA were dead against this idea and the very fact that it had been proposed provoked a sharp deterioration in relations between the European wing of football administration, FIFA, and its other continental affiliates. Its main proponent was Sepp Blatter, the man being groomed by Pelé's great foe, FIFA president for life

Chris Horrie

João Havelange, to succeed him when he retired in 1998 after twenty-four years in the job. Its main opponent was UEFA president Lennart Johansson, who was planning to stand for the post on an anti-corruption 'clean-up' ticket. In addition to Pelé's allegations of corruption in Havelange's power base, the Brazilian Football Federation, there had been a series of scandals in the African and Asian federations which also tended to support Havelange.

For his part, Blatter accused UEFA of wanting to keep the TV millions they received from the Champions' League. The money FIFA would get from the World Club Championship, in contrast, would be shared by all FIFA's national affiliates including the many penniless, and in some cases corruption-afflicted, associations in Africa and Asia. The proposal immediately became an issue in FIFA's murky internal politics and one of the main planks in Blatter's election campaign.

In June 1998 Blatter won the election by a margin of 111 votes to 80 and replaced Havelange as supreme ruler of world football. Johansson immediately called foul and, after reports that at least twenty delegates had been seen receiving envelopes full of cash from FIFA officials at the Meridien Hotel in Paris, demanded that an independent commission be established to investigate allegations of bribery. Blatter said that the election was over and there was no need for an investigation – and left it at that. Others in FIFA were more expansive. Jack Warner, a FIFA vice-president and head of the North and Central America Football Federation, told the press that money had indeed been handed over as an 'advance' against the annual $250,000 a year FIFA paid to poorer affiliates as their share of TV rights money: 'Some countries wanted a portion of the $250,000 paid earlier than scheduled. Some wanted $50,000, some $40,000, others less.' Warner was backed up by one of FIFA's vice-presidents, the Scottish FA delegate David Will, who said that stories of money changing hands for votes were mere 'rumours and hearsay'.

Unfortunately for Will, within a few months he was caught up in a cash for votes scandal, though he was the innocent victim rather than the perpetrator. In December 1998 FA chief executive Graham Kelly and chairman Keith Wiseman resigned from their positions after it was discovered that they had approved a £3.2 million non-repayable loan to the Welsh FA in return for the Welsh vote in an election to replace Will with an English nominee as the FIFA vice-president from Britain.

With Blatter in control of FIFA, the plan for the World Club Championship went ahead. It had been scaled down from the thirty-two-club three-week competition to be played in Saudi Arabia, to a more modest made-for-TV event involving eight clubs: Corinthians and Vasco da Gama from Brazil; Raja Casablanca, the African champions; Real Madrid; Asian champions Al Nasr of Saudi Arabia; Nexaca of Mexico City, winner of the North American Cup; South Melbourne, champions of Oceania; and Manchester United, who received the invitation to join the competition as European Champions in June 1999.

The problem was that by taking part in the tournament United would be out of the country in January when the fourth round of the FA Cup was due to take place. There ensued much agonizing over whether they should take part or stay at home and defend the FA Cup they had so recently won as a part of their epoch-shattering treble. The United board later claimed they had considered opting for the FA Cup but had been put under pressure by the FA and the government to take part in the World Club Championship. That the FA should back the competition said a lot. The FA was supposed to be not only the guardian of the FA Cup competition itself, but also of the concept of equal treatment and level playing fields for the whole sport. It also meant that the FA was breaking its own rule, specifically clause 16.2.13 of the *Blueprint for the Future of Football* which set up the Premiership. The clause states in black and white:

> It will be mandatory that all clubs in the Football Association Premier League enter the FA Challenge Cup.

When it came to money, it seemed, the FA would just make up the rules as it went along. It was feared that upsetting FIFA would reduce the FA's government-backed bid to host the 2006 World Cup in England and Manchester United complained that they had been placed in an 'impossible position'.

But the competition did have its attractions from a commercial point of view. Even before the Sky takeover bid, United had adopted a corporate strategy that involved making United a world brand to rival Nike and Coca-Cola. They were targeting untapped and emerging markets for football such as South Africa, China, Japan, Australia, the USA and the Middle East where, in tandem with the development of pay-TV, football in general and Manchester United in particular, was developing into a consumer craze.

In the summer of 1999 the United PLC had announced a plan to set up a McDonald's style chain of virtual reality theme parks branded as 'Theatre of Dreams' in Singapore, Hong Kong, Malaysia, Thailand and China.

This was followed by a series of exhibition games in the Far East, culminating in a match against a South China side in Hong Kong, watched by 40,000 and broadcast to many millions. Then came the old-style champions of South America versus Champions of Europe one-off World Championship match.

As usual the one-off World Championship game, in which United played Palmeiras of Brazil, attracted little interest in England and the rest of Europe. But it was a huge TV ratings hit in Japan, where it was staged, and throughout much of the rest of the world. Unlike some of the clubs United would later meet in the FIFA tournament, Palmeiras were a half-decent side, having managed to hang on to a few Brazilian and other South American stars. Their overall rating would have been that of a mid-table Premiership side perhaps Newcastle or Aston Villa, but certainly less of a challenge than Bayern Munich, the team United had already beaten to become champions of mere Europe and not the whole world. United won the match with a single goal from Roy Keane who was in the news for demanding a new post-Bosman contract from United which would make him the first Premiership player on wages of more than £50,000 a week. The game and its aftermath produced some strange scenes: man of the match Ryan Giggs struggling down the tunnel carrying a giant Toyota car key twice his size, Japanese fans not only dressed in replica kits, but also tottering on replica football boots complete with studs, and huge queues to buy Manchester United merchandise of all sorts, amid salvos of camera flashlights every time David Beckham appeared, or came near the ball during the game. After this Japan and China were reported to be in the grip of 'Beckham mania', helped by association with his wife Victoria, the pop star.

This taking part in the FIFA club competition would give United additional exposure to global markets, even though the games would be considered meaningless by traditional fans. But the traditional fans were measured only in millions rather than tens or hundreds of millions, back in the UK.

For the United board it was a simple commercial calculation. Would they get more money from playing in the FIFA tournament or the FA Cup? As a PLC, with responsibilities to shareholders, they were not in a position to do anything else. While they could, and sometimes did, make donations to charities, these had to be declared. A commercial decision deliberately to forgo profit justified only by some nostrum such as honoring the history of the game was out of the question – possibly even illegal under the companies act.

Since the English FA was encouraging United to withdraw from the FA Cup and go to Brazil (though it had no power to actually make them do so), the United board's first concern was how much compensation they would get. A run through the rounds to reach the FA Cup final was worth around £5 million, which they would now not get. Any hesitation the board might have had was about the compensation issue, where talks dragged on for days before Sports Minister Tony Banks intervened, 'begging' United to go to Brazil so as not to upset FIFA in the run-up to England's World Cup bid. That seemed to settle it, even though a few months later the new sports minister, Kate Hoey, changed tack, describing the decision to pull out of the FA Cup as 'shabby'.

Public anger and condemnation were immediate. The FA Cup, it was said, would be devalued, even rendered meaningless, if the holders did not take part. The whole point of the FA Cup was that it united all the clubs in the land, from tiny outfits which were not much more than Sunday-league pub teams to those in the Premiership. It was also a vital financial lifeline for smaller clubs, especially those in the lower depths beneath the Premiership – in fact, the only remaining mechanism for redistributing a fraction of the Premiership millions downwards towards the small clubs.

Each year a clutch of Second and Third Division, and even some non-league, clubs made it through the qualifying rounds to be included in the third- and fourth-round draws. If they drew a big club they were guaranteed 'a big payday', as it was called, a share of the takings at a Premiership ground – a once-in-a-generation windfall which, except for selling players, was the only chance many clubs had of staying in business.

After Kate Hoey's about-face, Bobby Charlton got caught up in the row, asking the United board to reconsider or come up with some sort of compromise, and talking about the club's 'responsibility to the history of the game'. One possibility was for the club to field the reserves in the FA Cup and the first team in Brazil. But the FA objected to this, saying it would set a worrying precedent. The obvious danger was the constant and ever-growing one of match-fixing. Once it had been established that a team could field anything other than more or less their best players, crooked clubs might gain the right to field a side of old-age pensioners in return for a bribe. The other possibility, of United sending their reserves to Brazil (sensible in a way because they would be facing teams mainly of a far lower standard than the average Premiership reserve side) was not even discussed.

General disgust intensified when more details of the tournament became clear. The only clubs lined up for the competition who had genuinely world-class players were Manchester United and Real Madrid, and everything appeared to be seeded to produce a Manchester United–Real Madrid final after a series of meaningless matches in two parallel qualifying groups of four. United and Real Madrid were seeded in separate groups with two fairly successful Brazilian sides, Vasco da Gama and Corinthians. Vasco da Gama had hired three world-class players, Romario, Jorginho and Junior Baiano, specifically for the contest. Without them the team had a distinct feel of being the South American equivalent of Bolton Wanderers.

Then there were the obvious make-weight teams. In United's group both the also-rans, South Melbourne and Nexaca, the Mexican champions of North and Central America, happened to represent the essentially English-speaking world. Both of Real Madrid's opponents, meanwhile, were from the Arab-speaking world, Raja Casablanca, the African champions, and Al Nasr of Saudi Arabia. A measure of the weakness of United's opponents was that Necaxa had qualified for this contest of global supremacy by beating the champions of Costa Rica in the North American champions final staged as a minor cable TV event in Las Vegas. South Melbourne had an average home gate of 8,500, similar to a typical English Second Division club and not that much more than those lucky losers Darlington.

Once they arrived in Brazil the Manchester United contingent preserved some dignity by hardly bothering to play and, it seemed to some, refusing to take the whole circus seriously, instead treating it as a handy mid-season holiday. 'We're using it as exercise to revitalize the players,' Alex Ferguson told reporters. 'We've had a bit of quality training and the sun on the players' backs.

It's an advantage at this time of year.' For the record, basically fielding their reserve team after all United drew their first game against Necaxa, lost the second to Vasco da Gama 3–1 and beat South Melbourne 2–0. The competition was won by Corinthians who beat fellow Brazilians Vasco da Gama on penalties after drawing 0–0 in the final. Real Madrid managed only to come fourth after losing to Nexaca, also on penalties. Results ran so counter to form that some people laying bets would have made a lot of money.

Back in England the consensus was that the FA Cup had indeed been devalued by the actions of United, the FA and FIFA. Above all, the glory of the club's treble achievement had been tarnished. The reality was that when it mattered the board of United PLC cared little about any of the three competitions involved. They had abandoned the FA Cup and had been threatening a possible breakaway from the Premiership and UEFA Champions' League to play in Berlusconi's Super League, even as they were winning the trophies. When United rejoined the FA Cup the following season and were knocked out in the fourth round by unfancied West Ham United, there was such glee at the fat cats' undoing that the story made the front page of all the tabloids.

Market research showed that fully one half of the people in England who watched football at all now regarded themselves as nominal Manchester United supporters, but among the other half, whoever they supported, United were increasingly despised. A behind the scenes video was made by the PLC to celebrate participation in the World Club Championship and to show the board striking various heroic poses. It sold in predictably huge quantities to the captive audience of United addicts, but it must have been the first football video to include thrilling footage of a besuited chief executive making a slide-show marketing presentation to corporate clients. Balance to the pervading tone of self-congratulation was provided by an interview with a couple of Leeds United fans, eating chips while slouching away disconsolately from Old Trafford after another defeat.

'What it felt like today,' they said between munches, 'was that a team which is still basically a football team from Leeds was up against a multinational corporation.' Then one of the fans thought for a moment and added with over-the-top but matter-of-fact cold hatred, 'It was a victory for evil.'

Immediately after the tournament Brazilian football was again engulfed by accusations of match-fixing and other forms of corruption. The country's congress placed numerous figures in the Brazilian game under investigation, including officials at Corinthians and Vasco da Gama. For years Corinthians had been managed by Wanderley Luxemburgo, but he had left the club in 1997 to manage the national team. Under investigation from the Brazilian congress he admitted large-scale tax evasion and then faced additional charges of fixing matches and taking kickback bungs on transfers of players to European clubs. Despite all the revelations, after the tournament Luxemburgo returned to take his position as club manager. Vasco's president was also called upon to explain where the money from multi-million transfers of players, including that of World Cup star Bebeto, to European clubs had gone. Soon after that star defender Junior Baiano tested positive for performance-enhancing and other drugs including cocaine. He claimed that somebody had slipped something into his drink without him knowing. Corinthians were meanwhile asked to explain how their star player, Edu, who played in the World Club Champions' final against Vasco, had turned up in England following his transfer to Arsenal carrying a forged Portuguese passport.

As the official Senatorial investigation into what was called the 'black box' of football corruption broadened out in the spring of 2000, Sepp Blatter threatened to throw Brazil out of the 2002 World Cup unless it was called off. But the senators ploughed on, using special powers to look into bank accounts and private company papers not available to the police. The deeper the investigators delved, the more the trail led to a single source – the global brand which had sponsored the Brazilian national team to the tune of $300 million and which was now starting to play an increasingly large role in the English Premiership.

The company was one of the most famous in the world: Nike.

1998–99 season

The season started with 1997–98 champions Arsenal and runners-up Manchester United joint favourites, with Chelsea, now managed by former player Gianluca Vialli after the departure of Ruud Gullit to become manager of Newcastle, tipped as having an outside chance. The early leaders turned out to be Aston Villa, despite the departure of their leading goalscorer Dwight Yorke, who moved to Manchester United at the start of the season. Chelsea took over the lead after Christmas, but Arsenal and United were beginning to close the gap. United had faltered at the start, and lost 3–2 at home to Middlesbrough in December. But that was to be their last defeat of the season. Newcastle, recently contenders under

Chris Horrie

Keegan, were nowhere. Manager Ruud Gullit complained that Kenny Dalglish had left him with a 'relegation team' that was not only no good, but also boring. He promised to introduce 'sexy football'. Rival fans were less than impressed. During Newcastle's away defeat at Anfield, jubilant Liverpool fans chanted 'you can stick your sexy football up your arse' for the whole of the second half.

Meanwhile, Tottenham fans were amazed and dismayed to find George Graham, a man they still completely identified with their great rivals Arsenal, appointed as Spurs' manager. Even when Graham achieved the modest success of winning the Worthington Cup (now routinely called the 'worthless cup' because Manchester United and Arsenal refuse to take it seriously, often choosing to field their reserve teams), the Tottenham fans could not bring themselves to mention his name. Arsenal fans had made the chant 'Arsène Wenger's red and white army' popular. The Tottenham version was to be 'Man in a raincoat's blue and white army'.

By the spring the championship had turned into a two-horse race between United and Arsenal, who were neck and neck. Arsenal were grinding out results, whereas Ferguson's team sometimes turned on the style. They beat Nottingham Forest 8–1, a record away win, with Ole Gunnar Solskjaer coming on as a substitute thirteen minutes before the end and scoring four goals before the final whistle. The ground resounded with the United fans' 'Alan Shearer was f***ing dearer' chant which the PLC liked so much (since it praised their financial acumen) that they produced a sanitized version to be played pre-match at Old Trafford: 'Alan Shearer was much, much dearer'. By this time United were advancing towards winning the treble of the Premier League, the FA Cup and the Champions' League. They reached the final of the FA Cup against Gullit's Newcastle (which turned out to be a push-over) by winning a semi-final replay against Arsenal *at Villa Park. The score was 1–1 at full-time with Schmeichel saving a penalty from Dennis Bergkamp in the final minute of injury time. Ryan Giggs scored what was instantly adjudged by the tabloids to be the 'greatest goal of all time', winning the game in extra time. He picked up the ball on the half-way line, dribbled past four or five Arsenal defenders in the penalty box and drove the ball past David Seaman, leaving the entire Arsenal team stunned with disbelief. The treble was completed when United beat Bayern Munich 2–1 in Barcelona in the final of the Champions' League, even though they had not qualified as champions. For most of the game they were 1–0 down, but won with two goals in the last minute of normal time. It was the team's thirty-third consecutive game unbeaten.*

20.
A Great Year for English Football

Not many people paid much attention, but if they had, residents of the inner Manchester suburb of Longsight would in the winter of 1995 have seen the strange sight of a fully grown man falling to his knees in the street and bowing, forehead touching the pavement Muslim-prayer style, before an advertising hoarding. The man kept repeating the action over and over until the police arrived to move him on.

The object of his adoration was a 20-foot poster of Eric Cantona, arms folded, eyes blazing with his trademark 'f*** you' gaze of contempt, overhanging brow furrowed, designer-stubbled chin jutting forward. It was an advertisement for Nike, Cantona's personal sponsor, emblazoned with the slogan:

1966 WAS A GREAT YEAR FOR ENGLISH FOOTBALL – ERIC CANTONA WAS BORN

The poster was so effective in generating publicity that it would later be remembered along the Wonderbra 'Hello Boys!' poster as capable of causing traffic accidents. It went up on relatively few sites around the country, all of them as near as possible to football grounds. Acres of free publicity was generated. As part of the hype it was reported that hoardings were vandalized within minutes of the poster going up – either by Manchester United fans trying to steal the picture or by rivals attempting to deface it. Manchester City fans, generally the winners in the Mancunian mordant wit stakes, circulated leaflets with graffiti suggestions – cross out 'English

Football' and insert 'morons' or 'wankers' or 'f***ing bastards'.

Much has been written about the appeal of the enigmatic Cantona, 'le Brat', the Premiership bad boy, football philosopher, style icon, poet, artist, troubled soul, darling of a new type of more intellectual, middle-class football supporter. He was described as the club's 'talisman'. It was not until his arrival that United finally won the championship after almost thirty years. When he was out of the team, serving one of his many suspensions for foul or violent play culminating in the long ban after the famous kung fu attack on an abusive Crystal Palace fan, the team seemed lost, treading water, waiting for the return of the Supremely Gifted One, the greatest United player since George Best – the most loved since Denis Law.

As a player Cantona was invaluable. But in the age of the Premiership kicking a ball was only one aspect of a player's value to a club such as Manchester United. Increasingly important was the potential for merchandising. With Cantona there were problems. Unlike some of the other players, he would not co-operate with the tackier aspects of United's mushrooming trashy trinkets business. Ryan Giggs might agree to be featured on a life-size duvet cover or put his signature on a pair of plastic flip-flops. But not Eric Cantona. After his sudden retirement from football, Cantona complained that the Manchester United merchandising machine had tried to 'buy his soul'. There was another potential source of tension along the commercial lines. Eric Cantona belonged to Nike; Manchester United belonged to Umbro, one of Nike's deadliest rivals in the £2.7 billion-a-year replica shirt market. Eventually, after the Frenchman had left the club and retired from football, the two companies would end up battling with each other in a squabble over rights to exploit the Manchester United brand.

Nike hardly needed Manchester United while they had Cantona. In the age of sponsorship, the old sporting cliché that no single player is bigger than the club was starting to look threadbare. As a marketing proposition Cantona, handled properly, might bring in as much merchandising revenue as the rest of United's players put together – and without the tedious and costly business of having to run a football club. Alan Shearer had been a much hotter property than Blackburn Rovers, especially to the increasingly important global audience that Nike in particular was interested in. Jürgen Klinsmann was bigger than Spurs, Gianfranco Zola bigger than Chelsea, Juninho much bigger than Middlesbrough and Benito Carbone in a different league from short-term Premiership franchisees Bradford.

Nike got behind promoting the cult of Cantona, detaching his image from Manchester United's as much as possible. Borrowing a trick from their operations with baseball stars in the US, in 1997 they filmed an advert featuring Cantona playing alongside the company's second and third most important English footballers, Ian Wright and Robbie Fowler, possibly the most hated players at Old Trafford at the time, in a spoof Nike pub kick-about team. The whole thing was set to streetwise pop music, Blur's 'Park Life', thus achieving the image the company wanted to promote of 'bad boy f*** you' Nike stars together against the establishment.

This was followed by television adverts on a daring but feelgood anti-racist theme, featuring Cantona, Ian Wright and Les Ferdinand, which created a lot of free publicity. The next masterstroke, after Cantona's ban for attacking a supporter, was a cinema-only advert showing him attacking fans in what was described as a 'tongue in cheek' way. In the run-up to Euro 96 he appeared alongside all of Nike's European stars in a mini horror film, showing the forthcoming contest as an extremely violent fight between Team Nike – Cantona well to the fore – and a gang of armoured neanderthals (i.e. Adidas and Umbro). And when Cantona started his sideline career as a film star while still on United's books, his first movie, a light farce in which he played an adulterous French rugby player, was so stuffed with Nike product placement that some reviewers said it was little more than a feature-length advert for the company.

Nike had emerged as a major company in the 1970s, marketing a new type of lightweight moulded-rubber running shoe which, according to the their official mythology, had been invented when the company's founder had poured molten rubber into a waffle-iron. By 1974 Nike's 'waffle sole' design was the best-selling running shoe in America. From the start the company adopted an anti-establishment stance, tracking the rock and roll, hippie and student counter-culture trend of wearing sloppy, informal clothes at a time when anything less than smart dress and shiny shoes was still seen as a form of rebellion. From the start the company was careful to associate itself with cool, no bullshit anti-establishment sportspeople such as the American athletics star Steve Prefontaine and tantrum-throwing tennis champion John McEnroe. The other key element of what was to be Nike's huge success was established. Production was moved to low-wage, non-union dictatorships in the Far East, starting with Taiwan and Korea. By 1980 the former hippie dress style of training shoes and jeans had become ubiquitous throughout the world.

The market was vast. But a training shoe is a training shoe – even though Nike's offering was indeed a very good and comfortable type of shoe – so holding and gaining market share became mainly a matter of what economists were starting to call 'product differentiation'. This was achieved in 1979 with the introduction of the supposedly revolutionary air-cushion sole which, when combined with massive marketing and expensively bought endorsement from a series of top athletics and basketball stars, made Nike stand out from the crowd. The company was one of the first to understand and take advantage of the opportunities for opening up worldwide markets by using the potent alliance of television and sport – athletics to begin with. By 1980 Nike had the endorsement of every world-record running champion from 800 to 10,000 metres, and had grown to take 50 per cent of the shoe market. The performance of multiple gold medal-winning runner Carl Lewis in the 1984 Olympics, and the widespread TV advertising campaign associated with his success, established the brand worldwide at a time of consumer mania for designer-label goods, boosting revenue to just under $1 billion a year.

The real breakthrough came in 1985 when Nike signed the basketball player Michael Jordan, and launched a new range of 'Air Jordan' shoes. Because of basketball's associations with hip young urban blacks the brand became an essential fashion item and the ultimate totem of anti-establishment success, much prized by the pop music movement based on the New York rap and hip-hop scene. The company's marketing efforts were innovative, brilliant – and ruthless. One tactic was to hunt down the trendiest and most fashion-conscious youths in cities such as New York and Chicago and give them free shoes, so as to create demand from their peers. Another was to constantly alter and update the styles with minute changes to design detail to create extra demand. It was the same trick used by the Premiership clubs, the constant changes to shirt designs, which had created so much anger among parents in England. The difference was that even Manchester United issued only three designs per year; Nike had more than 200.

The company hired film-maker Spike Lee, a key figure in the black American counter-culture, to make adverts featuring Jordan and his shoes. By 1991 Nike had branched out from shoes into sports apparel – all stamped with its simple tick-like logo, instantly recognizable. In a global market Nike was a product with no language barriers, and revenues reached $3 billion. In the USA the shoes, now made in Indonesia and Vietnam at a unit cost of just a few pence, were selling at the rate of 200 pairs per minute at a retail price of £120 a pair. The high cost of the shoes itself became part of the marketing campaign. After reports of muggings and even murders in which victims had been robbed of their Nike shoes instead of their wallets, the company ran pre-Christmas adverts showing a notorious basketball 'bad boy' mugging Father Christmas and demanding that he hand over the precious footwear. The advert ended with a terrified Santa being pinned against the wall, telling a dwarf helper 'give him the shoes'. It ended, as all Nike ads, with the slogan 'just do it'.

Surveys showed that many customers thought that much of the money was going to the stars they saw endorsing Nike on TV and so they did not mind making a contribution. Some of the money did go to the stars, but a lot more went to Nike and to the retailer. High profit margins ensured they kept Nike to the fore and squeezed the opposition. Chief executive Phil Knight was on course to make an estimated personal fortune of $5 billion by the end of the century.

Plenty of people in the past had worked out ways to make money out of sport. But by the mid-1990s Nike had hit upon a way of turning something even more potent into cash – it had become the worldwide symbol of the fight for black consciousness, racial equality and even black supremacism. These feelings were so emotionally charged that, in the old cliché, if anyone could find a way of bottling and selling them they would make a fortune. It seemed as though Nike had been able to do just that. It was as if they had come up with exclusive exploitation rights to the Christian crucifix, the hammer and sickle and the black power coiled fist salute rolled into one.

American athletics and other sports had always been a hotbed of racial politics and tension. Many had been segregated until the 1960s. And a type of segregation continued. Basketball and athletics, Nike's original base, were seen as basically black sports, whereas the official national sport of baseball was predominantly white. Black American sporting prowess provided an all-too-obvious living link back to the era of slavery. Black Americans were descended from slaves chosen by slave traders for sheer muscle power. Then only the strongest and fittest survived the death-camp conditions of the slave ships. It was little wonder that on average black Americans inherited a greater predisposition to physical strength than the population as a whole.

After the success of the Michael Jordan campaign, Nike ran a massive TV advertising campaign in the USA, using films cut in the style of an MTV rap music video and featuring dozens of black basketball stars known to be millionaires thanks to Nike sponsorship saying 'thank you' to Jackie Robinson, who was the first black baseball star. The unmistakable impression was that it was Nike that was somehow being thanked for the achievement. The company also became a sponsor of a national civil rights museum devoted to Martin Luther King. Top executives named Nelson Mandela as their all-time hero and role model. Nike became sponsors of Spike Lee's enormously hyped film about Malcolm X, and company products featured prominently in the film *White Men Can't Jump*, produced by Rupert Murdoch's Fox organization.

But other side to Nike was starting to gain attention by the mid-1990s – the stark contrast between its radical chic, pro-underdog and world-liberating image with the reality of its sweatshop employment practices. In 1997 the story broke of how twelve low-paid women workers at a factory making Nike shoes in Vietnam were hospitalized after being made to run laps round the plant in the hot sun until they dropped from exhaustion. The women were being punished because they had not worn regulation shoes to work.

The news was followed by the publication of a devastating investigation into Nike's Vietnamese sweatshops, conducted by Thuyen Nguyen, a Vietnamese-American former vice-president of the Bankers Trust Company. He found that Nike had moved much of its production to Vietnam because the country provided the cheapest and most strictly controlled workforce in the world. Ninety per cent of production workers were women or girls and they were paid about £1 a day. They were allowed one visit to the toilet and one glass of water per eight-hour shift and could be beaten or physically punished if they broke the rules. If they spoke to each other while

Chris Horrie

working, bosses would tape their mouths shut. While Nike was presenting itself around the world as the most reliable champion of racial equality, the campaigners found that most of the company's managers in the Vietnamese sweat-shops were Taiwanese or Korean, well known for the con-tempt they displayed to the 'racially inferior' Vietnamese. The company said they would do what they could to stop this kind of abuse happening, but claimed to be doing a lot of good for the local economy, providing work where there would have been none, and maintained they had little control over local employment practises.

At least in terms of money being spent, the publicity Nike was creating for itself by investing in English football paled into insignificance compared with its activities in Brazil. Association with the world champions was more than the obvious desire to be teamed up with success. The fact was that after winning the World Cup in the USA in 1994, the Brazilian team had been adopted by millions of Americans as an unofficial substitute for the decidedly average US national side.

Nike paid an undisclosed but vast sum – reports vary between $200 and $400 million though the exact amount remained a closely guarded secret – to become the spon-sors and kit-makers to the Brazilian national side on a renewable ten-year contract. The association with the feelgood aspects of the Brazil myth – Pelé and the beautiful game – was a Nike brand manager's dream come true. The company also became the sponsor of Brazil's great-est star, the photogenic, gap-toothed twenty-year-old striker Ronaldo, who was instantly given the Michael Jordan treatment – only this time, thanks to football's greater global reach, on a worldwide scale. Ronaldo, the ill-educated and dirt-poor black kid from the slums who, thanks to Nike, defied racism and poverty and became one of the most worshipped figures in the world.

And so Nike lined up to slug it out with its arch-rival Adidas during the 1998 World Cup in France. Brazil, the team that most of the minority of Americans who were interested in soccer were likely to support alongside the US national team (also kitted out by Nike) would be wearing their logo. On one level, the competition was to be played out as Nike versus Adidas. In addition to the USA and Brazil, Nike had signed up plucky and romantic Holland, stylish Italy, African heroes Nigeria, and important-market Korea. Adidas had almost everyone else, including Germany and the host country, France.

Everything went according to plan and the tournament, stained by the now standard accusations and allegations of match-fixing and bribery, produced a final between Nike's Brazil and Adidas's France. Then the controversy exploded. Against all expectations Brazil were thrashed 3–0. Ronaldo played for the full ninety minutes, and to most of those watching it seemed that he was completely unfit. According to some he could hardly move and appeared to be in a daze. It was known that Ronaldo had played in earlier games with a slightly torn leg muscle – the estimated 1,000 journalists assigned to follow his every movement had at least found that out. The standard procedure in such cases was to give players pain-killing injections to get them through all or part of games as important as this.

But what actually happened to Ronaldo in the hours before the 1998 World Cup final was to remain a secret as closely guarded as the exact figure paid by Nike to the Brazilian football federation and the precise undertakings given by the Brazilians in return. Various versions of events began to circulate. One rumour was that Ronaldo had broken up with his girlfriend on the night before the match and was feeling too upset to play. But the most widely believed story, sourced by some journalists to unnamed members of the Brazilian team who played in the game and experienced the pre-match drama, was that Ronaldo had been given such a massive dose of pain-killers on the evening before the match that it had caused a convulsive fit.

On the morning of the game Brazil's manager, Zagalo, had checked the striker's condition and decided that he was in no condition to play. But then, and, according to one account, with the French team already out on the pitch going through their warm-up routine, Zagalo had been overruled on the orders of Brazilian officials because of the amount of money Nike had paid with the intention of putting Ronaldo, a living, breathing (though at this point barely walking) Nike advert in front of the one-off two billion TV audience for the final. Brazil had played badly not only because they had in effect only ten men but also, according to the rumours, because arguments had gone on right until the last minute as to whether or not Ronaldo should be in the starting line-up. Another problem was that Zagalo had changed the tactics to suit Edmundo, the striker he had picked to instead of Ronaldo, and there was no time to change them back. In no version of the conspiracy theories that circulated later were Nike directly accused of ordering Zagalo to put their player on to the pitch.

Whatever the exact details of the Ronaldo saga, Brazil's defeat and the player's inexplicably poor performance drew the spotlight on to Brazil's sponsorship deal with Nike. Scrutiny became more intense when it was dis-covered that Nike had been given rights to schedule at least five matches a year featuring the team for marketing purposes. In the first year of the contract, in the run-up to the World Cup in France, Brazil played five times in the USA, including a match against America's national team which, unbelievably, Brazil lost (thus, in the minds of many Americans half-interested in the sport, making the USA the soccer champions).

The endless series of matches played for Nike seemed to have a draining effect on the Brazilian national team. The programme included meaningless games in markets Nike was keen to open up, including Thailand and Wales. In 2000, after the Brazilian side was knocked out of the Olympic Games football tournament by a Cameroon team reduced to nine men, coach Wanderley Luxemburgo was sacked, opening up a can of worms. The team had already lost World Cup qualifiers against Paraguay and Chile. Under investigation by the Brazilian congress's special commission on football corruption, Luxemburgo confessed to charges of evading taxes and faced allegations of throwing games by selecting substandard players and taking kickback bungs on transfers of players to European clubs.

As the investigation continued it came to focus increasingly on the deal between the Brazilian football federation and Nike which, investigators complained, was 'an affront to Brazilian sovereignty' because it gave so much power over the affairs of the team to the company. The commission's chairman, Aldo Rebelo, said that Brazilian football and its players had been 'treated just as a commodity. Football cannot be reduced to this. This is the death of football.' Ronaldo was called to give evidence, but he said little, and not much more light was shed on the matter of Nike's involvement in his World Cup final appearance. João Havelange, the departed FIFA president, who remained an important figure in the Brazilian

Chris Horrie

federation, refused to disclose details of the Nike contract, claiming that he had never read the document.

The investigation continued for months, uncovering tax evasion and transfer kickbacks, widespread use of performance-enhancing drugs, procedures for signing youth players on lifelong contracts on 'slavery' wages, links to organized crime and misappropriation of funds on a massive scale. At many clubs supposedly amateur directors were found to have helped themselves to millions. When money from sponsorship and pay-TV came rolling into Brazilian football in return for saturation exposure which led to many matches being played in almost empty stadiums, many in the management and administration of the game had simply channelled it straight into their personal bank accounts.

But the investigators were still unable to penetrate the secrecy surrounding the Nike contract, and there was no indication that Nike had been involved in, or had condoned, any illegal activities. Sepp Blatter, Havelange's hand-picked successor as head of FIFA, threatened to throw Brazil out of the World Cup unless congress stopped 'interfering with the internal affairs' of the Brazilian football federation. This was a potent political threat – no politician in Brazil would stand much chance of re-election if they were to be held responsible for a World Cup ban – whatever the justice of the case. The investigators backed off and then, after months of prevarication, the Brazilian federation changed tactics. In February 2001 its chairman, Ricardo Teixeira, Havelange's son-in-law, declared that the investigation was no longer needed and should be suspended. The reason was that he was planning 'a revolution of transparency to restore the shine of Brazilian football' which would start by inviting previously vilified arch anti-corruption campaigner Pelé to 'put his name forward' as the man to replace him when he retired in 2003. Teixeira said: 'Pelé is a symbol of what Brazilian football stands for. I've already revised some of my own concepts and one of the main conclusions is that I was very wrong to set the CBF apart from Brazilian football's greatest star: Pelé.' The statement was interpreted by some as a call for an amnesty, and by others as the defenders' tactic of booting the ball into row Z of the stand during a threatening attack.

One of the most cherished notions of the football fan, screamed from the terraces during periodic outbreaks of sack-the-board fan power militancy, punctuating thousands of contributions to football phone-ins and printed in hundreds of fanzines and pamphlets: 'At the end of the day without the money we pay for tickets the clubs would not exist.'

Football's faithful could be forgiven for having this impression. After all every year since the start of the age of the Premiership ticket prices had increased well ahead of the rate of inflation and sometimes massively so. By 1995 tickets cost roughly six times more than they did twenty years previously, even after inflation had been taken into account. Fans were aware that transfer fees had gone through the roof and wages had risen enormously since the start of the Premiership. In fact from the mid-1990s many of the favourites among the dying art of the football chant concerned the players' wages. Alan Shearer was jeered with chants of 'One greedy bastard . . . There's only one greedy bastard . . . That's Alan Shearer . . .' Arsenal fans entertained themselves with the song 'He gets £50 thousand quid . . . he scores for Real Madrid' to mark Roy Keane's arrival in the £50,000 post-Bosman category and to rub in the fact that his first action after signing had been to score an own goal that helped put his team out of the 2001 Champions' League. Chelsea supporters, facing the highest and most rapidly escalating ticket prices in the Premiership, were forever being told by Ken Bates that the money was being used to bring top-class players to Chelsea 'to compete with the best in Europe' and that they should therefore stop moaning.

Television was the main new source of revenue, but as the age of the Premiership wore on others started to become almost as important. Leading the way were shirt sponsors and replica kit manufacturers. Liverpool had a deal with Reebok which brought in £6.5 million a year, roughly the same amount generated by the sale of 12,000 season tickets. Manchester United's 1996 £42 million deal with Umbro was worth around 20,000 fans in the Old Trafford stadium, every game.

And in October 2000 United switched the replica contract to Nike for a reported sum of $430 million – more than the best guess of the amount of money Nike put into Brazil. It was also reported that Nike would take charge of United's growing chain of shops and megastores and that the two companies would make a joint attack on markets such as the Far East and above all the USA itself.

Now that Nike was paying as much as the fans, the company's executives were at least as entitled as the fans to take the view that since the club depended on their money it ought to do what they wanted.

1999–2000 season

After Manchester United's treble in the previous season all the talk now was that the team had such a vast wealth of resources that no other side stood a serious chance of beating them to the championship. The usual pattern of a team becoming dominant then falling away for a few years as players aged and the side was rebuilt, had apparently been broken. United were now using a squad rotation system which meant that the team consisted not of eleven players and eleven substitutes and understudies that would be used in emergencies, but of thirty international players, any one of whom would have been an automatic choice for more or less any other team. The growing gap between United and the rest of English football was underlined by the club's decision to withdraw from the FA Cup and play instead in a made-for-TV FIFA World Club Championship held in Brazil in January. There was widespread disgust that the holders of the FA Cup would pull out in this way and Brian Clough popped up to lambast United for going to Brazil, saying: 'I hope they all get diarrhoea.' The team returned from the Brazilian tournament refreshed, tanned, with a game in hand and only three points behind a revived Leeds United led by manager David O'Leary. Manchester United powered ahead until April, when they were knocked out of the European Cup by 2000 winners' Real Madrid. They won their sixth title in eight years with a 3–1 away win against Southampton. By then the nearest challengers were Liverpool who were thirteen points behind. United ended up winning the league by the record margin of eighteen points. Arsenal were again the runners-up.

In December 1999 Chelsea became the first Premiership club to field a team composed entirely of foreign players, in an away game against Southampton. Manager Gianluca Vialli had signed twenty-two foreign players since taking over from Ruud Gullit at the start of the previous season.

21.
Bursting Bubbles

The tenth anniversary of Graham Kelly's *Blueprint for the Future of Football* came and went in March 2001, almost unnoticed. If anything, the document that heralded the new age with its talk of a 'League of Equality', cheap access to games, the promotion of fan power and the diversion of vast sums to the game's grass roots was a profound embarrassment to the FA. Visitors to the FA's headquarters were met with blank stares if they asked for it, and it took the organization's official historian a couple of hours to find a copy buried somewhere in the filing system.

By 2001 Kelly himself had parted company with the FA having, in his own words, been 'forced to fall on [his] sword' by the FA council. The cause of his abrupt and unwilling departure was a 'cash for votes' scandal, involving secretive payments of £400,000 a year from the English FA to its Welsh equivalent, intended to secure their support for England's ultimately doomed bid for the rights to stage the 2006 World Cup. There was never any indication that Kelly – and FA chairman Keith Wiseman, who was also caught up in the scandal – had been doing anything other than furthering the cause of English football as they saw it. The objection was that they had caused embarrassment to the FA, had failed to keep club chairmen informed and had acted in a generally ham-fisted way.

By December 1998 there were powerful voices in the Premiership and the FA calling for change at the top. Kelly and Wiseman had already clashed with some of the big club chairmen over the TV contract and the attempted

Media Partners European league breakaway. There had also been a slanging match with Ken Bates of Chelsea, who complained that he and the FA council had not been properly consulted over the appointment of an FA 'sleazebuster' to enforce the FA's rules on transfer deals after the traumas of the 'bungs' affair. And Kelly was under pressure after England's poor performance in the 1998 World Cup in France and the subsequent scandal over team manager Glenn Hoddle's controversial *World Cup Diary*.

After members of the FA council got hold of an invoice from the Welsh FA sent to Kelly by mistake (it should have been sent to the Sports Council, through whom the money was being siphoned) they decided to act. Kelly and Wiseman were unceremoniously given the boot by Geoff Thompson, the FA vice-chairman and the man seen by many as the voice of the big clubs. Kelly got a £375,000 payoff and was allowed to keep his company car.

Kelly and Wiseman were not replaced until March 1999 by which time Peter Leaver, chief-executive of the Premier League, had also been shown the door. His plan to set up the Premier League's own pay TV channel instead of selling the rights to Sky was fraught with difficulties, but held the possibility of massively increasing the Premiership's TV income by cutting out the middleman. It would also have the advantage, from Leaver's point of view, of making the Premier League the new paymaster of English football, restoring the its fading authority over Manchester United and the other big clubs at a stroke. To help him carry out his master plan Leaver had hired former Sky TV chiefs Sam Chisholm and David Chance as consultants, each on wages of $1 million (£666,000) a year, plus bonuses if the scheme came off. But it did not and Leaver was forced out after a row over the amount of money he had offered the former Sky executives.

The departure of Kelly, Wiseman and Leaver left all the effective power in the hands of the big clubs and Sky, who consolidated their position by holding on to their stake in Manchester United and buying into a string of other clubs including Sunderland, Leeds, Chelsea and Manchester City.

Underlying all the arguments was a struggle over who really owned football and who should control it. Kelly, Wiseman and Leaver looked to the model of the American NFL where the central organisation had the power to grant franchise licences to individual clubs lucky enough to be asked to take part. This was the idea at the centre of Kelly's *Blueprint* – the famous 'League of Equality' which would modernize the game, organize centralized merchandising, marketing and TV exploitation, and distribute a large part of its income to the grass roots, looking after supporters and giving priority to the needs of the England national team.

It had not worked out like that, even when Kelly and the rest of the old guard were still in charge. When Kelly left all power passed to the big clubs: they didn't even bother to replace him for a period of three months. After that there was a straightforward attempt to place the Premier League in charge of the whole of English football by means of a proposed 'merger' with the FA, abolishing its separate existence.

It was therefore unsurprising that Kelly's *Blueprint* had been forgotten at the FA headquarters. The central idea that Premier clubs – as a condition of playing in the competition – would continue to support the FA Cup had been abandoned when Manchester United opted out in order to play in FIFA's made-for-TV World Club Championship. On almost every other point the vision set out in the *Blueprint* had been ignored.

The promise, echoing the Taylor report on Hillsborough, that clubs should not use their new all-seater Premiership stadiums to put up prices had been entirely overlooked. A survey showed that by the start of the 2001–02 season ticket prices had more than doubled in the second five years of the Premiership decade, with the most expensive tickets – reaching £70 for an individual seat – on sale at Newcastle United's refurbished leisure complex.

One of the original architects of the Premier League, Irving Scholar of Tottenham, had been laughed at a decade earlier when he suggested that the business of attending a football match should be like a trip to the opera – an expensive special occasion rather than part of the weekly routine. But Scholar's vision had come to pass. The average Premiership match ticket was now £25. Tickets for the Royal Opera House could be had for only £23. Instead of the game's new riches being used to feed the grass roots and the national team the money was increasingly concentrated in the hands of a few. But by the time of the tenth anniversary even the richest clubs were finding it hard to keep up.

In October 2000, despite increased ticket prices and extra TV money worth £16 million earned by reaching the quarter-finals of the Champions League, Chelsea reported a £3.5 million loss. Much of the damage to the club's balance sheet had been caused by frantic activity in the transfer market, designed to keep the club in Europe. Manager Gianluca Vialli had spent almost £60 million during his thirty months in charge. When the team's performance dipped – threatening Chelsea's chances of European qualification – Vialli was abruptly shown the door. But by this stage news of yet another managerial sacking hardly raised an eyebrow. Few Premiership managers could now expect an extended run at their job, and the fashion for sacking managers had spread throughout the entire professional game. In the calendar year 2000 there had been forty-eight changes of manager across the four divisions (of the ninety-two league managers in place at the start of the Premiership, seventy-two had left the game completely by the start of 2001–2002 season and were, for the most part, unemployed).

Meanwhile, Ken Bates shrugged off the losses – and the much more threatening long-term debt caused by the creation of the Chelsea Village – by saying it was just the cost of doing business. The position was eased when, a few weeks later, he announced a £24 million sponsorship deal with Emirates airlines. Bates talked of seed corn investment which would reap a golden harvest in the future. But the scale of Chelsea's debts were huge and could only be paid off if Bates's optimistic forecasts for increased TV money, merchandising and ticket prices were borne out.

By January 2001 Manchester United itself – established as the world's richest club with an annual turnover of £110.9 million – announced that it was going to lay off half its merchandising staff in order to relieve pressure on declining profits. The grand plan to establish a world-wide 'brand' and a chain of shops to go with it was stalling badly. The following month the Dublin branch of United's international chain of Planet Hollywood-style Red Café outlets closed with heavy losses. An associated Dublin branch of its Manchester United Superstore – described by one Irish journalist as '10,000 square feet of tat' – was also failing to thrive. If United's merchandising could not do well in Dublin, a hotbed of support for the club, it was unlikely to thrive anywhere else. Soon after this, United handed over much of its merchandising operation to its new shirt sponsor, Nike, in a joint marketing and merchandising deal with the New York Yankees, designed to take on the world.

And it wasn't just United experiencing a merchandising downturn. Professor Tom Cannon, a football economist and advisor to the board of Everton, forecast an average fall of 15 per cent in merchandising income for Premiership clubs as consumer resistance began to set in. The clubs, he said, were starting to pay the price for 'overkill and greed'. Manchester United had changed its strip fourteen times since the launch of the Premiership, meaning that a truly devoted fan would have shelled out around £1,000 for replica shirts alone. 'The bubble has burst as far as merchandising is concerned. People are not desperate to be associated with their clubs anymore,' Professor Cannon said.

Even more worrying was the decline in football's ability to attract new pay TV subscribers, which reduced the amount of money Sky and the other pay TV operators were willing to pay.

In 1996 Sky had paid £670 million for a four-year deal. But at that time Chisholm was still running Sky and the company had faced little effective competition. In 2000 they would face much more determined rivals in the form of ITV subsidiary OnDigital (later renamed ITV Digital) and the cable operator NTL. Most commentators expected the price to go up to as much as £2 billion.

By the spring of 2000 the superprofits that Sky had

made on the back of football had evaporated. The company's plan to use 'live and exclusive' Premiership games to sell the next generation of digital TV subscriptions had fallen apart. The magic no longer worked. Sky ended up having to give away its digital set-top boxes. The result was reported losses running at over £70 million a year and a halving of the company's share price at a time when the rest of the stock market was still booming. When the new rights deal was completed in June 2000, Sky paid only £1.1 billion – still a huge sum, but almost £1 billion less than the amount anticipated only a few months earlier.

The disappointing Sky deal was offset – slightly – by a greatly increased deal for edited highlights, previously packaged as the BBC's *Match of the Day* programme on Saturday night. ITV won the auction with a bid of £183 million, against the £90 million first offered by the BBC. BBC Director General Greg Dyke simply did not think that the highlights were worth the extra £90 million a year, despite the good ratings. *Match of the Day* was already the BBC's most expensive programme: when the cost of buying the highlights was divided by the number of viewers they got, the cost worked out at a controversial 11.4p per viewer per hour. The Corporation's rule of thumb was that no programme should cost more than 10p per viewer/hour and more than 85 per cent of the programmes met the target. Dyke was willing to push up the budget for Match of the Day to 18p, but no further.

Dyke, more than most, knew what he was talking about. In the 1980s he had virtually created what became the Premiership when he had been in charge of ITV sport. He had also served on the board of Manchester United, advising on TV rights. For the first time since the birth of the Premiership an important TV executive was saying that football was over-rated, over-priced, and not worth buying.

The Premiership chairmen's decision to go for ITV's money rather than the BBC's reputation and proven audience soon began to look short-sighted. There was real anger that the BBC's *Match of the Day* – a national institution and a firm favourite with football fans – would now disappear from the airwaves, probably never to return.

As it turned out, ITV's version of *Match of the Day* – called *The Premiership* – started off as a ratings and critical disaster. It was shown at 6pm in the evening, was riddled with adverts and had the look and feel of a light entertainment 'tea time' show made for children or young teenagers. The start time was too early for many fans who would still be making their way home from games.

The show attracted around four million viewers – less than half the hoped-for audience. Such a dramatic impact on the weekly routines of millions of fans could have done little to counter the decline in loyalty and the feeling among many that they were being taken for mugs – or the growing, all pervasive complaint that football was now 'all about money'.

The big clubs reacted by concentrating on European competitions where, after twisting UEFA's arm with the threat of a European breakaway league, they were more or less guaranteed qualification to the Champions League and a larger number of lucrative televised games. But many of the extra games were frankly unappealing and drew smaller than anticipated TV audiences. Meanwhile, the fact that a team needed only to finish somewhere in the top five or six places in the Premiership in order to play 'in Europe' made the league even less competitive and took a lot of the shine off winning the trophy itself.

The domination of the competition by Manchester United had made many matches boring or, at least, lacking in passion and interest for the paying supporters inside the stadiums. It was often said that Manchester United fans were so used to winning that they rarely bothered to cheer their team with much enthusiasm. Alex Ferguson complained that the fans were no longer doing their bit to get behind the team and were more interested in sitting quietly and eating packets of crisps. Team captain Roy Keane went one further, saying that the match day atmosphere inside Old Trafford was now dominated by 'the drinks and prawn sandwich brigade' brought in by the stadium's corporate entertainment operation.

The big clubs reacted to these various woes by reverting to the refrain that the smaller clubs were enjoying a free ride on their coat-tails and 'bleeding' them dry, threatening their ability to compete in Europe. If the value of TV rights was no longer rocketing, the argument ran, it was because there were lots of Premiership matches featuring unfashionable clubs who were still entitled to a share of the TV money, even if they were doing relatively little to generate an audience. By October 2001 the Manchester United chief-executive was reportedly campaigning for a sixteen-club Premiership consisting of fourteen English clubs plus Glasgow Rangers and Celtic.

Kenyon wanted six clubs – Ipswich, West Ham, Leicester and Blackburn were mentioned in the press – to be put to the sword before negotiations for the next TV deal in 2004 began. That way the league could offer the pay TV operators a higher proportion of 'event-like' games with the added surprise, and exciting extra ingredient, of Scottish participation. 'Part of our responsibility is in continuing to evolve the sport positively,' Kenyon said, adding: 'There was a critical shift in 1991–92 when the Premier League was formed. To suggest there isn't another shift in another hundred years is unreal. People don't like change, but change is necessary.'

But a more fundamental problem was starting to threaten the economics of the Premiership – the potentially ruinous escalation in players' wages. Tens of millions were now needed by every club just to tread water. Transfer spending in the Premiership in the year to January 2000 had reached £423 million, taking the total for the previous five years to almost £1.8 billion. The simple fact was that any club spending less than £20 million on players – or with a squad wages bill of less than £500,000 a game – was likely to find itself slipping down the table. To have a good chance of staying at the top Manchester United's Alex Ferguson, facing his last season before retirement, decided that the club had to spend £42 million on just two players, the striker Ruud Van Nistelrooy and midfielder Juan Sebastian Veron. Even then, as the season started, United started to lose a lot of matches and it was realized that the club might have to spend as much again strengthening its leaky defence.

In the first half of the Premiership decade, increased income from TV and merchandising, along with injections of cash from City flotations, had made the leading clubs extremely profitable and their share prices had rocketed. But after the high point of 1996 – when media companies like Sky, Granada and NTL were queuing up to buy into football – the clubs had saddled themselves

Chris Horrie

with debt and heavy overheads in the form of stadium redevelopment schemes, transfer fees, marketing and catering overheads and – above all – players' wages. Everything was based on the assumption that the good times would continue.

But by the start of the 2001–2002 season a survey revealed that average Premiership squad wages had reached almost half a million a year for each player. Almost every club had at least two players who were on £25,000 a week or more. This particular genie had been let out of the bottle by clubs like Chelsea who found they could pick up international stars from Europe on 'free' Bosman transfers, paying out most of the multi-million fee they would previously have expected to pay in the form of wages. Established players then got in on the act, demanding parity in an inflationary cycle that put the Weimar Republic to shame.

United's Roy Keane had a lengthy dispute with the club, threatening to leave unless he was granted wages amounting to more than £100,000 a week and an anticipated £15 million over the period of a renewed three-year playing contract. Sol Campbell, switching from Tottenham to Arsenal, demanded a similar deal. Potentially the biggest earner was David Beckham. He employed two separate teams of lawyers and advisors with the aim of making sure he got even more than Keane and Campbell.

United's chief executive had talked about the 'critical shift' which had taken place with the formation of the Premiership. What this amounted to was a concentration of the football industry's growing income into the hands of a few clubs. That shift followed the irresistible commercial logic that once football had been re-themed as a TV spectacle, most of the TV money would go to the teams which drew the biggest TV audience.

Now a second shift was taking place. There was still much rhetoric that no individual player was as important as the club he played for, but that reality was starting to change. The clubs themselves relentlessly hyped individual stars as the key to their merchandising activities – especially those aimed at a younger and more capricious audience. Led by Nike, the shirt and boot manufacturers boosted the trend, marketing individual players as one-off geniuses, promoting them on TV like pop stars and members of 'Team Nike'. Previously, a young football fan would think of themselves as a Manchester United or Newcastle supporter, who then developed a liking for a favourite player. But by the end of the Premiership decade it was just as likely that he or she would be a David Beckham or Alan Shearer fan, who then backed Manchester United or Newcastle because that was the team the star happened to play for.

Players and their agents began to argue that the TV audience was increasingly being generated by them as individuals, and no longer entirely by the team or club. Sky and the tabloids were pushing things in the same direction, billing games like Manchester United vs Arsenal as contests between Vieira and Keane; Chelsea vs Liverpool as Hasselbaink vs Owen. When the big clubs wanted to whip the smaller clubs into line over TV rights, they had always been able to threaten to walk away saying, basically, that without Manchester United, Arsenal and Liverpool the Premiership was worth nothing to TV. Now things were set to move on another stage. Beckham, Keane and Giggs could threaten to walk away, saying without them Manchester United was worth nothing to

Chris Horrie

TV. The revolutionary thinking was that individual players would end up getting most of the money coming into the game, just like TV performers or stars of non-team sports such as golf or boxing. Some commentators, like former BBC1 and Channel Four boss Michael Grade, said footballers might end up selling their services to the highest bidder week by week in a world of made-for-TV matches promoted like boxing matches.

It was against this background that, in October 2001, the players' union – the Professional Footballers' Association – threatened to strike against a reduction in the amount of money it got as its direct cut of money paid by Sky for rights to screen matches.

The fact that the union got any money at all from television was a strange state of affairs, but it suited the clubs and the TV companies nicely. Since the 1950s individual players had waived their potential right to individual 'appearance money' in televised matches in favour of a lump sum payment to their union. The arrangement was an extension of the old device of the 'players' pool' where any extra money coming the way of the team from newspaper interviews or team photos had been paid into a common fund and shared equally. By custom and practice 5 per cent of any extra money clubs got from televised games was paid into the fund in lieu of appearance money paid to individual players.

Naturally, the union had supported this arrangement because the money was used to pay its own officials, as well as to fund various welfare schemes. When the sums of money to be had from TV were not great (and when players did not have teams of razor-sharp contract lawyers working for them) nobody paid much attention. But under the renewed Sky deal in 1996 the 5 per cent had amounted to £7.5 million over five years – a significant sum. Both Sky and the clubs had every reason to think this 'alms-giving' was cheap at the price, since it avoided the nightmare issue of appearance money and game-by-game payments to individual star players of the sort made to other TV performers.

But just a few days into the 2001–2002 season, the Premiership started to poke at this particular hornets' nest by proposing to cut the PFA's money by £2.3 million or just 1 per cent of the new deal agreed with Sky. The union immediately balloted its members recommending strike action if the league failed to restore the 5 per cent. After a brief period of brinkmanship the strike threat was withdrawn and a compromise was negotiated.

And so, in many ways, the story of TV and football – the crucial relationship which underlies every aspect of the Premiership – had come full circle.

Almost half a century earlier players had threatened to strike when, in 1956, ITV first offered to pay money to show League football on television. The players wanted a bonus for appearing on TV; and if they didn't get it they would impose a 'total ban' on televised football. Their argument was that if they were TV performers, they should be paid as TV performers. The strike never happened, and the players never got their appearance money, because the club chairmen of the time rejected the offer to televise live games, and kept doing so for another thirty years.

In 1956 the club chairmen saw TV as a pandora's box which would increase the gap between rich and poor clubs, create a generation of unfit, stay-at-home 'armchair supporters', leave the sport prey to the whims and fashions of the entertainment industry and push up top players' wages to ruinous levels.

And in 1956 the maximum wage earned by any football player in England was £15 per week.

2000–2001 season and start of 2001–2002 season

2000-2001 was another victory parade for Manchester United who lost a string of matches towards the end of the season – once the title was theirs – but still finished ten points clear of second placed Arsenal. They had been eighteen points clear at the end of May, before the run of bad results in meaningless games started. It was the third consecutive season that United and Arsenal had finished in first and second position. The season before that, 1997–98, they had switched positions with Arsenal coming first (by one point) and United second. United had won the title seven times since the start of the Premiership. Only two dropped points in nine years had prevented them from making a clean sweep. United manager Alex Ferguson announced that he was going to retire at the end of the next season and had a noisy dispute with the club about his future role and how much he would be paid. The squabble was settled to Ferguson's satisfaction and the hunt began for his replacement. It seemed likely the United would look abroad, following the example of Arsenal, Liverpool and the England national team.

Liverpool, restored to superpower status by a French manager, came third. The team also won the FA Cup, UEFA Cup and League Cup 'treble'. The main surprise of the season was the performance of Ipswich Town who, after winning promotion in the previous season and spending relatively modest sums on transfers and wages, came fifth. The other newly promoted teams – Bradford and Manchester City – were relegated – an especially hard blow for City to bear, given the continuing domination of United. City had based most of their hopes on former 'World Footballer of the Year' George Weah, a prime example of the post-Bosman trend of individual stars hiring themselves out for short spells on vast wages before moving on. On signing for City Weah had said: 'I will come here and give everything. I think we will go into Europe'. City fans had taunted visiting United supporters at the Manchester derby by holding up a banner saying 'Welcome to Manchester'.

There were signs at the start of the 2001–2002 season that United's grip on the Premiership might be starting to slip. For years the club had been fielding a second string team in the League Cup, and it still rankled that they had pulled out of the FA Cup two seasons earlier. It now seemed that they were treating the Premiership with similar disdain, fielding as many as eight reserve team players in league games against 'unfancied' opposition, saving the stars for European games. The strategy sometimes worked but, early in the season, they frequently slipped up, dropping points and apparently leaving the competition looking more open than it had been for many years.

With United in difficulty and clouds gathering around the value of TV rights and merchandising, it seemed that the Premiership and the 'football industry' was heading for new and more threatening waters.

Chronology

The 1980s and before

1885: Professionalism legalized.

1888: Football League founded.

1905: First £1,000 transfer: Alf Common from Sunderland to Middlesbrough.

1928: First £10,000 transfer: David Jack from Bolton to Arsenal.

1948: Len Shackleton's record transfer from Newcastle to Sunderland was subject to a kickback bung paid to the Sunderland chairman.

1955: In the run-up to the launch of commercial television ITV begins to offer large sums of money to individual clubs such as Manchester United, Aston Villa and Newcastle for rights to show their League matches live on Saturday afternoons.

1955: Stanley Seymour of Newcastle United proposes a breakaway made-for-TV Wednesday evening 'ITV Floodlit League' in order to capitalize on television money.

1955: In response to offers of money from ITV for live football, the Football League's ninety-two chairmen vote for a complete ban on live matches. The decision marks the start of a thirty-year battle between generally 'pro TV' big clubs and generally 'anti-TV' small clubs. Live coverage of League football remains banned until 1982.

1955: First European Cup competition set up partly to cater for the TV industry's growing demand for live football.

English champions Chelsea decline invitation to participate after pressure is applied by the League and FA.

1956: Manchester United's 'Busby Babes' team win the League and, despite official displeasure, play in the European Cup. The competition draws record TV audiences in the UK which, Busby says, makes Manchester United 'a household name throughout the universe'.

1956: The Professional Footballers' Association sides with the League authorities and threatens to strike if additional evening televised live games are introduced without bonus payments and a lifting of the FA's £15-a-week maximum wage. Influential ('pro-TV') club chairman Tommy Trinder of Fulham says with considerable foresight: 'Football players are now TV stars and should be paid as such.'

1957: 'Busby Babes' win the League championship for the second season in a row, but miss out on the League and Cup double by losing in the FA Cup final to Aston Villa.

1957: A Manchester United home tie against Borussia Dortmund in the European Cup draws a crowd of 75,000. Away games in the new made-for-TV competition continue to break all-time UK viewing records on ITV. Granada TV pay for floodlights to be installed at Old Trafford to allow more TV-friendly evening games and conclude a deal to pay United the unprecedented sum of £2,500 per live game.

1958: Most of the Manchester United 'Busby Babes' die in the Munich air crash.

1960: After campaigning by Burnley chairman Bob Lord, the Football League reject a massive £150,000-a-year offer from ITV for live League games.

1961: First £100,000 transfer: Denis Law from Manchester City to Torino.

Chris Horrie

1961: The PFA players' union led by chairman Jimmy Hill of Fulham bring about an end to the maximum wage.

1961: Tottenham Hotspur become the first club to win the League and Cup double in the twentieth century, fielding the first million-pound football team.

1964: Two former England players, Tony Kay and Peter Swan, together with David Layne and Dick Beattie, found guilty of match-fixing and jailed. As a result fixed odds betting on individual games curbed.

1964: After initial hostility from the League to televised football, BBC begins to broadcast *Match of the Day*. First programme features highlights of Liverpool–Arsenal (3–2) at Anfield. The show is an immediate hit and is soon being watched by fully a quarter of the adult TV audience.

1965: The Football League attempts to pull out of *Match of the Day*, blaming it for a decline in attendance at smaller clubs.

1966: England win the first World Cup of the television age. The Wembley final is broadcast to a worldwide audience of 400 million.

1968: Manchester United become the first English club to win the European Cup. George Best, the team's biggest star, is voted British 'Footballer of the Year' (and in 2000 was to be voted 'Footballer of the Century').

1969: Matt Busby retires from football management.

1970: FA Cup final between Leeds and Chelsea gets a record UK TV audience of 20 million.

1973: Cup Winners' Cup final: AC Milan 1 – Leeds 0. Milan had 'bought' the German referee.

1974: Manchester United relegated to Division Two.

1978: Three Scottish officials, referee John Gordon and two linesmen, suspended after suspected involvement in match-fixing. They accepted gifts of clothes from AC Milan despite being the officials at the UEFA Cup tie between Milan and Levski Spartak of Sofia. Milan won 3–0. The Milan officials claimed this was normal practice.

1979: First £1 million transfer: Trevor Francis from Birmingham City to Brian Clough's Nottingham Forest.

1980: Chairman of Manchester United Louis Edwards dies of heart attack, one month after it was alleged on Granada TV's *World in Action* 'The Man Who Bought United', that he was involved in dodgy share deals to buy Manchester United and in operating a cash slush fund to offer inducements to young players.

1980: Lazio and AC Milan both to be relegated for their part in match-fixing scandals. Lazio players Bruno Giordano banned for life and Lionello Manfredonia heavily implicated. Later in the year property developer Silvio Berlusconi buys AC Milan and within a few years becomes one of the most influential men in European football.

1983: Forty-three members of Hungarian crime syndicate go on trial for involvement in match-fixing.

1983: English First Division clubs allowed to keep all home gate receipts (except in FA Cup), widening the gap between rich and poor clubs.

1984: FC Porto bribe Romanian referee in European Cup Winners' Cup semi-final against Aberdeen.

1984: Anderlecht bribe referee in UEFA Cup, defeating Nottingham Forest in the semi-final.

Chris Horrie

1985: Dino Viola, chairman of Italian club Roma, found guilty of attempting to give a £40,000 bribe to the referee in a Cup Winners' Cup semi-final against Dundee. Roma later banned from European competition for a year as a result.

1986: Yiorgos Chrisovitsanos and Yiorgos Rigas jailed for one year after being convicted of attempted bribery while at AEK Athens.

1986: Italian authorities announce investigation of over eighty top-flight games after allegations of match-fixing and bribery.

1986: Yugoslav football authorities nullify the result of the First Division championship after twelve of the eighteen teams are alleged to have rigged the last games of the season.

1986: *Sunday Times* alleges that Argentina bribed Peru on a national level through the supply of free grain and a $50 million line of credit to ensure Argentina made it to the final of the World Cup in 1978, which they won. Argentine Admiral Carlos Lacoste, then vice-president of FIFA, named in the accusations. It was also alleged players were on drugs. Journalist Carlos Ares exiled himself to Spain after his life was threatened by Lacoste.

1986: Twelve Italian clubs including Napoli, Udinese and Bari indicted for 'sporting fraud' in conjunction with illegal betting.

1988: Whole year of crisis meetings and TV rights negotiations after soon-to-launch satellite pay-TV operator BSB offers £47 millions for rights to live First Division football. Greg Dyke of ITV responds with a plan to launch an 'ITV ten' league with a smaller number of clubs, each getting as much as they would have done from the satellite operator. A compromise is reached with ITV paying much more to screen a limited number of live Sunday *Big Match* league games. But the arguments, resentments and divisions created lead directly to the launch of the Premier League.

1989 (February): Sky TV re-launched by Rupert Murdoch and available in the UK. But without football there are not many takers and the operation is soon losing millions and threatening to sink the entire Murdoch media empire.

1989 (April): Hillsborough disaster.

1989 (May): Bordeaux versus Napoli in UEFA Cup. Three German officials received £35,000 between them.

1990

7.04: New FA chief executive Graham Kelly (who has arrived from the Football League) presents a plan for unifying the FA and the Football League to the FA council. It is rejected.

17.08: Football League enlarges First Division to twenty-two clubs, as proposed by Ken Bates of Chelsea and Ron Noades of Crystal Palace. The FA, Graham Taylor and Graham Kelly, are opposed. Conflict between FA and League is predicted.

16.09: Maxwell makes firm bid to buy Tottenham Hotspur.

1991

8.04: Graham Kelly presents his *Blueprint for the Future of Football* to the FA council. A breakaway 'premier division' of eighteen clubs is formed by clubs resigning from the league First Division. At least twelve clubs, including all the Big Five, say they are ready to join. After a wrangle the number of clubs is increased to twenty. The Premiership is born.

22.05: Manchester United is floated on the stock market, valued at £47 million. The club's chairman, Martin Edwards, makes a personal fortune of about £20 million.

14.06: Four more clubs sign documents of intent to resign from the Football League First Division and set up the Premier League. All hopes that the Football League can presuade clubs not to breakaway now disappear.

20.06: Armed with Jack Walker's money, Blackburn make a £2 million bid for Gary Lineker of Tottenham, but are rebuffed.

22.06: Alan Sugar and Terry Venables complete their £7.25 million takeover bid for Tottenham Hotspur. Venables becomes chief executive and Sugar chairman. Venables and Sugar tell the world that they will have joint control and equal power, but Sugar has secretly underwritten Venables' 50 per cent of the purchase price. They begin to fall out almost at once.

17.07: The clubs resigning from the First Division to set up the Premier League sign a founder member document committing them to play in the Premier League from the 1992–93 season onwards. The Football League was not consulted, even though the Premier League expected the League to take relegated teams. There would be no promotion from the Second Division (to be renamed the First Division) for a number of seasons until the Premier League was reduced to eighteen clubs. The Football League launches legal action aimed, first, at preventing the breakaway and, secondly, at gaining £6 million a year compensation for the next fifty years.

31.07: Robert Maxwell, having sold most of the club's best players, completes the sale of Derby County to new chairman Brian Fearn. Having been rebuffed by Manchester United, Maxwell is locked into a takeover battle fought over Tottenham Hotspur. The main motivation is expected increases in cash from TV rights sales.

13.08: The Third and Fourth Division clubs threaten to boycott the FA Cup if the FA does not compensate them for the formation of the Premier League.

17.08: The Football League Management Committee has collapsed since several members are chairmen of Premier League clubs who are now disqualified from voting. Bob Murray of Sunderland emerges as the leader of an anti-Premiership campaign, circulating a plan to boycott and isolate the Premiership clubs. He also promises to back a threatened PFA players' strike.

19.08: Manchester United and Tottenham issue stock market statements predicting better profits now that Premier League is going ahead. Robin Launders, United's finance director, signed in the close season from the motor dealer Reg Vardy, argues that additional money will flow to the Premier League clubs through television fees and sponsorship, whereas 'at the moment we have a modest share relative to our pulling power'.

29.08: David Moores takes over as chairman of Liverpool, replacing Noel White.

5.09: FA chief executive Graham Kelly threatens to get the courts to close down the Football League if certain clubs led by Sunderland continue to try to disrupt plans for the Premiership.

14.09: Kenny Dalglish signs Mike Newell of Everton to Second Division Blackburn Rovers for £1.1 million, the first of a wave of multi-million signings designed to ensure Blackburn joins the upcoming bonanza of the Premier League.

19.09: The FA and the Football League reach a settlement. Instead of compensation of £6 million a year for the next fifty years they had asked for, the League accepted a 'humiliating' £2 million a year from the FA and £1 million a year from the Premier League clubs for five years only. Within a few days the Premier League has a green light to go ahead at the start of the next season, with the existing twenty-two First Division clubs and reduced to twenty clubs and not eighteen as at first planned. The first job of the Premiership is to obtain a new TV contract. ITV and Sky begin to court the FA and individual clubs. The deadline for the TV deal is set for April 1992, a few months before the start of the season.

1.10: Manchester United PLC maiden results. Profits strongly up because of extra revenue (30 per cent ticket-price increase) and TV income from Cup Winners' Cup, achieved with more moderate activity in the transfer market.

8.12: Rick Parry from the Manchester branch of accountant Ernst and Young is appointed interim chief executive of the Premier League.

9.12. Bill Fox, the Football League chairman and chairman of Blackburn Rovers, dies, giving complete control of the club to Jack Walker. Fox's death is seen by many as signalling the end of the old order in the Football League, now very much secondary to the FA and its new Premier League.

23.12: George Graham receives a £140,500 'bung' from Norwegian transfer agent Rune Hauge. Another £285,000 is to be paid in August 1992. Graham later returned the money, claiming it was an 'unsolicited gift'.

1992

2.02: Eric Cantona signs on loan to Leeds United after walking out of Sheffield Wednesday.

5.02: Kevin Keegan brought in as manager of Newcastle. The team is in danger of relegation to the Third Division.

14.02: Premier League confirms Rick Parry as chief executive.

19.02: Alan Shearer scores on his England international debut in a 2–0 victory over France at Wembley.

2.03: Date of invoice to Tottenham from First Wave Management £10,000 for 'merchandising'. In reality this is commission paid for arranging the transfer of Andy Gray to Tottenham.

26.03: Ken Bates buys a 27 per cent stake in Cabra Estates, the owners of Chelsea's Stamford Bridge stadium site. At the time Cabra were planning to develop the site as a housing estate.

11.05: Sir John Hall buys a controlling 51 per cent of Newcastle. The club, managed by the recently arrived Kevin Keegan, finishes twentieth in Division Two. Hall persuades Keegan to remain as manager with a promise of large funds to buy players and achieve a quick entry to the new Premier League.

Chris Horrie

18.05: Sky buys the rights to show the Premier League for £304 million in a five-year deal. The BBC gets highlights to be shown in *Match of the Day*. ITV is defeated and threatens legal action over the way Sky conducted the negotiations with Premier League chief executive Rick Parry and chairman Sir John Quinton. In reality Sky paid only £190 million after the company failed to reach certain targets for sales overseas and subsidiary rights.

22.06: Denmark are the surprise winners of the European Championship, beating Holland in the final. Peter Schmeichel of Manchester United is the great hero after saving a penalty taken by Marco Van Basten in the semi-final.

1.07: World transfer record is set by AC Milan's £13 million transfer of Gianluigi Lentini from Torino. It is later revealed that the transfer was subject to a massive bung payment.

8.07: A bout of transfer frenzy in advance of the first Premiership season starts when Blackburn sign Stuart Ripley for £1.3 million.

14.07: Arsenal sign John Jensen for £1.1 million from Brondy. Manager George Graham took a £425,000 unsolicited gift from the proceeds, which he later paid back to Arsenal.

26.07: Blackburn sign Alan Shearer for a record £3.6 million. Shearer turned down a move to Manchester United and said that he was going to Blackburn 'to win trophies'.

15.08: (Saturday) The first Premier League season kicks off. Favourites Arsenal are beaten 4–2 at home by Norwich.

16.08: (Sunday) First live Sky match. Liverpool are beaten 1–0 by Nottingham Forest. The scorer is Teddy Sheringham.

17.08: (Monday) First live Sky evening match. Manchester City and QPR draw 1–1 at Maine Road.

19.08: George Graham receives a further £285,000 cash bung from the agent Rune Hauge as an unsolicited gift showing gratitude for signing so many of Hauge's players.

28.08: Spurs sign Teddy Sheringham from Nottingham Forest for £2.15 million. The transfer was subject to a £50,000 cash bung given to officials at Forest.

28.08: ITV sign a four-year deal with the new Football League First Division worth a minimum of £25 million for seventy Sunday *Big Match* live programmes.

26.11: Manchester United sign Eric Cantona from Leeds for £1.2 million.

15.12: Ken Bates pays £16.5 million to the Bank of Scotland for an option to buy Stamford Bridge for Chelsea at any point in the next twenty years. The deal is the green light for Bates's redevelopment of Stamford Bridge as the Chelsea Village shopping and hotel complex. Chelsea will also play at a stadium developed as part of the Village.

1993

1.02: Arsenal sign Martin Keown from Everton for £2 million, a club record for a defender. A bout of huge transfer fee inflation begins, fuelled by money from the TV deal with Sky and the expectation, even among smaller clubs, that players can be resold at a huge profit.

26.04: Brian Clough, manager of soon-to-be-relegated Nottingham Forest announces his intention to retire from management at the end of the season.

3.05: Manchester United confirmed as the first champions of the Premier League after winning their first league championship for twenty-six years.

8.05: After Liverpool's last home game of the first Premiership season the Kop is demolished.

14.05: Shortly before the first anniversary of his joint takeover of Tottenham with Terry Venables, Alan Sugar and the Tottenham Hotspur PLC board removed Venables from his job as chief executive. Venables obtains a High Court injunction and is reinstated pending a hearing.

30.05: First Premierships season final table:

1	Manchester United	84 pts
2	Aston Villa	74 pts
3	Norwich City	72 pts

Relegated:
Crystal Palace (49); Middlesbrough (44); Nottingham Forest (40)

Promoted from Division One:
Newcastle; West Ham; Swindon

1.06: A *Financial Times* review of the first Premiership season declares it to be 'an outstanding financial success'. Clubs have spent £75 million on ground improvements, with 75 per cent of the cost being met by the Football Trust. The cheapest seats at English grounds cost as much as 50 per cent more than the standing tickets they replace. The fans are paying more but attendances have climbed in every season from 1985–86 to 1992–93, from 16.5 million to 20.66 million. Individual big clubs are profiting. In 1989 Liverpool won the First Division championship and turnover was £4.77 million with profits of £145,000. In 1993 the club finished mid-table but turnover was £17 million and profits were £1.6 million. Between 1990 and 1993 Manchester United's turnover rose from £11.6 million to £25.3 million.

10.06: The bitterly contested attempt by Alan Sugar to remove Terry Venables from his job as chief executive at Tottenham results in 2600 pages of sworn statements, including the allegation that Venables had told Sugar that Brian Clough of Nottingham Forest was a man who 'liked a bung'. Eventually this led to an FA investigation revealing that bungs were widespread at some English clubs. The High Court upholds Sugar's right to get rid of Venables, who loses his job four days later and is banned for a while from even entering White Hart Lane.

10.07: Legia Warsaw, regular participants in the European Cup, are stripped of their Polish championship after a match-fixing scandal is uncovered. At the same time match-rigging scandals are reported in Cyprus, Spain and Georgia. In the Georgian case UEFA found Dynamo Tbilisi guilty of attempting to bribe the referee in a match against Linfield.

12.07: Marseille's Jean-Jacques Eydelie confesses to offering bribes to players in the French league to throw games in favour of Marseille, helping them to win the championship and, subsequently, the European Cup.

19.07: Manchester United sign Roy Keane from Nottingham Forest for £3.75 million. Seven years later his estimated value is £20 million.

19.07: Ryan Giggs of Manchester United signs a boot sponsorship deal with Reebok worth £325,000 over three years as brand wars between sports shoe and clothing manufacturers hot up. Nike sponsor Eric Cantona and Umbro the United team as a whole.

11.08: The FA warns clubs that they face fines if they suffer floodlight failures. The danger is that criminals will turn off the lights in the second half to freeze the results needed for betting scams. In the Far East the result stands if the game has lasted more than sixty minutes.

3.11: Manchester United's 'Welcome to Hell' UEFA Champions' Cup match in Istambul results in a 0–0 draw, exit from the European Cup and a suspension for Eric Cantona, who accused the referee in the match of taking a bung.

30.11: The Premier League establishes a three-man commission of inquiry to investigate the possibility of bungs in the Sheringham transfer from Nottingham Forest to Tottenham, as well as in forty other transfers mainly involving the movement of Scandinavian players to the Premier League.

1994

4.01: Liverpool goalkeeper Bruce Grobbelaar lets in three goals in a 3–3 draw against Manchester United at Anfield. It is later alleged that Grobbelaar was paid by betting interests to fix the result.

20.01: Matt Busby dies, aged eighty-four.

31.01: Roy Evans is appointed manager of Liverpool. One of his first actions is to give Bruce Grobbelaar a free transfer.

22.04: After a year's deliberation, the French league relegate last year's European Cup winners Marseille after proof of match-fixing in the league. Club president Bernard Tapie and three Marseille players are suspended from any involvement in football for two years.

2.05: Manchester United win their second consecutive Premiership championship and a few days later win the FA Cup and thus do the double. But the one-time fifteen-point lead is reduced to only eight points. Blackburn and

Newcastle see a return on their heavy investment in players by finishing second and third respectively.

7.05: On the last day of the season Everton escape relegation after coming back from a 2–0 deficit against Wimbledon to win 3–2. It is later alleged in court that Wimbledon goalkeeper Hans Segers accepted money to let in goals. He denied the charges but was disciplined for taking money from Far Eastern betting syndicates to forecast matches.

30.05: Second Premiership season (1993–94) final table:

1	Manchester United	92 pts
2	Blackburn Rovers	84 pts
3	Newcastle United	77 pts

Relegated:
Sheffied United (42); Oldham Athletic (40); Swindon Town (30)

Promoted from Division One:
Crystal Palace; Nottingham Forest; Leicester City

9.09: Inland Revenue investigation into £15 million worth of signing-on fees paid to foreign players. In an amnesty negotiated between the FA and the Inland Revenue, Sheffield Wednesday, for example, paid nearly £1 million in back tax, Norwich paid £600,000 and Spurs £200,000. Weeks later top clubs pay a one-off payment of £30 million to clear estimates of unpaid tax.

9.11: FA begin investigation into allegations of match-fixing surrounding Bruce Grobbelaar. Mark Lawrenson also claims he was offered £25,000 to concede a penalty against Panathinaikos, but refused.

12.11: Paul Merson admits he is a reformed cocaine

addict. Former Manchester United and Aston Villa manager Ron Atkinson later claims that drug abuse is widespread in English professional football.

2.12: FIFA admits that transfer irregularities have become a global problem, with the number of cases they have been asked to investigate doubling this year. The British FA are investigating three managers, including Arsenal's George Graham, who may have taken kickback bungs on transfers.

1995

12.01: Andy Cole transferred from Newcastle to Manchester United for £6 million plus the counter-transfer of Keith Gillespie.

25.01: Eric Cantona attacks fan with kung fu kick at a match against Crystal Palace. He receives a long ban and is sentenced to a period of community service by a Magistrates' Court.

21.02: George Graham leaves his job at Arsenal after the club fails to renew his contract ahead of the publication of the Premiership report into bungs. Arsenal says Graham has 'failed to act in the best interests of the club'. Graham described both Arsenal's decision and the Premier League inquiry as a 'kangaroo-court judgement' which he would 'contest vigorously'.

6.03: Referee Ken Aston claims that a Far Eastern betting syndicate is trying to fix Premiership matches. Aston claimed he was approached in Singapore and offered cash for names and addresses of leading players and referees.

7.03: The Premier League charge Graham over 'illegal payments and misconduct'.

12.03: Malaysian league bribery scandal breaks. One hundred and fifty players arrested, fifty-eight admit match-fixing. Malaysian authorities say source of corruption is Singapore.

15.03: Bruce Grobbelaar, Hans Segers and John Fashanu arrested by police investigating allegations of match-fixing.

19.04: FIFA investigate World Youth Tournament in Malaysia after allegations of attempted match fixing.

30.05: Third Premiership season (1994–95) final table:

1	Blackburn Rovers	89 pts
2	Manchester United	88 pts
3	Nottingham Forest	77 pts

Relegated:
Crystal Palace (45); Norwich (43); Leicester City (after one season) (29); Ipswich Town (27)

Promoted from Division One:
Bolton Wanderers; Middlesbrough (Premiership reduced from twenty-two to twenty clubs for next season)

26.07: Only four of the twenty Premiership clubs are keeping the same strip this season. There are complaints that the clubs are exploiting fans with frequent strip changes designed to cash in on the 'pester power' of children.

30.07: Accountants Touche Ross's annual report on football finance shows a widening gap in the finances of Premiership and First Division clubs. Premiership clubs in the 1993–94 season enjoyed an average 27 per cent increase in revenue and made average operating profits (excluding transfer activity) of £1.86 million while all football league clubs averaged increasing losses.

11.08: FIFA suspend Rune Hauge as an agent for two years because of his role in the George Graham bungs affair.

12.08: The first day of the 1995–96 season. The influx of foreign players into the Premiership (and to a lesser extent, the First Division) in the 1995 close season has included (in addition to the players mentioned above, Gullit, Ginola and Bergkamp) Savo Milošević (Aston Villa, £3.5 million); Georgi Kinkladze (Manchester City, £2 million); Marco Boogers (West Ham, £1 million); Marc Degryse (Sheffield Wednesday, £1.5 million); Andrea Silenzi (Nottingham Forest, £1.8 million); Ned Zelic (QPR, £1.25).

15.08: Fast-food chain McDonald's sign £1.75 million two-year sponsorship deal with the Premiership.

25.08: Manchester United sell Andrei Kanchelskis to Everton for £5 million after a long wrangle over the proportion of the fee to be given to Kanchelskis's former club Shakhtar Donetsk under a sell-on agreement.

20.09: Jean-Marc Bosman wins his 'contract freedom' case at the European Court of Justice. The Football League predicts many smaller selling clubs will go bust and that up to 75 per cent of professional footballers will have to be made redundant.

30.09: Sky announces that the introduction of digital broadcasting technology will allow it to operate up to 300 channels and offers to show all English Premiership matches live and simultaneously on different channels on Saturdays and Sundays.

2.11: Matthew Harding, the millionaire who helped rescue Chelsea by lending £25 million to the club, is forced off the board of Chelsea Village, owners of Chelsea Football Club, by Ken Bates as part of a long-running power struggle and feud between the two men.

28.11: Bernard Tapie, president of former European Champions' Marseille, is jailed for match-fixing.

15.12: The European Court of Justice quashes an appeal by FIFA and UEFA against the Bosman ruling, and in its verdict emphasizes even more clearly that clubs are not allowed to demand transfer fees for players at the end of their contracts and that, in principle, all players should be able to move as freely as possible between clubs at will.

30.12: Alan Shearer of Blackburn becomes the first player to score 100 goals in the Premiership.

1996

7.02: A UEFA summit in Geneva agrees to expand the Champions' League to thirty-three clubs within the next two seasons. Two clubs, winner and runner-up, from the seven major European domestic leagues (including the Premiership) will qualify for the competition. The Premiership is represented by Manchester United, Arsenal and Liverpool who all vote for the changes.

23.02: Newcastle, six points clear of Manchester United at the top of the Premiership, strengthen their squad by signing David Batty from Blackburn for £3.75 million. The deal takes Newcastle manager Kevin Keegan's spending on players to £44 million in four years.

29.03: Chelsea floated on the Alternative Investment Market as 'Chelsea Village'.

2.05: Glenn Hoddle is appointed England manager. His place as Chelsea manager is taken by Ruud Gullit.

11.05: Manchester United beat Liverpool 1–0 in the FA Cup final to achieve their second League and Cup double.

31.05: Fourth Premiership season (1995–96) final table (reduced from twenty-two to twenty clubs):

1	Manchester United	82 pts
2	Newcastle United	78 pts
3	Liverpool	71 pts

Relegated:
Manchester City (38); QPR (33); Bolton Wanderers (after one season) (29 pts)

Promoted from Division One:
Sunderland; Derby County; Leicester

6.06: The FA sign a new £670 million four-year contract with Sky for live and exclusive coverage of the Premiership.

8.06: England hosts Euro 96, the European championships. The pop song 'Three Lions' spawns the chant 'football's coming home' and becomes a hit and the England team do well under Terry Venables who has already announced that he will resign (to be replaced by Glenn Hoddle) after the championship in order to deal with his tortuous business and legal affairs.

1.07: The FA announces an English bid to host the 2006 World Cup.

25.07: The media group Caspian complete their £16 million takeover of Leeds United.

29.07: Newcastle sign Alan Shearer for a record £15 million.

9.09: Nineteen months after resigning as Arsenal manager, George Graham becomes manager of Leeds United.

22.09: Arsène Wenger is introduced to the press as the new manager of Arsenal.

3.10: As widely expected UEFA officially announce that two English clubs (champions and runners-up) will qualify for the Champions' League from the start of the next season.

22.10: Matthew Harding, deputy chairman of Chelsea, dies in a helicopter crash. His great rival Ken Bates later said that he could not really find it in himself to feel regret.

1.12: Rick Parry, chief executive of the Premiership, resigns in order to take over as chief executive at Liverpool. He is replaced in February 1997 by Peter Leaver QC, a former director at Alan Sugar's Tottenham Hotspur.

7.12: Nike agrees to pay an undisclosed sum, reported to be between $200 and $400 million, to sponsor the Brazilian national football team for ten years. Nike announces its intent to become the major player in a world replica football shirt and football boot market now worth £2.7 billion per year.

1997

14.01: Kevin Keegan resigns as manager of Newcastle after five years, complaining that bankers and financial interests have too much power at the club. He is replaced by Kenny Dalglish.

16.01: Newcastle announce plans for a stock market flotation aimed at raising up to £50 million in capital, valuing the club at around £100 million.

18.05: With Manchester United confirmed as champions for the fourth time in five seasons, Eric Cantona announces his retirement from football.

29.05: Mohammed Al Fayed, owner of Harrods, buys a controlling stake in Fulham after an attempted partnership with Ken Bates to run Chelsea and develop the Chelsea Village hotel and shopping complex.

30.05: Fifth Premiership season (1996–97) final table:

1	Manchester United	75 pts
2	Newcastle United	68 pts (GD: +33)
3	Arsenal	68 pts (GD: +30)

Relegated:
Sunderland (after one season) (40); Middlesbrough (39); Nottingham Forest (34)

Promoted from Division One:
Bolton Wanderers; Barnsley; Crystal Palace

28.07: David Mellor is appointed to head a Football Taskforce set up by the New Labour government elected in May 1997 to look mainly into consumer rip-offs in the football industry.

30.07: Arsenal sell shirt manufacturing rights to Nike for £40 million.

5.08: Arsenal chairman Peter Hill-Wood announces that the club's wage bill has increased from £8.7 million to £13.3 million in a single year and warns that players' wages are spiralling out of control in the wake of the Bosman ruling.

8.08: The retrial of Hans Segers and Bruce Grobbelaar on match-fixing charges ends at Winchester Crown Court. The players are acquitted, though they have admitted breaches of FA rules in accepting money for forecasting the results of games.

15.09: Sir John Hall announces his retirement from Newcastle United. His capital gains from involvement in the club are more than £100 million.

19.09: The FA publishes its 500-page report into corruption and bungs in the English game based on investigation of a selected number of transfers, mostly involving Rune Hauge. Robert Reid QC talks of a 'cult of dishonesty' in the business dealings of English football. In addition to bungs Reid uncovered instances of false invoicing and illegal use of agents.

22.09: Anderlecht are banned for one year from taking part in any European competition they qualify for, after it is finally established that the club bribed a referee in order to win a UEFA Cup semi-final against Nottingham Forest in 1984.

27.09: Manchester United announce the launch of MUTV, a satellite and cable channel developed with Sky and Granada TV. The club has appointed TV mogul Greg Dyke to the board to advise on their television activities. The channel will not show live United games, which are exclusively contracted to Sky Sports until at least 2002.

30.10: Sir John Smith, former deputy commissioner of the Metropolitan Police completes a two-month inquiry into gambling in football. He concluded that 'widespread betting . . . is damaging the integrity of professional football'. He found that at some clubs players and executives were betting on their team to lose. David Davies of the FA responds by promising a clamp-down.

3.11: Premiership match between West Ham and Crystal Palace called off after sixty-five minutes with the score at 3–3. It is later discovered that the floodlights had been tampered with, police believe, by Far Eastern gangsters trying to freeze the drawn result for purposes of defrauding bookmakers.

13.11: The Premiership signs a £100 million three-year contract with Mark McCormack's TWI and Canal Plus, the French pay-TV operator, for rights to sell live Premier League games around the world.

23.12: Floodlight failure at Selhurst Park match between Arsenal and Wimbledon is investigated by police as another instance of match-fixing by Far Eastern betting syndicates.

1998

12.02: Chelsea dismiss manager Ruud Gullit and replace him with Gianluca Vialli as player-manager. The reason is Gullit's demand for a salary in excess of £1 million a year 'netto' (the Italian term for payment after tax).

14.03: A Sunday newspaper prints an account of Newcastle chairman Freddie Shepherd and director Douglas Hall sitting in a Spanish brothel boasting about ripping off fans with high replica shirt prices, selling Andy Cole to Manchester United in full knowledge that he had a long-term injury and calling Newcastle women 'dogs'. Twenty days later, after a huge outcry, Shepherd and Hall resign. But after an interval of four months they regain their places on the board.

5.05: Manchester United sign defender Jaap Stam from PSV Eindhoven on a seven-year contract worth £1.75 million a season and for a fee of £10.75 million. The fee is equivalent to the entire transfer turnover of League Divisions Two and Three combined.

30.05: Premier League rejects Sky's proposal to televise

live matches on a pay-per-view basis next season, due to concerns over financial terms and a plan to move some matches from Saturday to Sunday.

30.05: Sixth Premiership season (1997–98) final table:

1	Arsenal	78 pts
2	Manchester United	77 pts
3	Liverpool	65 pts

Under new UEFA regulations both Arsenal and Manchester United qualify for the UEFA Champions' League.

Relegated:
Bolton Wanderers (40); Barnsley (35); Crystal Palace (33) (all after one season)

Promoted from Division One:
Charlton Athletic; Nottingham Forest; Middlesbrough

30.06: England eliminated from the World Cup in France by Argentina on penalties after drawing 2–2. The game produces a record UK TV viewing figure of 28 million.

12.07: France win the World Cup final against Brazil featuring a distinctly groggy Ronaldo who, it is widely suspected, was forced to play while ill, under pressure from Nike who are his and the Brazil team's sponsor. He later denied the allegation, but the debate over the role of Nike continued in Brazil.

6.08: The Dutch-based company Media Partners offer Manchester United and Arsenal £100 million a year to play in a proposed breakaway 'European Super League' backed with £2 billion capital and the support of American merchant bank J.P. Morgan. Manchester United, Liverpool and

Chris Horrie

Arsenal entertain the idea, but much depends on whether or not Media Partners can sign up other top clubs.

6.08: Accountants Deloitte Touche claim that since 1993 Premiership and other English clubs have spent more than £250 million buying foreign players.

14.08: David Beckham signs a new five-year contract at Manchester United putting him on minimum wages of £1 million a year.

24.08: UEFA say they will not be the governing authority for Media Partners' proposed Super League if it goes ahead. They counter-attack by suggesting that many more English clubs could play in the existing Champions' League or UEFA Cup.

27.08: Kenny Dalglish leaves Newcastle United after eighteen months in charge. His place is taken by Ruud Gullit, who is reportedly on wages of £1 million a year and promises to bring 'sexy football' to Newcastle.

6.09: Sky TV's plan to buy Manchester United is leaked to a Sunday newspaper.

8.09: The Manchester United board accept an improved takeover offer of £625 million from Sky. The club's capital valuation at stock market flotation seven years previously was £47 million. If the sale goes ahead Manchester United chairman Martin Edwards stands to make as much as £80 million personal profit.

26.09: Paolo Di Canio knocks referee Paul Alcock to the ground after being shown the red card while playing for Sheffield Wednesday against Arsenal. He receives an eleven-match ban.

29.09: Whether or not the takeover by Sky goes ahead,

Manchester United announce a plan to open a chain of 150 'Red Café' merchandising outlets and travel agents around the world, with many planned for China and the Far East, described as making the club 'the McDonald's of world football'. A £30 million expansion of Old Trafford providing an extra 12,400 seats and estimated extra gross revenues of more than £8 million a year are also planned.

30.10: Sky's takeover bid for Manchester United Football Club is referred to the Monopolies and Mergers Commission.

10.11: FA appoint former South Yorkshire policeman Graham Bean as 'Sleazebuster' – i.e., one-man regulation enforcement department.

16.11: Manchester United make arrangements for the Belgian side Antwerp to become a subsidiary 'feeder' club.

16.11: Scandal at the FA as the Welsh FA reveal they were given an £3.2 million 'non-repayable loan' over eight years in return for voting for the FA's nominee, Keith Wiseman, to become the British Isles vice-president of UEFA and take a seat on the UEFA executive committee, instead of the incumbent Scottish FA representative David Will.

15.12: Resignation of Premiership architect and FA chief executive Graham Kelly after internal investigation finds that the 'cash-for-votes' loan to the Welsh FA was an improper use of English FA funds. Keith Wiseman is given a unanimous vote of no-confidence and resigns shortly afterward, admitting a 'grave error of judgement'. The Welsh FA are now describing the money as a 'gift' which they were not obliged to repay.

18.12: NTL buys a 6.3 per cent stake in Newcastle United

for £10 million, and announces their intention to mount a full takeover bid if Sky are allowed to buy Manchester United.

1999

2.02: A survey by accountants Deloitte & Touche finds that Manchester United PLC is the richest football company in the world in terms of revenue. Turnover to the end of the 1996–97 season was £87.94 million. The second richest club was Barcelona with turnover of under £60 million.

11.02: Three Malaysians and a Charlton security guard are arrested after the men are found tampering with Charlton's floodlight power system in attempt to rig a floodlight failure for betting purposes. This is the fourth betting syndicate-related floodlight problem in two years.

12.02: Security checks at all ninety-two league grounds to ensure no more 'devices of darkness' are in place – after three men appeared in court charged with attempting to sabotage floodlights. Three games during the 1997–98 season in which half-time floodlight failures caused the matches to be abandoned, are being investigated. The games took place at West Ham, Derby and Wimbledon.

27.02: Sky shows its first pay-per-view football match, the Division One game between Oxford United and Sunderland, at a cost of £7.95 per subscriber.

11.03: Premiership chief executive Peter Leaver and chairman Sir John Quinton are forced to resign after giving multi-million consultancy fees to Sam Chisholm and David Chance, lately of Sky TV, without consulting club chairmen.

10.04: Sky's attempt to acquire Manchester United is

blocked by the government, as the Competition Commission said it would have given Sky an unfair advantage in sports rights negotiations.

14.04: In an FA Cup semi-final replay at Villa Park Ryan Giggs scores what was described by many in the press as 'the goal of the century' against Arsenal.

22.04: Cable company NTL drops plans to bid for Newcastle United in the wake of the government block on Sky's takeover of Manchester United.

7.05: Manchester United announce plan to set up a chain of amusement parks in Singapore, Hong Kong, Malaysia, Thailand and China, possibly using virtual reality technology to 'reproduce the experience' of visiting Old Trafford.

26.05: Manchester United complete a unique treble of national championship, FA Cup and European championship by beating Bayern Munich 2–1 in the Champions' League final in Barcelona. United scored two goals in the last few seconds of the game.

30.05: Seventh Premiership season (1998–99) final table:

1	Manchester United	79 pts
2	Arsenal	78 pts
3	Chelsea	75 pts

Relegated:
Charlton Athletic (36) (after one season); Blackburn Rovers (35); Nottingham Forest (after one season) (30)

Promoted from Division One:
Sunderland; Bradford; Watford

21.06: Manchester United announce that they will take part in FIFA's World Club Championship in Brazil in January 2000 and will therefore pull out of the FA Cup.

22.06: A survey shows that 172 foreign players will take part in the Premiership in the 1999–2000 season compared with sixty-three in 1995.

13.07: The ITV company Granada buys a 10 per cent stake in Liverpool, becoming the club's second largest shareholder.

23.07: Manchester United launch a new navy blue and black away strip, the sixteenth new design in eight years.

24.07: Manchester United play a South China side in Hong Kong before a crowd of 40,000. The game is part of a pre-season tour of China amid 'Beckham mania'. There is much talk of Manchester United only just beginning to tap vast worldwide revenues for their brand.

22.08: Sky launch 'Sky Sports Interactive' which allows pay-TV subscribers to switch between cameras and call up factual information on the screen.

31.08: Sky buys a 9.1 per cent stake in Leeds United for £13.8 million.

1.09: Sky acquires a 9.1 per cent stake in Leeds United's parent company, Leeds Sporting, for £9.2 million, and becomes the exclusive media agent for the club.

6.11: Sky buys a 9.9 per cent stake in Manchester City.

18.12: Sky acquires a 5 per cent stake in Sunderland for £6.5 million, and will also become the club's media agent for five years.

2000

5.01: A survey reveals that Premiership clubs spent £348

million on players in the calendar year 1999, taking spending in the decade of the 1990s to £1.8 billion.

17.02: Manchester United's capital valuation reaches £800 million – a twenty-fold increase since flotation in 1991.

4.03: Sky buys a 9.9 per cent stake in Chelsea and finances aspects the club's development activities for a total payment of £40 million.

10.03: Liverpool sign Emile Heskey from Leicester City for £11 million.

1.04: First reports appear in the press that fourteen European clubs are to establish a central organization to co-ordinate activities and, possibly, form a breakaway European league. The new organization has taken the title Group of 14, or G–14, and consists of Manchester United and Liverpool from the Premiership, along with Real Madrid, Bayern Munich, Juventus, Barcelona, AC Milan, Inter Milan, Borussia Dortmund, Paris St-Germain, PSV Eindhoven, Ajax, Marseille and Porto. There are now four putative European super league organizations in operation: UEFA, the semi-official European Leagues Co-Ordinating Committee, G–14 and the remnants of the Berlusconi–Media Partners operation.

18.04: Rupert Murdoch proposes a new breakaway European super league to be run by pay-TV operators Kirsch of Germany, Canal Plus of France and Telephonica of Spain. Sixteen clubs are to be invited to join, each guaranteed £15 million a year, plus performance bonuses.

22.04: Manchester United win the Premiership by a record margin of eighteen points. It is their sixth championship title in eight years. In the two seasons they did not win they came second by one point in each case.

Chris Horrie

8.05: A survey shows that Premiership players' wages increased by 31 per cent during the 1999–2000 season, reaching a total of £397 million a year.

30.05: Eighth Premiership season (1999–2000) final table:

1	Manchester United	91 pts
2	Arsenal	73 pts
3	Leeds United	69 pts

Relegated:
Wimbledon (33); Sheffield Wednesday (31); Watford (after one season) (24)

Promoted from Division One:
Charlton Athletic; Manchester City; Ipswich Town

14.06: Premiership sells rights to Saturday night TV highlights package to ITV in a three-season deal worth £183 million, outbidding the BBC who therefore lost the right to screen *Match of the Day*.

15.08: The annual Deloitte & Touche Premiership audit reveals that average Premiership player wages have reached £350,000 a year, compared with £37,000 a year for Division Three players. The firm predicts that during the season the average salary will reach £100,000 a week – working out at something like £1,000 per player, per minute and £10,000 per team per minute.

18.08: Jack Walker, owner of Blackburn, dies of cancer.

21.08: Manchester United chief executive Peter Kenyon says that the club has no plans to participate in any European Super League and will continue to support UEFA and the Champions League.

12.09: Ken Bates of Chelsea sacks manager Gianluca Vialli.

The former player/coach had spent £57 million on (mostly foreign) players during his thirty months in charge.

22.10: Brazilian authorities begin investigation into the effects of the Brazilian national team's sponsorship deal with Nike.

09.11: Manchester United captain Roy Keane says that the atmosphere at Old Trafford has been ruined by 'the drinks and prawn sandwich brigade' brought in by the stadium's corporate entertainment operation.

06.12: Manchester United PLC annual report puts turnover at £110.9 million, confirming that the club is by far the richest in the world. Only Bayern Munich (turnover £83.5 million) comes close.

2001

04.01: A survey shows that Premiership transfer spending in 2000 was £423 million, taking the total for the previous five years to almost £1.8 billion.

16.01: Alex Ferguson announces that he intends to retire as manager of Manchester United at the end of the next season and begins a noisy argument with the club over his future role.

07.02: Manchester United sign a marketing and merchandising agreement with the New York Yankees baseball team as a first step to attacking the American 'soccer market'.

30.05: Ninth Premiership season (2000–2001) final table.

1	Manchester United	80 pts
2	Arsenal	70 pts
3	Liverpool	69 pts

Chris Horrie

Relegated:
Manchester City (after one season) (34); Coventry City (34); Bradford City (after one season) (26)

Promoted from Division One:
Fulham; Blackburn; Bolton Wanderers

Select Bibliography

Ian Bent, et al, *Football Confidential*, BBC, 2000

Mihir Bose, *Manchester Unlimited*, Orion, 1999

—— *False Messiah – The Life and Times of Terry Venables*, Andre Deutsch, 1997

Matt Busby, *Soccer at the Top*, Sphere, 1973

Denis Campbell, Pete May and Andrew Shields, *The Lad Done Bad – Sex, Sleaze and Scandal in English Football*, Penguin, 1996

Peter Chippindale and Susanne Franks, *Dished! The Rise and Fall of British Satellite Broadcasting*, Simon & Schuster, 1991

Neville Clarke and Edwin Riddell, *Sky Barons – The Men Who Control Global Media*, Methuen, 1992

Brian Clough, *Clough – The Autobiography*, Corgi, 1996

David Conn, *The Football Business*, Mainstream, 1997

Michael Crick, *Manchester United – Betrayal of a Legend*, Pelham, 1989

Kenny Dalglish, *Dalglish: My Autobiography*, Hodder and Stoughton, 1996

Niall Edworthy, *The Second Most Important Job in the Country*, Virgin, 1999

Alex Ferguson, *Managing My Life – My Autobiography*, Hodder and Stoughton, 1999

The Football Association, *Blueprint for the Future of Football*, Football Association, 1991

The Football League, *One Game, One Team, One Voice*, Football League, 1990

Alex Fynn and Lynton Guest, *Out of Time – Why Football Isn't Working*, Simon & Schuster, 1994

Chris Horrie

George Graham, *The Glory and the Grief*, Andre Deutsch, 1995

Sean Hamil, et al, *A Game of Two Halves? – The Business of Football*, Mainstream, 1999

Alan Hardaker, *Hardaker of the League*, Pelham, 1977

Harry Harris, *The Ferguson Effect*, Orion, 1999

—— *Ruud Gullit: The Chelsea Diary*, Orion, 1998

HMSO, *The Hillsborough Stadium Disaster – Final Report by Lord Justice Taylor*, Cmd 962, 1990

Chris Horrie, *Sick as a Parrot – The Inside Story of the Spurs Fiasco*, Virgin, 1992

Chris Horrie and Steve Clarke, *Citizen Greg*, Simon & Schuster, 2000

Chris Horrie and Adam Nathan, *L?ve TV*, Simon & Schuster, 1999

Matthew Horsman, *Sky High*, Orion, 1997

Simon Inglis, *League Football and the Men Who Made It – The Official Centenary of the Football League*, Collins, 1988

Kevin Keegan, *Kevin Keegan by Kevin Keegan*, Arthur Barker, 1977

Simon Kuper, *Football Against the Enemy*, Phoenix Press, 1995

Glenda Rollin and Jack Rollin (eds.), *Rothmans Football Yearbook 2000–2001*, Headline, 2000

Hans Segers, *The Final Score*, Robson Books, 1998

Graham Sharpe, *Gambling on Goals – A Century of Football Betting*, Mainstream, 1997

Alan Shearer, *Alan Shearer: Diary of a Season*, Virgin, 1995

Bruce Smith, *Premier League Record File*, Virgin, 2000

Phil Soar, *The Encyclopedia of British Football*, Marshall Cavendish, 1987

Stefan Szymanski and Tim Kuypers, *Winners and Losers*, Penguin, 2000

Brian Woolnough, *Ken Bates – My Chelsea Dream*, Virgin, 1998

David Yallop, *How They Stole the Game*, Poetic Publishing, 1999

Index

Chris Horrie

Chris Horrie

Chris Horrie

Chris Horrie